LISTED STOCK OPTIONS

The Hands-On Study Guide for Investors & Traders

REVISED EDITION

Carl F. Luft & Richard K. Sheiner

McGraw-Hill

New York San Francisco Washington, D.C. Auckland Bogotá Caracas Lisbon London Madrid Mexico City Milan Montreal New Delhi San Juan Singapore Sydney Tokyo Toronto

McGraw-Hill

A Division of The McGraw-Hill Companies

ISBN 1-55738-520-3

Printed in the United States of America

9 0

CONTENTS

Preface

This book has been written for the conservative and prudent investor. Our primary goal is to show the investor how stock options can be used to reduce risk and stabilize return. While it is true that some option strategies are extremely risky, it is also true many option strategies provide the investor with a powerful risk management tool. Thus, our secondary goal is to debunk the myth that all option investment strategies are too complex for the average investor to understand, and too risky for the average investor to undertake. Whether you are a neophyte option investor, or one who has been active in the options market for years, we feel that this book will make worthwhile reading.

In the early chapters, we introduce option basics, the mechanics of the options market, and the fundamental properties of both call and put options. Later chapters introduce various option strategies that increase in complexity. The strategy chapters rely heavily on actual market examples where graphs and worksheets are used to clarify and augment the presentation. The worksheets are designed to provide the investor with ample opportunity to become familiar with all phases of the individual strategies. We feel that mastering the worksheets will give the average investor the confidence to use the various option strategies as a means of effectively managing one's risk without unduly sacrificing one's return.

We gratefully acknowledge the support of Dr. Geoffrey Hirt, Chairman of DePaul University's Finance Department; and the DePaul University Faculty Research Council. We also wish to thank Elliot Katz for his valuable insights, and Mr. Thomas F. Mucha and Mr. Arnaud Burin des Roziers for their many hours of research and computer assistance. We especially thank our wives and children for their unqualified support.

Carl F. Luft
Richard K. Sheiner

Chapter One

INTRODUCTION TO OPTIONS

Introduction

An *option* is the right, not the obligation, to buy or sell some asset at some point in the future. A *call* option grants the right to buy the asset, while a *put* option grants the right to sell the asset. When an option is exercised the underlying asset changes hands at a price known as the *striking* or *exercise* price. Options can be classified further as being either European or American. A *European* option can be exercised only at maturity, while an *American* option can be exercised at any time up to, and including, the maturity date. Active trading of equity options occurs on five exchanges in the United States. These exchanges are: the Chicago Board Options Exchange (CBOE); the American Stock Exchange (AMEX); the Philadelphia Stock Exchange (PHLX); the Pacific Stock Exchange (PSE); and the New York Stock Exchange (NYSE). All equity options traded on these exchanges are American options; there are no exchange traded equity options which are European in nature.

Combining these concepts yields the specific definitions for call and put options. An *American call option* grants the owner the right to purchase the underlying asset on or before the maturity date for the exercise price. An *American put option* grants the owner the right to sell the underlying asset on or before the maturity date for the exercise price. A *European call option* grants the owner the right to purchase the asset for the striking price only at maturity. A *European put option* grants the holder the right to sell the underlying asset for the striking price only at maturity.

The trading price for the option is commonly referred to as the *premium*. Thus, if one purchases a put option, then one pays the premium. If one sells, or writes, a put option then the premium is collected. All premiums are paid at the time of the sale.

It is important not to confuse the option's premium with the option's exercise or striking price. The exercise price is the price at which the underlying asset changes hands. For example, if an investor paid a five dollar premium for a call option with a forty dollar striking price and then exercised the option, the investor would purchase the stock from the call writer at a price of $40 per share. In general, stocks trading at less than $25 per share have striking prices listed at $2.50 increments. Stocks with values between $25 and $200 per share will have striking prices listed in $5.00 increments, while stocks trading at values greater than $200 per share will have striking prices listed with $10.00 increments.

Option Maturities

All exchange traded equity options mature according to one of three standard expiration cycles. These cycles are termed the January sequential cycle, the February sequential cycle, and the March sequential cycle and are structured so that option expirations can occur as far out as eight months, as well as monthly. All three cycles are designed to satisfy the demand for shorter maturity options by creating options with maturities of approximately thirty and sixty days. The shorter maturities provide more flexibility by guaranteeing that the investor will have the opportunity to establish positions in one- or two- month options in these stocks, while the longer maturities make it possible for the investor to establish positions that can be left intact for at least six months.

In October of 1990 the Chicago Board Options Exchange and the American Stock Exchange began trading Long-term Equity Anticipation Securities, LEAPS. In June of 1991 the Philadelphia Stock Exchange began trading LEAPS, followed by the Pacific Stock Exchange in October of that year. Finally, the New York Stock Exchange began trading Long-term Equity Anticipation Securities in January of 1992. These instruments were created to satisfy investors' needs for long-term maturity options. LEAPS are options on individual stocks that grant the right to buy or sell one hundred shares of the underlying stock at a specified striking price, on or before a given date up to three years in the future. LEAPS that are traded on the American Stock Exchange, the Chicago Board Options Exchange, the Pacific Stock Exchange, and the Philadelphia Stock Exchange have maturities that extend up to two years, while the Long-term Equity Anticipation Securities traded on the New York Stock Exchange have maturities of up to three years.

Quite often the terms "class" and "series" are used when discussing options. These terms simply relate the concepts of striking price and maturity to specific options. An *option class* refers to the type of option written on a single underlying stock. Thus, exchange traded options have two separate classes, one for puts and one for calls. An *option series* is a subset of an option class. All options with the same striking price and maturity date constitute a series. Since virtually all option classes have three maturity dates, there are at least three series of options for each class. For example, if there are four exercise prices and three maturities, then there are three series of options for that class.

The Options Market

In Exhibit 1–1, option price quotations from the Monday, October 4, 1993 *Wall Street Journal* are provided. Note that the prices are quotes for the prior day's trading. In this case, the quotes are the closing prices for the options traded on Friday, October 1, 1993. Since these prices are for the previous day's final trade, it is very unlikely that an investor would be able to transact in the options market at these prices. However, to keep the following explanation as simple as possible, these final prices are used without reservation.

LISTED OPTIONS QUOTATIONS

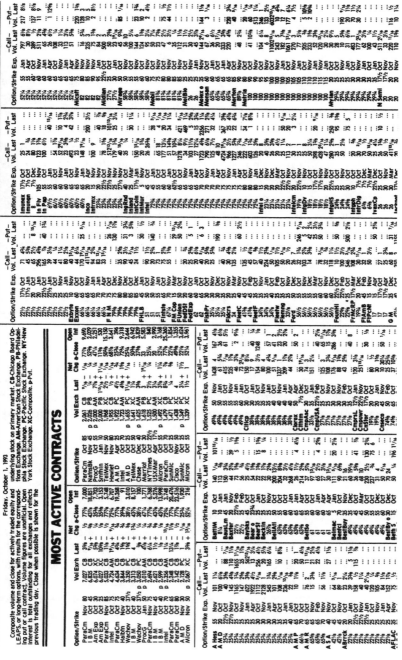

Friday, October 1, 1993

Composite volume and close for actively traded equity and LEAPS, or long-term options, with results for the corresponding put or call contract. Volume figures are unofficial. Open interest is total outstanding for all exchanges and reflects previous trading day. Close when possible is shown for the underlying stock on primary market. CB-Chicago Board Options Exchange. AM-American Stock Exchange. PB-Philadelphia Stock Exchange. PC-Pacific Stock Exchange. NY-New York Stock Exchange. XC-Composite. p-Put.

MOST ACTIVE CONTRACTS

Option/Strike				Vol	Exch	Last	Net Chg	a-Close	Open Int
ParaCm	Nov	80		7,027	CB	3⅜	– ½	77⅞	7,000
I B M	Oct	45		6,835	CB	9/16	+ ⅜	43⅞	18,851
Am Exp	Oct	30		6,074	XC	5⅜	– ¼	35⅜	7,703
Am Exp	Oct	25		6,027	XC	10⅜	– ⅛	35⅜	3,153
ParaCm	Nov	85		5,033	CB	1⅛	– ½	77⅞	5,748
Intel	Oct	75		4,724	AM	1 9/16	+ 9/16	72¾	6,707
ParaCm	Oct	75		4,634	CB	4¾	– ¾	77⅞	19,268
Halbtn	Nov	40		3,844	CB	1⅝	+ ¾	39⅜	91
Wachov	Oct	37½		3,350	PC	1⅝	– ⅜	38½	3,010
I B M	Oct	40		3,313	CB	4	+ 1¾	43⅞	8,157
Wachov	Oct	37½	p	3,050	PC	⅜	– ¼	38½	100
ProcG	Jan	50	p	3,010	AM	4⅛	+ ¼	47¼	1,771
ParaCm	Nov	75		2,694	CB	6¼	– ¾	77⅞	6,768
I B M	Nov	45		2,621	CB	1½	+ ⅝	43⅞	5,276
I B M	Oct	40	p	2,599	CB	⅛	– ⅛	43⅞	13,998
Intel	Oct	70	p	2,356	AM	1¼	– 13/16	72¾	3,748
ParaCm	Oct	65		2,248	CB	13¼	– 1⅛	77⅞	20,476
ParaCm	Oct	80		2,142	CB	1⅞	– ½	77⅞	23,516
A M D	Nov	30		2,128	PC	1	– 1/16	25¾	1,930
Micron	Nov	50	p	2,067	XC	3⅜	+ 1 3/16	52¼	216

Option/Strike				Vol	Exch	Last	Net Chg	a-Close	Open Int
ParaCm	Oct	85		2,061	CB	9/16	– 1/16	77⅞	9,690
NatnsBk	Nov	45	p	2,026	PB	¼	– ¼	52⅜	2,029
ProcG	Oct	55	p	2,000	AM	7⅞	+ ¼	47¼	2,251
SmthIn	Jan	10		2,000	PB	1 15/16	+ 1 1/16	11⅜	530
TelMex	Nov	50		1,968	XC	2½	– 1/16	50⅜	15,150
Hewlet	Nov	80		1,955	CB	½	+ 1/16	68⅞	3,641
A M D	Apr	25		1,922	PC	4½	– ¾	25¾	396
Intel	Oct	70		1,723	AM	4⅜	+ 1⅝	72¾	9,318
A M D	Oct	25	p	1,655	PC	1 1/16	+ 1/16	25¾	2,644
TelMex	Oct	50		1,641	XC	1¼	...	50⅜	6,942
Chase	Dec	40	p	1,625	AM	3⅝	...	37⅜	3,839
Marriot	Oct	30		1,618	PB	3	+ 1 9/16	33	5,583
NYTimes	Oct	22½		1,525	PC	2½	+ ¼	25¼	840
USXMar	Apr	17½		1,500	AM	3¼	...	20	2,990
Micron	Oct	55	p	1,492	XC	3⅞	+ 1¼	52¼	3,168
ParaCm	Oct	70		1,479	CB	8¾	– ⅞	77⅞	25,360
SunMic	Oct	25		1,471	PC	¼	– ⅝	22⅛	1,854
Cisco	Nov	50		1,438	XC	4	...	49⅜	1,355
SunMic	Oct	25	p	1,349	PC	3¼	+ 1½	22⅛	3,624
Micron	Oct	55		1,339	XC	1½	– 1	52¼	3,961

Option/Strike		Exp.	-Call- Vol.	-Call- Last	-Put- Vol.	-Put- Last
A Hess	55	Nov	101	1¼	...	...
A M D	20	Oct	100	6⅛	...	...
25¾	22½	Oct	40	3⅝	88	7/16
25¾	22½	Nov	145	4⅜	110	1⅛
25¾	25	Oct	1165	1¾	1655	1 1/16
25¾	25	Nov	147	2⅝	35	1⅞
25¾	25	Jan	622	3⅝	562	13/16
25¾	25	Apr	1922	4½	13	3¼
25¾	30	Oct	1112	5/16	256	4½
25¾	30	Nov	2128	1	20	5⅛
25¾	30	Jan	545	1¾	165	6¼
25¾	30	Apr	101	2⅝	...	...
25¾	35	Oct	108	1/16	10	8⅞
25¾	35	Jan	236	13/16	...	...
25¾	40	Jan	22	⅜	...	...
A M P	65	Oct	10	1⅛	20	1
66⅛	70	Oct	...	...	50	4⅛
A M R	65	Oct	76	2	11	13/16
65⅝	65	Nov	15	3⅜	21	2⅛
65⅝	65	Feb	...	...	22	4⅛
65⅝	70	Nov	56	1⅛	...	...
A S A	40	Nov	...	...	27	1⅛
42⅛	45	Oct	64	3/16	...	...
42⅛	45	Nov	89	1	...	...
ABrrck	20	Oct	23	2¼	...	...
22⅛	20	Jan	39	3⅜	5	1⅛
22⅛	22½	Oct	158	½	115	⅞
22⅛	22½	Nov	40	1¼	...	...
22⅛	22½	Jan	40	2 1/16	...	...
22⅛	25	Oct	120	¼	...	...
22⅛	25	Nov	105	⅝	...	...
22⅛	25	Jan	84	1⅛	...	...
22⅛	25	Apr	152	1⅞	...	...
AFLAC	35	Nov	75	½	...	...

Option/Strike		Exp.	-Call- Vol.	-Call- Last	-Put- Vol.	-Put- Last
BattlM	10	Oct	140	1/16	101	15/16
8¼	10	Jan	113	⅜	...	...
BausLm	45	Jan	150	3¾	...	...
Baxter	20	Nov	44	2⅞	39	½
22½	22½	Feb	73	1⅝	5	1⅝
22½	25	Feb	56	¾	...	...
Baybks	45	Oct	25	4½	...	...
Bear o	23¾	Oct	54	1⅝	...	...
BearSt	25	Jan	22	1⅝	15	1⅝
Beckln	25	Oct	22	1⅞	8	¼
26⅞	25	Nov	30	2⅜	...	...
BellAtl	50	Oct	200	13½	...	...
63⅜	55	Oct	204	8⅜	...	...
63⅜	60	Oct	32	3½	...	...
63⅜	60	Jan	268	4⅛	...	...
63⅜	65	Jan	26	1½	4	4⅛
63⅜	65	Apr	214	2⅜	...	...
BellSo	55	Oct	37	5⅞	...	...
61	60	Oct	97	1 3/16	...	...
61	60	Jan	65	2½	4	2⅝
61	60	Apr	27	3⅛	...	...
61	65	Apr	30	1 3/16	...	...
Belmac	5	Jan	111	5/16	20	2⅛
Benfcl	70	Oct	90	6⅝	...	...
BestBuy	35	Nov	21	16	...	...
49¾	35	Dec	60	19⅛	...	...
49¾	45	Oct	36	5⅝	41	⅞
49¾	45	Mar	68	10	...	...
49¾	50	Oct	230	2½	130	2¾
49¾	55	Oct	237	¾	75	6
49¾	55	Dec	31	4	...	...
49¾	60	Oct	50	5/16	...	...
BestBy o	30	Dec	70	24	...	...
Beth S	15	Oct	50	¼	196	1 1/16

Option/Strike		Exp.	-Call- Vol.	-Call- Last	-Put- Vol.	-Put- Last
49⅜	50	Nov	1438	4	167	4⅛
49⅜	50	Jan	61	5¾	36	6⅛
49⅜	55	Oct	415	7/16	61	5½
49⅜	55	Nov	235	1⅞	...	...
49⅜	55	Jan	46	3⅞	2	9⅛
49⅜	60	Jan	73	2 3/16	...	...
Citicp	30	Oct	150	8¼	...	...
38⅜	30	Jan	17	9	40	¼
38⅜	35	Oct	154	3½	1248	⅛
38⅜	35	Nov	80	4	...	...
38⅜	35	Jan	100	4¾	57	1
38⅜	40	Oct	51	5/16	41	2
38⅜	40	Nov	1337	1	23	2½
38⅜	40	Jan	209	1⅞	20	2⅞
38⅜	40	Apr	44	2⅞	...	...
Clorox	50	Apr	...	...	50	2
Clthtm	7½	Dec	30	1 9/16	...	...
CmpAsc	30	Oct	74	3	...	...
33⅛	35	Jan	151	2¼	...	...
CmpUSA	22½	Feb	...	...	40	2⅛
27⅛	25	Oct	125	3	65	11/16
27⅛	25	Nov	108	3¾	15	1⅞
27⅛	30	Oct	176	5/16	286	3⅜
27⅛	30	Nov	88	1⅜	...	...
27⅛	30	Feb	43	2⅝	...	...
27⅛	35	Oct	...	...	40	8
CmprsL	12½	Jan	120	3⅛	...	...
Cmpuwr	22½	Nov	251	15/16	...	...
CnStor	17½	Oct	...	...	30	⅛
19⅞	20	Oct	80	½	...	...
19⅞	20	Jan	30	1⅝	...	...
Cnseco	45	Nov	10	30¼	50	1/16
74⅝	50	Feb	25	25¾	...	...
74⅝	65	Oct	37	10⅜	...	...

Option/Strike		Exp.	-Call- Vol.	-Call- Last	-Put- Vol.	-Put- Last
22½	17½	Oct	71	4¾	...	...
22½	17½	Jan	45	5⅜	...	...
22½	20	Oct	65	2½	8	15/16
22½	20	Jan	296	4⅜	...	...
22½	22½	Oct	165	⅞	40	1¾
22½	22½	Jan	39	3⅛	...	...
22½	25	Oct	44	¼	...	...
22½	25	Nov	41	1¼	...	...
22½	25	Jan	80	2⅛	...	...
Exbyte	10	Nov	40	1 5/16	...	...
Exxon	60	Oct	44	6¼	...	...
66¼	65	Oct	170	1 9/16	25	5/16
66¼	65	Nov	411	13/16	...	...
66¼	65	Jan	94	2¾	...	...
66¼	70	Jan	83	13/16	...	...
66¼	70	Apr	33	1 5/16	...	...
F N M	75	Oct	...	...	26	7/16
79⅝	75	Dec	...	...	130	1⅞
79⅝	80	Nov	35	2⅝	...	...
79⅝	80	Dec	90	3½	31	3¾
79⅝	85	Oct	45	3/16	3	5⅜
79⅝	85	Dec	24	1½	...	...
FHLB	45	Jan	...	...	30	½
51	50	Oct	90	1½	...	...
51	50	Nov	20	2¾	140	¾
51	55	Jan	73	1	...	...
FIntste	65	Oct	75	2⅞	...	...
67¼	70	Nov	55	1⅜	...	...
FM Cop	15	Mar	...	...	29	13/16
FUnion	50	Oct	...	...	50	2¾
FedDSt	20	Nov	20	¾	...	...
FedExp	60	Oct	25	2⅜	5	1
62	60	Jan	20	6⅛	...	...
62	65	Oct	40	5/16	6	3
FishPr	30	Oct	20	5⅜	...	...
35¼	30	Nov	25	5⅜	...	...
35¼	30	Dec	...	...	190	⅜
35¼	35	Oct	40	¾	...	...
Fldcrs	20	Nov	30	4⅜	...	...
24	25	Mar	135	2⅛	...	...
FleetC	40	Nov	...	...	60	2½
41⅜	45	Oct	135	½	...	...
41⅜	45	Feb	45	4⅛	...	...
FleetF	35	Oct	57	⅝	...	...
34⅞	35	Nov	40	1½	...	...
34⅞	35	Jan	224	2⅜	...	...
34⅞	40	Oct	50	1/16	...	...
Fleetw	25	Feb	105	1½	...	...
Flemng	35	Oct	50	3/16	...	...
33⅛	35	Nov	20	½	...	...
Ford	50	Dec	26	7	...	...
56½	55	Oct	32	1¾	246	9/16
56½	55	Nov	103	2⅞	5	2
56½	55	Dec	14	3⅜	42	2¼
56½	55	Mar	...	...	25	3½
56½	60	Oct	78	3/16	50	3¾
56½	60	Nov	32	¾	...	...
56½	60	Dec	118	1¼	...	...
FounHl	22½	Oct	10	1½	50	⅝
22⅝	22½	Feb	100	3½	...	...
22⅝	25	Oct	546	3/16	500	2⅛
FrMcRP	17½	Mar	108	2¾	...	...
19¾	20	Dec	30	11/16	...	...
FtAmB	45	Feb	32	1	...	...
FtPcNt	15	Nov	50	3½	...	...
17	15	Apr	...	...	50	2⅞
17	17½	Oct	27	1	...	...
17	17½	Apr	25	3¾	...	...
G M	35	Dec	60	8	31	7/16

Option/Strike		Exp.	-Call- Vol.	-Call- Last	-Put- Vol.	-Put- Last
Imunex	17½	Oct	25	1	...	...
Imungn	7½	Oct	24	¾	...	...
8	7½	Dec	80	1⅛	...	...
In Flv	105	Nov	123	1⅞	...	...
In Pap	55	Oct	100	6½	...	...
60½	55	Jan	...	...	40	15/16
60½	60	Oct	54	1⅞	...	...
60½	60	Nov	52	2 9/16	10	1⅞
60½	60	Jan	23	3⅜	4	2¾
60½	65	Oct	493	¼	42	3⅞
60½	65	Nov	23	½	...	...
60½	65	Jan	148	1 9/16	...	...
Inco	20	Apr	...	...	200	3½
Infrmx	15	Nov	100	9	...	...
23¾	20	Nov	...	...	40	⅞
23¾	22½	Oct	78	1⅝	18	⅝
23¾	22½	Nov	512	13/16	101	13/16
23¾	25	Nov	179	1¾	25	3¼
23¾	27½	Nov	40	15/16	...	...
IngRnd	40	Oct	35	¼	...	...
Inland	25	Mar	...	...	30	1¼
IntCoin	17½	Jan	150	1 5/16	...	...
IntMur	5	Nov	20	1¾	...	...
Intel	45	Oct	26	26⅜	...	...
72¾	45	Jan	...	...	28	3/16
72¾	55	Oct	65	18	4	1/16
72¾	60	Oct	177	13¼	20	1/16
72¾	60	Jan	51	14⅜	34	1¼
72¾	62½	Oct	57	10¾	...	...
72¾	65	Oct	1278	8¼	421	5/16
72¾	65	Nov	34	9½	469	1¼
72¾	65	Jan	103	11⅛	5	2⅝
72¾	65	Apr	27	12¼	15	3¾
72¾	70	Oct	1723	4⅜	2356	1¼
72¾	70	Nov	790	6⅛	271	2⅞
72¾	70	Jan	125	7½	32	4¼
72¾	70	Apr	48	10	...	...
72¾	75	Oct	4724	1 9/16	367	3⅝
72¾	75	Nov	966	3½	25	4⅞
72¾	75	Jan	1227	5⅜	22	6¾
72¾	75	Apr	246	7¾	...	...
72¾	80	Oct	222	7/16	34	7⅛
72¾	80	Nov	603	1¾	1	8⅞
72¾	80	Jan	126	3⅝	...	...
Intel o	15	Dec	20	8	...	...
23¼	20	Nov	40	3⅝	...	...
23¼	20	Dec	26	3⅝	...	...
23¼	20	Mar	20	4½	...	...
23¼	22½	Oct	25	1¼	50	5/16
23¼	22½	Nov	113	2	20	1
Intelcm	20	Oct	30	1	3	2¼
19⅛	22½	Nov	25	1	...	...
IntgDv	10	Nov	25	8	...	...
18½	15	Oct	50	3¼	...	...
18½	17½	Oct	398	1⅜	20	9/16
18½	17½	Nov	428	2 5/16	...	...
18½	20	Nov	47	1¼	...	...
IntgHS	22½	Oct	280	2⅜	250	⅜
24⅝	25	Oct	35	1	95	1⅝
24⅝	25	Nov	50	2⅛	...	...
24⅝	30	Oct	...	...	75	5
Intgph	10	Oct	20	⅝	...	...
IntrDig	7½	Oct	30	3/16	...	...
6⅜	7½	Dec	70	½	...	...
6⅜	7½	Mar	50	15/16	...	...
IvaxCp	22½	Dec	25	4¼	...	...
26	25	Oct	26	1⅝	10	½
26	30	Nov	50	½	...	...
26	30	Mar	411	13/16	...	...

Option/Strike		Exp.	-Call- Vol.	-Call- Last	-Put- Vol.	-Put- Last
52¼	55	Jan	797	6⅛	217	8⅛
52¼	55	Apr	30	8½	...	...
52¼	60	Oct	389	½	137	8⅛
52¼	60	Nov	511	2⅛	11	9
52¼	60	Jan	65	4⅜	...	...
52¼	60	Apr	26	6½	1	12⅝
52¼	65	Oct	108	¼	...	...
52¼	65	Nov	33	1¼	...	...
52¼	65	Jan	113	3⅛	...	...
52¼	65	Apr	51	5⅜	...	...
Micsft	75	Nov	...	...	220	1⅜
82	80	Nov	16	5¾	128	3
82	85	Nov	235	3	10	5
82	90	Nov	75	1⅜	2	8½
82	95	Jan	84	2	...	...
Midlan	22½	Oct	500	5	...	...
27½	25	Oct	50	2⅝	...	...
27½	30	Jan	23	1 9/16	...	...
Mirage	50	Oct	45	9¾	85	1/16
58¾	50	Nov	56	10	...	...
58¾	55	Oct	100	5¼	...	...
58¾	55	Nov	144	6	23	1¾
58¾	60	Oct	124	1⅜	10	2
58¾	60	Nov	95	3¼	2	4½
Mobil	75	Oct	50	7¼	...	...
81¾	75	Nov	23	7⅜	...	...
81¾	80	Oct	47	2½	75	½
81¾	80	Nov	6	3½	44	1½
81¾	85	Oct	35	¼	...	...
81¾	85	Nov	112	1⅛	...	...
MolBio	25	Oct	31	1½	...	...
26	25	Nov	30	2½	...	...
26	25	Jan	45	3⅞	...	...
Molex o	35	Nov	144	2 9/16	144	1⅛
Monsan	60	Oct	67	6	3	1/16
65¾	60	Jan	36	6½	...	...
65¾	65	Oct	20	1 7/16	...	...
65¾	65	Jan	333	3⅝	...	...
65¾	65	Apr	220	4⅝	220	3¾
Morton	85	Oct	...	...	40	5/16
89⅞	90	Nov	48	2¾	...	...
Motrla	80	Oct	...	...	20	1/16
100	90	Oct	41	10⅜	60	¼
100	90	Nov	...	...	513	1¼
100	95	Oct	104	6¼	246	1
100	95	Nov	6	8	133	2½
100	100	Oct	11002	15/16	6032	13/16
100	100	Nov	243	5	10	4¾
100	100	Jan	182	7⅜	12	7
100	105	Oct	1061	1 3/16	177	6¼
100	105	Nov	270	3	4	7½
100	105	Jan	77	5⅛	...	...
100	110	Oct	205	⅜	5	10⅛
100	110	Nov	233	1⅝	2	10¾
100	110	Jan	52	3⅝	...	...
100	115	Nov	120	13/16	...	...
100	115	Jan	30	2¼	...	...
Mylan	20	Oct	30	9½	...	...
29¾	25	Oct	28	5	...	...
29¾	25	Nov	10	5⅝	190	9/16
29¾	25	Jan	31	6⅛	20	1⅛
29¾	30	Oct	483	1	70	1½
29¾	30	Nov	177	2 3/16	30	2¼
29¾	30	Jan	62	3⅛	...	...
29¾	35	Oct	100	¼	...	...
29¾	35	Jan	43	1½	...	...
N Semi	17½	Oct	511	2 7/16	...	...
20	17½	Nov	33	3⅛	...	...
20	20	Oct	220	11/16	116	½
20	20	Nov	110	1⅝	10	1¼

The "MOST ACTIVE CONTRACTS" section of Exhibit 1–1 presents the data for the most actively traded contracts across all exchanges. Note that this section's format differs from that used on the rest of the page. In the "MOST ACTIVE CONTRACTS" section column one provides the name of the underlying stock, column two supplies the maturity month, and column three provides the striking price for the option. If the option is a call option, then column four is blank. If the fourth column shows a "p," then the option is a put option. The fifth column furnishes the option's trading volume for the prior day. Observe that the volume ranges from 1,339 Micron Technology October 55 call option contracts to 7,027 Paramount Communications October 85 put options. Column six denotes the exchange where the option is listed. Columns seven, eight, and nine supply price information from the previous trading day. The seventh column gives the option's closing price for the day. Column eight shows the option's change in price from one day's closing to the next. The ninth column reports the underlying stock's prior day's closing price in its primary market. The final column presents the total open interest on all exchanges for each option. Open interest differs from volume in that open interest represents the number of outstanding positions in that particular series, while volume is the number of option contracts in the series that are exchanged between buyers and sellers. Since some options are listed on multiple exchanges the value in the tenth column represents the total number of open positions on all exchanges that list the option.

The second section of the quotation page provides data for all the listed options that were traded on the previous day. In this format, column one provides the name of the underlying stock and its closing price for that day. Column two supplies the striking price, and column three provides the maturity months for the options. The call options' trading volume is provided in the fourth column, and the fifth column supplies the call options' prior day's closing prices. Note that the data for the AMD November 30 call option are provided in this section and in the prior section. This is true for all of the most actively traded contracts. Column six denotes the put option trading volume, and the seventh column presents the put option's closing price information from the previous trading day. If there are no entries in a particular column, then it means no options were traded on the previous day. For example, no trading occurred in the Exxon January 65 and 70 put options on October 1.

It is important to realize that the option prices are expressed on a per share basis, but that each option controls one hundred shares. Thus, if one purchased a General Motors call option which has a striking price of 45 and a December expiration, then a premium of $156.26, or 1 9/16 points, is paid by the call buyer for the right to purchase one hundred shares of General Motors common stock, on or before the December expiration date, for a price of $45 per share. Conversely, the call option seller, or writer, collects a $156.25 premium and incurs the obligation to deliver one hundred shares of General Motors common stock at a price of $45 per share if the call option is exercised.

Exhibit 1–2 contains information regarding LEAPS and is interpreted in exactly the same manner as the second section of the quotation page in Exhibit 1–1.

Exhibit 1–2
WSJ Price Quotes for LEAPS 10/4/93

LEAPS — LONG TERM OPTIONS

Option/Stock	Strike	Exp.	Call Vol.	Call Last	Put Vol.	Put Last
ABarck	20	Jan 95	141	6⅛	...	...
22⅛	30	Jan 95	49	2¼	...	...
AMD	25	Jan 95	52	6½	...	...
AT&T	50	Jan 96	50	13¾	...	...
59	55	Jan 96	...	...	195	4⅛
59	60	Jan 96	15	7¾	...	...
59	65	Jan 95	12	3½	...	...
59	70	Jan 96	100	4	...	...
AbtLab	25	Jan 95	...	...	12	2
Alza	20	Jan 96	50	7¾	...	...
AmExp	20	Jan 95	500	15⅝	...	...
35⅝	30	Jan 95	23	7⅝	...	...
Amgen	30	Jan 95	11	14	...	...
39⅞	45	Jan 95	30	5¾	...	...
39⅞	55	Jan 95	13	2¾	...	...
Anheus	40	Jan 95	53	7⅞	...	...
AppleC	20	Jan 95	9	6⅝	13	3¼
22¾	20	Jan 96	44	7⅛	75	3¾
22¾	30	Jan 95	59	2⅞	...	...
22¾	30	Jan 96	31	4¼	22	10⅝
22¾	40	Jan 95	53	1⅜	14	17⅞
22¾	60	Jan 95	50	5/16	2	37⅝
22¾	60	Jan 96	30	¾	3	37¼
BankAm	55	Jan 96	11	4⅛	...	...
BellSo	50	Jan 95	240	11	...	...
BlockE	20	Jan 96	11	11	...	...
Boeing	30	Jan 95	118	10	10	¾
38¾	40	Jan 95	25	4	...	...
38¾	50	Jan 95	37	1¼	...	...
BerInt	20	Jan 96	36	4¼	...	...
BrMySq	50	Jan 96	54	10	5	4⅞
56	60	Jan 95	...	...	19	7¾
56	60	Jan 96	1	6	11	9⅝
ChmBnk	40	Jan 95	22	8¼	...	...
Chrysl	30	Jan 95	679	20¼	...	...
48⅞	40	Jan 96	14	15⅞	...	...
Chubb	60	Jan 95	...	...	20	¾
Cisco	50	Jan 95	24	12½	...	...
Citicp	20	Jan 95	20	18¾	...	...
38⅜	22½	Jan 96	...	...	42	15/16
38⅜	30	Jan 95	25	11	10	1½
38⅜	35	Jan 95	23	7½	10	3
38⅜	40	Jan 95	28	5	...	...
CocaCl	40	Jan 95	12	5⅞	257	3⅛
42	40	Jan 96	...	...	250	4⅝
42	50	Jan 96	50	3¾	15	9¼
ConrPr	10	Jan 95	10	2¾	25	2
10	15	Jan 95	15	1¼	...	...
Disney	30	Jan 95	27	10⅝	6	1¾
37⅞	50	Jan 95	131	1⅞	...	...
DuPont	55	Jan 95	85	1¾	...	...
Exxon	80	Jan 95	145	15/16	...	...
FedNM	70	Jan 95	20	15⅛	...	...
FordM	55	Jan 95	17	7⅝	5	6
GTE	30	Jan 96	112	8⅛	...	...
Glaxo	15	Jan 95	120	5¼	40	11/16
19	20	Jan 95	57	2¾	20	3⅝
19	25	Jan 95	133	1¼	186	6⅞
19	35	Jan 95	101	5/16	...	...
GnMotr	25	Jan 95	29	18	86	½
42½	30	Jan 95	106	14⅝	60	1⅜
42½	40	Jan 95	1193	8	448	4⅝
42½	40	Jan 96	18	10⅛	...	...
42½	45	Jan 96	12	8	...	...
42½	50	Jan 95	670	3⅞	5	10⅝
42½	50	Jan 96	512	6	1	11½
HmeD e	27½	Jan 95	30	14	...	...
Homstk	10	Jan 95	...	...	12	9/16
15.00	15	Jan 95	40	4⅝	...	...
IBM	40	Jan 96	106	9¾	76	4⅝
43⅞	45	Jan 95	191	6	10	6½
43⅞	55	Jan 95	113	2 13/16	11	12¾
43⅞	60	Jan 96	60	3⅝	...	...
43⅞	70	Jan 95	56	11/16	...	...
43⅞	85	Jan 95	73	5/16	...	...
IntGme	22½	Jan 95	...	...	20	11/16
IntPap	60	Jan 95	...	...	15	5¼
60½	60	Jan 96	...	...	15	6¼
Intel	42½	Jan 95	24	32½	...	...
72¾	50	Jan 95	45	27⅝	...	...
72¾	65	Jan 95	14	17⅝	...	...
72¾	65	Jan 96	28	22	...	...
72¾	72½	Jan 95	43	13¾	...	...
72¾	80	Jan 95	120	9⅞	...	...
72¾	80	Jan 96	162	14½	...	...
JohnJn	35	Jan 95	60	7	25	2¼
39⅛	40	Jan 95	50	4½	2	4¾
MMM	110	Jan 96	...	...	30	15⅛
Marriot	20	Jan 95	11	12⅝	11	½
MerLyn	100	Jan 95	150	14½	...	...
Merck	30	Jan 95	15	4¾	...	...
30⅞	30	Jan 96	101	6⅝	15	4½
30⅞	40	Jan 95	14	1 11/16	15	10
Micsft	80	Jan 96	12	20	...	...
Motorla	100	Jan 95	500	16	2	12⅛
100	120	Jan 96	500	14⅛	...	...
NatnsBk	60	Jan 95	11	3⅛	20	10⅝
Novell	15	Jan 96	25	8	...	...
18¼	25	Jan 96	28	3⅞	...	...
PacTel	35	Jan 96	...	...	51	13/16
54⅝	45	Jan 95	...	...	25	1¼
54⅝	45	Jan 96	...	...	25	2¼
PerCom	60	Jan 96	...	...	30	2 7/16
77⅞	65	Jan 95	...	...	20	3⅝
77⅞	65	Jan 96	...	...	30	3⅞
PepsiC	30	Jan 95	16	10⅝	...	...
38¾	35	Jan 95	40	7¼	...	...
38¾	40	Jan 95	50	4⅛	...	...
Pfizer	100	Jan 95	21	½	...	...
PhilMr	40	Jan 95	156	8	36	3
46	40	Jan 96	50	9¼	10	4⅛
46	50	Jan 95	241	3¼	...	...
46	50	Jan 96	23	5⅛	5	9⅛
46	60	Jan 95	399	1¼	...	...
46	80	Jan 95	10	¼	...	...
46	100	Jan 95	70	⅛	...	...
PlacrD	10	Jan 95	20	9⅝	...	...
RJR Nb	5	Jan 95	20	13/16	...	...
4½	5	Jan 95	15	13/16	10	15/16
4½	7½	Jan 95	119	5/16	12	3⅛
Sears	45	Jan 95	2	12	150	2¾
54⅞	55	Jan 95	15	6⅝	...	...
Sears o	65	Jan 95	50	12½	...	...
StorTch	25	Jan 95	31	8½	3	5¼
27⅛	30	Jan 95	30	6⅝	...	...
27⅛	40	Jan 95	14	4⅛	...	...
SunMic	35	Jan 95	14	1	...	...
Syntex	25	Jan 95	36	1	15	8¾
TelMex	45	Jan 95	20	10	...	...
50⅝	55	Jan 95	1000	5½	...	...
50⅝	55	Jan 95	15	5½	...	...
50⅝	60	Jan 95	20	3¾	...	...
Texaco	50	Jan 95	...	...	14	¾
TritEn	35	Jan 96	4	7	200	7
UCarb	15	Jan 95	15	4⅞	...	...
US Surg	20	Jan 95	...	...	11	3½
20⅞	25	Jan 95	34	3½	...	...
20⅞	30	Jan 95	3	2¼	20	10⅛
20⅞	45	Jan 95	125	½	...	...
UnCarb	17½	Jan 96	20	4⅛	20	2
Unisys	10	Jan 96	...	...	100	1⅜
12⅛	12½	Jan 96	...	...	50	2⅜
12⅛	15	Jan 95	38	1⅜	...	...
WMX Tc	25	Jan 96	10	8⅝	25	2⅛
30	30	Jan 95	51	4	15	3¼
WalMart	32½	Jan 95	10	1¼	...	...
WalMrt	30	Jan 96	14	3⅝	...	...
WellsF	100	Jan 95	51	35⅝	20	5
WstgEl	15	Jan 95	57	1 9/16	...	...
13⅛	17½	Jan 95	12	1	...	...

VOLUME & OPEN INTEREST SUMMARIES

AMERICAN	Call Vol:	6,448	Open Int:	489,141
	Put Vol:	913	Open Int:	306,602
CHICAGO BOARD	Call Vol:	5,651	Open Int:	516,889
	Put Vol:	3,205	Open Int:	611,285
PHILADELPHIA	Call Vol:	285	Open Int:	206,086
	Put Vol:	113	Open Int:	98,968
PACIFIC	Call Vol:	229	Open Int:	22,166
	Put Vol:	151	Open Int:	11,490
NEW YORK	Call Vol:	2	Open Int:	32,263
	Put Vol:	35	Open Int:	12,512
TOTAL	Call Vol:	12,615	Open Int:	1,266,985
	Put Vol:	4,417	Open Int:	1,040,857

Mechanics of Options Trading

THE CLEARING PROCESS So far, nothing specific has been said about trading exchange-listed options. To understand the market mechanics, one must have a grasp of how the Options Clearing Corporation (OCC) relates to the option market participants. The OCC guarantees the performance of all equity option contracts that are traded on all of the federally designated exchanges. Since there must be a buyer for each option sold, all option purchases and sales must match at the end of the day. The OCC facilitates this daily matching and in the process becomes the opposite party to all trades. This ability of the OCC to become the writer for every buyer, and buyer for every writer means that investors do not have to worry about contract performance or about locating someone to take an offsetting position. Thus, individual investors easily can create or liquidate positions unilaterally. While the ultimate guarantor of the option contract is the OCC, the investor has virtually no direct contact with the Clearing Corporation. Instead, it is the investor's brokerage house that must clear all trades through a member of the Options Clearing Corporation. Exhibit 1–3 illustrates the clearing process structure.

Exhibit 1–3 Clearing Process Structure

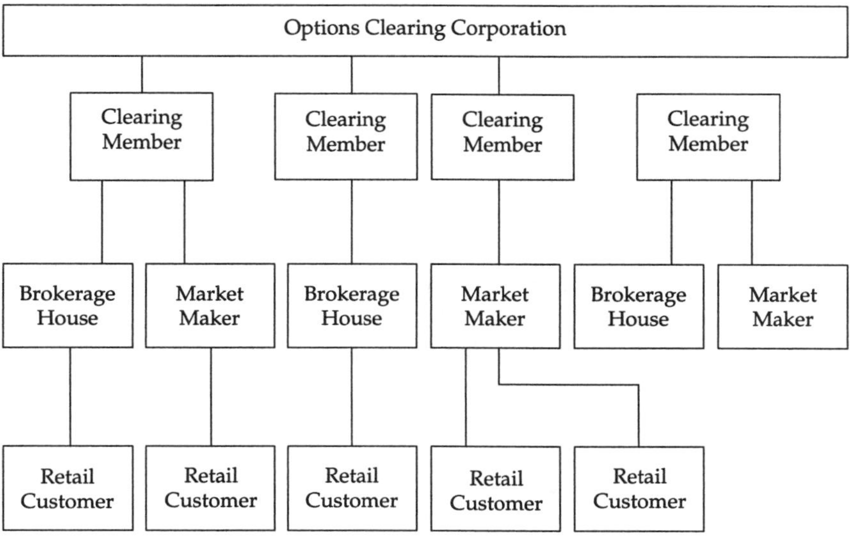

THE ORDER PROCESS On the floor of the Chicago Board Options Exchange (CBOE) there are three types of brokers that can execute trades: floor brokers, market makers, and order book officials. *Floor brokers* usually are salaried employees of brokerage houses and execute orders for public customers. *Market makers* trade for their own accounts and are prohibited from executing orders on behalf of public customers. *Order book officials* are employees of the Chicago Board Options Exchange and maintain a book of unfilled limit orders. Bid and Ask price information for the limit orders that are closest to the current market quote is constantly made available by the order book official to the floor brokers and market makers. If there appears to be little chance of a limit order being executed, then a floor broker may elect to place the order with the order book official. Once in the book, the exchange guarantees that when the market reaches the order's limit, the order will be executed based on its price and time of entry into the book.

When the investor places an option order with a brokerage house, certain information is required. The investor must specify whether a put or a call is to be bought or sold; the name of the underlying stock; the striking price; the expiration month; the type of order, market or limit; and whether or not it is an opening or closing transaction.

Basically, there are two types of orders, market and limit. A *market order* is an order to either buy or sell the option at the current market price, and it is executed immediately. A *limit order* is an order to buy or sell an option at a specified price or better. It is executed only if the market reaches the specified limit. However, if the market moves rapidly through the limit, then it may not be possible to transact at the specified price. Unless specified otherwise, all orders are *day orders,* i.e. good until the end of the trading day. However, the investor can issue instructions that the order remain in effect until cancelled. Hence the name *good till cancelled* (GTC). If an order is used to establish an initial position that increases the number of outstanding options, or open interest, in the market, then the order is classified as an *opening transaction.* Conversely, an order that cancels an existing position and reduces the number of outstanding options is known as a *closing transaction.*

After the order has been placed with the brokerage house it is transmitted to the exchange by telephone. A phone clerk then time stamps the order and gives it to a runner. The runner then delivers the order to the floor broker that the brokerage house uses for trading. If the order is a market order, then it will be executed immediately at the prevailing market price. The floor broker may transact with another floor broker, a market maker, or with the order book official. Once the trade has been completed the two brokers verify the transaction, then a copy of the verification is given to the runner who returns it to the phone clerk. The phone clerk time stamps the order and notifies the brokerage house. The brokerage house then notifies the investor about the terms of the trade and its completion. The typical elapsed time between order placement and confirmation by the brokerage house is ten minutes.

At this point, full payment for the option is due on the next business day, and the investor can expect written confirmation of the order from the brokerage house within five days. Exhibit 1–4 provides a schematic for the order process.

Exhibit 1–4 Order Process

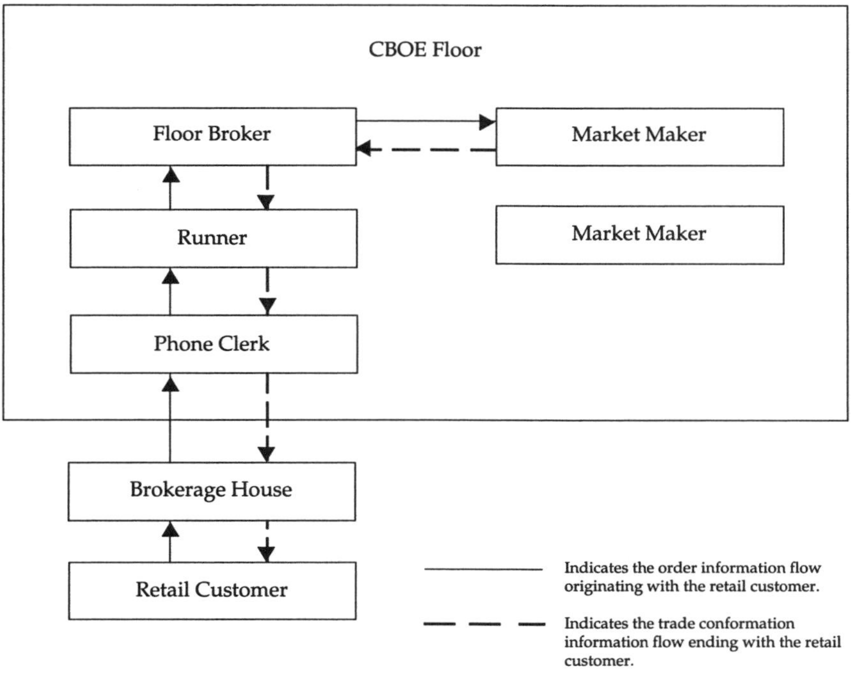

THE EXERCISE PROCESS When an option holder decides to exercise, the brokerage house is notified first. The brokerage house then uses its clearing member to inform the OCC. The OCC then randomly selects and notifies a clearing member, who has an open write position, of the assignment. If call options are being exercised then the assigned clearing member must deliver 100 shares of the underlying stock at the striking price for each option exercised, to the clearing member who is exercising the calls. For put options, the assigned clearing member must accept 100 shares of the underlying stock at the striking price for each option being exercised by the clearing member who initiated the process. Upon delivering shares to satisfy the call option's exercise, or receiving shares to satisfy the put option's exercise, the assigned clearing member will either deliver to, or receive shares from, one of its customers who is short a put or a call.

An investor may choose to exercise an equity option at any point in time during the option's life. However, notification of exercise must be given prior to 4:30 P.M. Central Time, on the third Friday of the option's expiration month. The reasons for this are twofold. First, the option's last trading day is the third Friday of the expiration month because the option expires on the following day, Saturday, at 10:59 A.M. Central Time. Second, the exchanges have imposed a notification deadline of 4:30 P.M. Central Time, on the option's last trading day. This deadline is only 90 minutes after trading options ceases on all exchanges at 3:00 P.M. Central Time.

LIMITS AND MARGIN REQUIREMENTS In addition to the trading and notification deadlines, the investor should be aware of position limits, exercise limits, and general margin requirements. The position and exercise limits are imposed to prevent manipulation of the option market. Margins are required to help insure contract performance.

A *position limit* requires that an investor, or group of investors, cannot own or have written more than a specified number of options that constitutes the same side of the market. One is considered to be on the same side of the market if one simultaneously writes calls and buys puts, or if one simultaneously buys calls and writes puts. In the first situation shares will be delivered if exercise of both puts and calls occurs. In the second case, shares will be accumulated from the exercise of both the puts and calls. Usually, *exercise limits* match position limits and can range from 3,000 to 8,000 contracts, depending on the stock's price and trading volume. Specific position and exercise limits can be obtained from the exchange on which the option is traded.

Margin requirements for options are subject to change and wide variation among brokerage houses. However, in general, option buyers must pay the full amount within one day of purchase. The reason is that the option itself is a leveraged instrument. For the price of an equity option, the investor can control 100 shares of the underlying stock. Option writers who do not own the underlying stock are required to deposit an amount equal to 15 percent of the current market value of the stock plus the entire call or put premium received. This margin may be posted in Treasury bills or cash. For writers who own the underlying shares the margins are much less, and can be posted in cash, Treasury bills, or shares of stock. Usually it is unwise to post a cash margin since one foregoes interest which is not lost if Treasury bills are used.

Some Investment Terminology

In the following chapters, certain terms which have unique meanings within the investment industry will be used to describe various option strategies. To achieve the greatest possible level of understanding of the strategies, one should be familiar with these terms.

MARKET FORECASTS The best starting point is the investor's outlook for market performance. If one is positive and optimistic about the markets in general, then one is considered *bullish.* A pessimistic investor is said to be *bearish,* while one who thinks that markets will exhibit very little movement either way is considered to be *neutral.* Bullish investors anticipate rising markets, bearish investors expect falling markets, and neutral investors think that markets will be flat.

Investors formulate their market forecasts in a variety of ways. However, the two most common methods of evaluating market conditions are fundamental analysis and technical analysis.

An investor who relies on *fundamental analysis* uses the relationships exhibited by basic economic, industry, and individual firm variables to assess the condition of the financial markets, specific industries, or of individual firms. For example, if an investor thinks that interest rates will increase because of rising inflation, and that a recession is likely, then the investor probably will be bearish on both the stock and bond markets.

An investor uses *technical analysis* if he or she relies on market-related data such as past prices, trading volume, the number of advancing shares, or short-selling activity to form an opinion about the markets in general, a specific industry, or a specific firm. The technician's goal is to discover the existence of price trends, and then to take positions that are designed to profit from these trends. Suppose an investor has found a stock that appears to have an upward price trend. Based on this trend, the investor may turn bullish and purchase the stock. The basic difference between technical and fundamental analysis is that pure technical analysis does not consider basic economic relationships; it relies solely on internal market data. On the other hand, fundamental analysis rejects isolated market data and focuses on the relationship of the basic underlying factors that determine a security's value.

SHORT SELLING Earlier in this chapter investors were described as being either option sellers or option buyers. It is less cumbersome and more consistent with industry practice to characterize an investor who has purchased an asset as being *long* the asset, and to characterize the seller of the asset as being *short* the asset. Thus, an investor who is bullish and who has purchased stock is long the stock, and an investor who has purchased an option is long the option. Conversely an option writer is considered short the option. The short stock position is rather complex and requires a detailed explanation.

Being *short stock* implies that the investor has sold stock. However, to be precise, this short position has been attained through a short sale. For a short sale to occur, three parties are needed: the stock's short seller, the stock's purchaser, and a lender of the shares to be sold short. The share lender is required because the short seller does not own the stock that is being sold.

The process begins with a bearish investor who believes that the stock's price is going to drop. In order to capture as much of the stock's current values as possible, the investor will short sell shares of the stock to the purchaser. At this point the seller has five business days to deliver the shares, while the stock purchaser has five business days to pay for the shares. To satisfy the delivery requirement the short seller will borrow shares from the share lender and deliver them to the share buyer. Now the share buyer is of no further consequence. Indeed, the share buyer probably neither knows nor cares that the shares were purchased from a short seller.

During the time period that the shares have been lent, the share lender demands compensation from the short seller in the form of interest. Furthermore, the short seller is required to pay all dividends to which the share lender is entitled. Finally, the share lender, which is usually a brokerage house, requires the short seller to deposit a portion of the sale proceeds. Thus, the short seller does not have full use of the sale proceeds and also must pay the share lender interest.

If the stock drops as anticipated, then the short seller will purchase enough shares in the market to close out the short position by replenishing the share lender's portfolio. The short seller profits by purchasing stock at a market price that is lower than the sale price, and low enough to cover all costs associated with the short sale transaction. If the stock rises, then the short seller will lose. The share lender will demand that the shares be replenished and the short seller has no choice but to purchase the stock at a market price that is higher than the sale price. If the short seller cannot fund the stock purchase, then the share lender, i.e., the brokerage house, has a legal right to demand that the short seller liquidate positions in other assets, such as stocks and bonds, in order to cover the short position. Obviously short selling is a very risky proposition since the potential for unlimited loss is quite high.

LEVERAGE The term *leverage* means that an investor can assume a position in a security by investing less than the full amount of the security's face value. Since a single option controls one hundred shares of stock, and enables the investor to benefit from price changes in the underlying security at a fraction of the security's cost, options are leveraged instruments. When an investor creates a highly leveraged position there is great potential for profit. However, like short selling, there is also the risk of a large loss. It is true that leverage magnifies an investor's return, but it is also true that leverage magnifies losses.

CAPITAL GAINS AND LOSSES The concepts of gains and losses must be understood within the context of capital assets, i.e., equities and their associated options. *Capital gains* are the gains resulting from changing values of stocks and options, while any losses that are incurred due to changing stock and option values are termed *capital losses*. Precise computation of these capital gains and losses depends upon the asset's cost basis. In general, the cost basis of any asset is the price for the asset plus all transaction costs that are paid at the time of purchase. This cost basis is used to determine the investor's capital gain or loss when the position is liquidated.

Conclusion

It is appropriate to conclude this chapter with two caveats. First, one should be aware that brokerage commissions have an extremely wide range within the industry. For this reason commissions will be ignored throughout the remainder of this book in both the discussion and examples. Second, before an investor undertakes any option strategy, a competent tax counselor should be consulted.

Chapter Two

THE PROPERTIES OF OPTION PRICES

Option Pricing Factors

A *stock option* is the right to buy or sell shares of stock on or before a specific date for a specific price known as the *exercise* or *striking price.* Given this definition, it follows that option prices are intimately related to: the underlying stock's price, the underlying stock's dividends, the volatility of the underlying stock's price changes, the time until the option matures, the option's exercise price, and interest rates. This chapter concentrates on the relationships of option prices to these six underlying factors.

Components of Option Prices

INTRINSIC VALUE Before one can comprehend fully the behavior of option prices, it is necessary to understand the concepts of intrinsic value, in-the-money options, at-the-money options, out-of-the-money options, and parity. These terms are most easily explained by using an approach that moves backward from an option's maturity to the present time.

Recall that a call option grants the owner the right, not the obligation, to buy shares of the underlying stock. Thus, at maturity a call option will be worth nothing or the difference between the current price of the underlying stock and the option's exercise price. This difference is known as the call option's *intrinsic value.* No other values are possible since no time remains in the call option's life. If the stock price is less than the exercise price, then a rational investor who owns the call option will not exercise the option because the underlying stock can be purchased in the open market at a price lower than the option's exercise price. Thus, the right to call shares at the exercise price is worthless, and the call option has no intrinsic value. However, if the underlying stock's price is greater than the option's exercise price, then the call option has intrinsic value and the option's owner can exercise the option and purchase shares of the underlying stock for the exercise price. At this point the investor can keep the shares or sell them for their current market price, which is greater than the exercise price. In this case, the right to call shares for the exercise price is worth the difference between the price of the underlying stock and the option's exercise price, or the call option's intrinsic value.

It is quite obvious that the call option's intrinsic value is determined by the relationship between the price of the underlying stock and the option's exercise price. If the price of the underlying stock is greater than the option's exercise price, then the call option has intrinsic value and is said to be *in-the-money.* If the stock's price is less than or equal to the option's exercise price, then the option has zero intrinsic value. Options are *at-the-money* when the stock price equals the option's exercise price. Call options are considered to be *out-of-the-money* when the stock price is less than the option's exercise price. For example, if Disney common stock is trading at a price of 40, then the Disney call options that have a striking price of 35 are 5 points in-the-money, or 40–35; the call options that have a striking price of 40 are at-the-money; and the Disney call options with a striking price of 45 are 5 points out-of-the-money, or 40–45.

The same logic used to determine a call option's price at maturity also can be used to determine the maturity value of a put option. However, one must remember that the put option grants the owner, or purchaser, the right to sell shares of the underlying stock at the exercise price, while the call option grants the owner the right to buy shares of the underlying stock at the exercise price. This fundamental difference in the nature of the put option and call option translates to a difference in their intrinsic values.

The put option, like the call option, will have one of two values at maturity; either zero or the difference between the exercise price and the underlying stock's price. Since the put option grants the right to sell shares at the exercise price, the put option will have a positive value at maturity if the price of the underlying stock is less than the put option's exercise price. In this case the put option owner will exercise the option by delivering shares of the underlying stock in exchange for the exercise price, which is greater than the stock's current market price. The right to sell stock at the exercise price is worth the difference between the exercise price and the stock's current market price, or the put option's intrinsic value. If the stock price is greater than the exercise price at maturity, then the put option is worthless and has no intrinsic value since a rational investor will not exercise the put option and sell shares at the exercise price when it is lower than the stock's current market price.

It is easy to see that the put option's intrinsic value, like the call option's intrinsic value, is determined by the relationship between the put option's exercise price and the market price of the underlying stock. Put options have positive intrinsic values, and are considered to be in-the-money, when the underlying stock's price is less than the exercise price. When the price of the underlying stock is greater than the put option's exercise price, the put option has no intrinsic value and is said to be out-of-the-money. If the underlying stock's price equals the put option's exercise price, then the put option is at-the-money, and has no intrinsic value. This can be illustrated by continuing with the Disney example. If Disney common stock is trading at 40, then the Disney put options that have a striking price of 45 are 5 points in-the-money, or 45–40; the put options with a striking price of 40 are at-the-money; and the Disney put options that have a striking price of 35 are 5 points out-of-the-money, or s35–40.

Notice that if a put option and a call option are written on the same stock, and have identical exercise prices, then they both will be at-the-money at the same time. Furthermore, when the call option is in-the-

Exhibit 2–1 Option Intrinsic Values

Call option intrinsic value = stock price – strike price
Put option intrinsic value = strike price – stock price

	Call Option	Put Option
Stock price > strike price	In-the-money	Out-of-the-money
Stock price = strike price	At-the-money	At-the-money
Stock price < strike price	Out-of-the-money	In-the-money

money, the put option is out-of-the-money; and when the call option is out-of-the-money the put option is in-the-money. These relationships occur because of the fundamental difference in the nature of the options, and because of the changes in the underlying stock's price. The option's exercise price does not change, it is fixed until the option contracts mature. These relationships are summarized in Exhibit 2–1.

TIME PREMIUM Up to this point the discussion has focused on the option prices at maturity. Now the emphasis will shift to option prices prior to maturity.

It is common practice within the industry to use the terms *premium* and *price* interchangeably. From the previous discussion, it follows that at the option's maturity its premium is either zero or its intrinsic value. Thus, at maturity the option's price, or premium, has only one component, its intrinsic value. Prior to maturity the option's premium will have a second component known as *time premium.* Consequently, the option's premium may be expressed as:

Option Premium = Intrinsic Value + Time Premium.

This general representation of option premium applies to both put options and call options. It is important to understand that the time premium is a component of the option's premium, or price. The time premium is not equivalent to the option's premium. When industry jargon is used to discuss options, time premium usually is stated explicitly. If one hears the term "premium" it should be interpreted as the option's price.

PARITY If an option is trading for its intrinsic value, then it is trading at *parity*. An option that is trading at parity has no time premium. At maturity, options will trade for either zero or parity. Prior to maturity, only deep in-the-money options have a chance of trading at parity.

Option premiums are sometimes quoted with respect to parity. For example, the price of a deep in-the-money call option with a premium of 21, an exercise price of 15, and an underlying stock price of 35, may be stated as 1 point above its parity value of 20, 35–15, if its premium is 21.

Behavior of Call Option Prices

RELATIONSHIP TO UNDERLYING STOCK PRICE The relationship between the call option's price and the price of the underlying stock is quite straightforward and easy to understand. The relationship is positive and is based on the fact that a position in a call option is a levered position in the underlying stock. If the stock price rises, then the value of being able to purchase shares at the exercise price also increases. Conversely, if the stock price drops, then the value of the right to purchase the option's underlying shares diminishes.

This positive relationship can prove to be quite useful if one feels bullish about a stock and wants to maximize the percentage gain in the near term. For example, suppose that an investor felt that Sears stock was going to rise by about 5 points prior to the next dividend payment date in three months. Assume that Sears currently is selling for 40 and the ninety-day at-the-money calls—i.e., call options with a striking price of 40—are trading at 2, then the investor can participate in the price movement of 100 shares of Sears stock by purchasing a ninety-day call option for a price of $200. If Sears stock rises 5 points in the next sixty days, then the investor's Sears call options that have an exercise price of 40 and a thirty-day maturity, will be worth approximately 5 ¼ points, or $525.

If the investor decides to close the option position and take the profits, then the percentage gain would be computed as:

$$\text{Percentage Gain} = \frac{(\$525 - \$200)}{\$200}$$

$$= 162\%$$

$$\text{Annualized Percentage Gain} = 162\% \times \left(\frac{12 \text{ months}}{2 \text{ months}}\right)$$
$$= 975\%$$

These percentage gains are much greater than the percentage gains enjoyed by an investor who had purchased 100 shares of Sears stock at 40 and then liquidated the position at 45. The stock investor's percentage gains would be computed as:

$$\text{Percentage Gain} = \frac{(\$4500 - \$4000)}{\$4000}$$
$$= 12.5\%.$$
$$\text{Annualized Percentage Gain} = 12.5\% \times \left(\frac{12 \text{ months}}{2 \text{ months}}\right)$$
$$= 75\%$$

It must be emphasized that the option investor's extremely large percentage gain is much riskier than the stock investor's percentage gain. The reason for this large disparity in the riskiness of the positions is that the option has a limited life and will mature in the near future, but the stock has an infinite life and will exist long after the option matures.

To see how the riskiness of these positions differs, assume that both investors have $4000 to invest in Sears stock. Once again assume that Sears stock is selling for $40, and that ninety-day at-the-money call options are selling for 2. The stock investor's $4000 results in a long position in 100 shares of Sears stock, $4000/$40, which have an unlimited life. The option investor's $4000 produces a long position in 20 at-the-money call options, $4000/$200, which will expire in ninety days. Suppose that during the next ninety days the price of Sears stock drops to $37. Both investors will suffer a loss, but the option investor will experience a much greater loss than the stock investor. After ninety days the value of the stock position is $3700, $37 × 100 shares, and the value of the option position is zero.

The option investor's position has expired worthless, since the call options were out-of-the-money at expiration. The percentage gains and losses for each position are:

$$\text{Stock Position Percentage Loss} = \frac{(\$3700 - \$4000)}{\$4000}$$
$$= -7.5\%$$

$$\text{Stock Position Annualized Loss} = -7.5\% \times \left(\frac{12 \text{ months}}{3 \text{ months}}\right)$$
$$= -30\%$$

$$\text{Option Position Percentage Loss} = \frac{(\$0 - \$4000)}{\$4000}$$
$$= 12.5\%$$

$$\text{Option Position Annualized Loss} = -100\% \times \left(\frac{12 \text{ months}}{3 \text{ months}}\right)$$
$$= -400\%$$

This example should make it quite clear that there is a tradeoff between the risk and return of investment alternatives. Prior to investing, one should always be well aware of the riskiness of the position as well as the position's potential return.

RELATIONSHIP TO CASH DIVIDENDS An inverse relationship exists between the call option's price and the underlying stock's dividends. This concept is easy to grasp given the prior discussion about the relationship between the call option's price and the stock's price. It is well known that on the ex-dividend date, the value of the stock declines by the amount of the dividend at the opening trade. Thus, it follows that the call option should drop in price since the stock's price is declining by the amount of the dividend.

Usually it is unwise for a call option owner to exercise the option before maturity since one forfeits the option's potential gain that is associated with an increase in the price of the underlying stock. This inverse relationship between the call option price and the cash dividend is important to both the call writer and call buyer since it can create circumstances where early exercise of the call option is optimal. For example, if the call option is deep in-the-money just prior to the stock's ex-dividend date, then it is quite probable that the call option owner will exercise the option to capture the dividend. The greater the value of the dividend, the greater the chance of exercise. This means that the call option writer will be assigned the obligation to deliver shares at the exercise price. If the writer wishes to avoid assignment, then the open short position in the call option must be covered by purchasing an identical call option before the end of the day's trading.

RELATIONSHIP TO VOLATILITY The third key factor that determines a call option's price is the *volatility* of the price changes in the underlying stock. The greater the volatility of the underlying stock, the greater the chance that the call option will gain intrinsic value and go deep in-the-money. If the call option is in-the-money at expiration, then it will be profitable for the call option owner to exercise the option.

This positive relationship between the call option's price and the underlying stock's price volatility should not be confused with the positive relationship between the stock price and the call option price; the two relationships are not identical. It is possible that a stock's price can increase and its volatility can shrink. For example, if a firm's stock is trading at $25 and the announcement is made that the firm has agreed to be taken over at $40 per share, and the deal will be consummated in thirty days, then the share price immediately will jump to $40 and remain there for the next thirty days. Since there is no reason for the stock to trade at any value less than $40, the stock's volatility is now virtually zero. In this example, the firm's call options with exercise prices of less than $40 will go in-the-money immediately and will be priced commensurate with their intrinsic values. However, during the next thirty days there will be very little price change in the option since the stock's price is fixed at $40 and the volatility has shrunk to zero.

This positive relationship between stock price volatility and call option prices implies that, in general, the greater the stock price volatility, the greater the call option's price. This relationship also provides insight as to why the riskier, more price-volatile stocks tend to have call option prices that are less stable than call option prices for more conservative stocks. Once again, the greater the stock's price volatility, the greater the risk. Thus, investors will require relatively greater returns before they will commit their funds to either the option or the underlying stock.

It should be mentioned that the stock price volatility is the only pricing factor that is not directly observable. Since the call option price is very sensitive to changes in the stock's price volatility it is crucial that accurate volatility estimates be obtained if one is attempting to speculate in mispriced options. However, since this book's primary objective is to provide guidance to the conservative investor, volatility estimating techniques will not be discussed.

RELATIONSHIP TO TIME TO MATURITY The relationship between call option prices and the fourth option pricing factor—time—is positive. Call options written on the same underlying stock that have identical striking prices but different maturities, will have different prices. Longer-term call options will have higher prices than shorter term call options. These greater prices for longer-term options reflect greater time premium values and should be expected to occur since the longer-term call options have more time to gain intrinsic value than do the shorter-term call options.

Since call options are *wasting* or *depleting assets,* the time premium will decay as time passes and the call options approach maturity. The closer the call option is to maturity, the more rapid the time premium's decay. This accelerating-decay process indicates that the market thinks that there is little chance of the call options gaining intrinsic value in the short time remaining until expiration. A diagram of the time premium's decay is given in Exhibit 2–2.

Exhibit 2–2 clearly shows that a call option is a depleting asset and highlights the fact that the time premium decay is quite small until about six weeks before expiration. Indeed, stock price volatility is much more important than time premium decay until about forty-five days from expiration. After that, the importance of the call option's remaining time until expiration increases dramatically, and has a much greater effect on the call option's price than before.

A subtle aspect of the relationship between the call option's price and time to maturity is that time premium is greatest for at-the-money call options. Call options that are either deep in-the-money or deep out-of-the-money have very small time premiums. The reason that large time premiums occur for the at-the-money call options and small time

Exhibit 2–2 Call Option Time Premium Decay

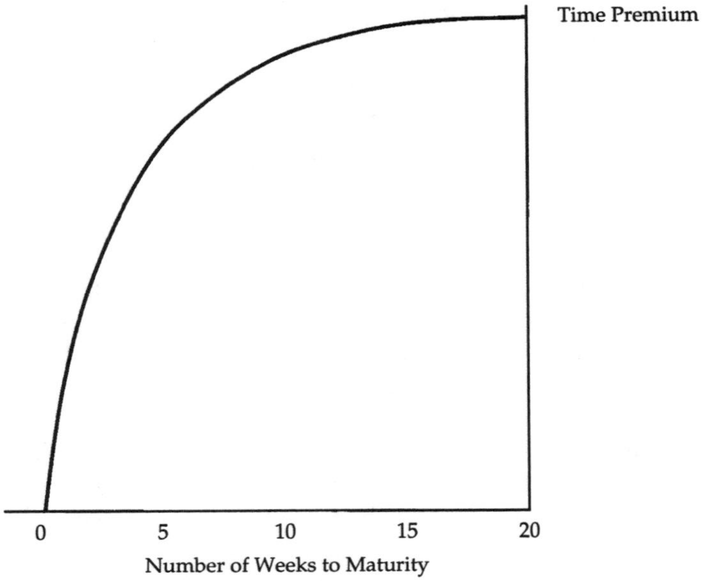

premiums occur for the far-from-the-money options is that a call option's time premium expresses the market's estimate of the likelihood that a call option will either gain or lose intrinsic value. The deep out-of-the-money call options' small time premiums indicate that there is little chance that the underlying stock's price will experience a large enough price increase to give the call option positive intrinsic value before expiration. The small time premiums for the deep in-the-money call options show that there is little chance that the price of the underlying stock will fall far enough to cause the call option to have zero intrinsic value before expiration. Finally, the large time premium for the at-the-money call options, which have a relatively long time until expiration, reflect the fact that it is highly probable that the underlying stock will rise so that these options will gain intrinsic value. However, if the price of the underlying stock does not change, then this time premium will decay rapidly as

Exhibit 2–3 Call Option Price Quotations WSJ 9/20/93

Option & NY Close	Strike Price	Calls–Last Oct.	Jan.	Apr.
IBM				
43 3/8	40	3 3/4	5	5 5/8
43 3/8	45	3/4	2 5/16	3 1/8
43 3/8	50	3/16	15/16	1 5/8

expiration approaches. Exhibit 2–3 uses IBM stock and call option prices to illustrate how time premium values differ.

The first thing to note about Exhibit 2–3 is that the data for the IBM options are arranged differently than in *The Wall Street Journal,* Exhibit 1–1 in the prior chapter. This figure contains data for nine IBM call options: three maturity months, October, January, and April; and for three striking prices, $40, $45, and $50. This arrangement highlights the relationship between option prices and time to maturity. Observe that if one holds the striking price constant, then the call options' prices increase with maturity. Since all of the IBM 40 call options have an intrinsic value of 3 3/8 points, 43 3/8 – 40, the higher prices for the January and April options occur because of greater time values for the longer-term options; 1 5/8 for the January 40 call option, 5 – 3 3/8, and 1 1/4, for the April 40 call, 5 5/8 – 3 3/8. If one reads down the October maturity column, then it is easy to see how the time premium shrinks for the far-from-the-money options. Specifically, the in-the-money October 40 call option's price of 3 3/4 is composed of 3 1/8 points of intrinsic value, 43 3/8 – 40, and only 3/8 point of time premium, 3 3/4 – 3 3/8, while the out-of-the-money October 45 call option's price of 3/4 has no intrinsic value, i.e., 43 3/8 is less than 45, but 3/4 point of time premium. Finally, note that the deep out-of-the-money October 50 call option has no intrinsic value, and only 3/16 point of time premium.

RELATIONSHIP TO EXERCISE PRICE The relationship between the call option's price and the fifth pricing factor—the exercise price—is negative. Call options written on the same stock and with identical maturities will have different values because of their striking prices. The deep out-of-the-money call options have high striking prices and low premiums since these options have relatively lower intrinsic values. Conversely, as call options go in-the-money they become more expensive. The call options with relatively low striking prices will have large amounts of intrinsic value that will be reflected in relatively higher call option prices. This inverse relationship between the call option's price and the exercise price is illustrated quite clearly in Exhibit 2–3. Notice that as one moves down the table, the exercise prices increase, but the call option prices decrease.

RELATIONSHIP TO INTEREST RATES The final relationship to be discussed is the positive relationship that exists between call option prices and unanticipated changes in interest rates. Simply stated, higher interest rates generally lead to higher call option prices, while lower interest rates result in lower call option prices. This positive relationship means that call option prices will move in the same direction as an unanticipated move in the interest rate, if the underlying stock price does not change. The logic for this relationship becomes clear if one recognizes that the call option buyer's leveraged position in the stock is being financed by a loan from the call option writer. The call option writer is postponing the benefits associated with converting the stock to cash by providing the call option buyer with the opportunity to take a levered position in the underlying stock. High interest rates translate to a high opportunity cost for the call option writer. Thus, the writer will demand a higher call option premium as compensation for the inability to take full advantage of the higher interest rates.

The concept of *present value* provides an alternative explanation for the positive relationship between call option prices and changing interest rates. If a call option is exercised at maturity, then one hundred shares of the underlying stock will be purchased for an amount equal to the option's exercise price. At any time prior to maturity, the call option's premium reflects the present value of the call option's exercise price, where the present value is computed by discounting the exercise price from the call option's maturity date to the present time at the risk-free rate of interest. Therefore, higher interest rates cause lower present values for the exercise price and greater call option intrinsic values. Lower interest rates have the opposite effect; higher present values for the exercise price and lower call option intrinsic values. It must be emphasized that one should not expect higher call option prices when interest rates increase if the price of the underlying stock drops. This relationship is predictable only if the stock price remains unchanged.

Behavior of Put Option Prices

This concludes the discussion of the relationships between call option prices and the pricing factors. Now the emphasis will focus on the behavior of put option prices with respect to the basic pricing factors. Recall that a put option grants the right to sell shares of the underlying stock for the exercise price on or before the option's expiration date. Although the put option differs fundamentally from the call option, the same pricing factors that determined the call option's price also determine the put option's price. Once again, the intrinsic value concept provides the key to understanding the behavior of option prices.

RELATIONSHIP TO UNDERLYING STOCK PRICE The relationship between the put option's price and the underlying stock's price is negative, just the opposite of the relationship between the call option's price and the price of the underlying stock. Remember that since a put option grants the right to sell shares at the exercise price, this privilege becomes less valuable to the put option owner as the stock price rises, and the put option loses intrinsic value. If the price of the underlying stock declines, the put option gains intrinsic value.

A major consequence of this inverse relationship is that there is an upper limit on the value of the put option that is equal to the put option's exercise price. This maximum value for put options occurs because the stock's price can never be less than zero. Thus, if a stock's value falls to zero, then the intrinsic value of the put option equals the exercise price—the option's exercise price minus zero, the current price of the stock. Conversely, there is no theoretical upper limit on the call option's value because there is no theoretical upper limit on the price of the stock and therefore no upper limit on the call option's intrinsic value.

Given the inverse relationship between the underlying stock price and the put option's price, it should be obvious that investors can use put options to profit from falling stock prices. For example, suppose that an investor was bearish and predicted a drop in the price of Bethlehem Steel stock within the next three months. By simply purchasing a six-month at-the-money put option on Bethlehem stock, the investor can benefit from any price decline that may occur. However, if the stock price fails to drop, or even rises, during the put option's life, then the investor's maximum loss is the price paid for the put option, i.e., the put option's premium.

RELATIONSHIP TO CASH DIVIDENDS The relationship between the put option's price and the underlying stock's cash dividends is positive. This is not surprising since the stock price will decline just prior to a dividend payment, which causes the put option to gain intrinsic value. The implication is that the put option holder will not exercise prior to the ex-dividend date since it would be foolish to sacrifice the resulting stock price decline and increase in intrinsic value. Furthermore, if two stocks are identical in all respects except their cash dividend payments, then the stock with the larger dividend will have a higher put option price since the stock with the larger dividend will experience a greater share price decline than the stock with the lower dividend.

RELATIONSHIP TO VOLATILITY A positive relationship exists between the third option pricing factor, stock price volatility, and the price of a put option. Note that this relationship is similar to the relationship that exists between the call option's price and the underlying stock price's volatility. Indeed, the same logic prevails for both the puts and calls: the greater the underlying stock's price volatility, the greater the chance that the option will gain intrinsic value and be profitable for the option's owner to exercise.

It is quite clear that large stock price declines will add intrinsic value to put option positions. Thus, stocks that have high volatilities will have relatively more potential for adding intrinsic value to put option positions than stocks with relatively low volatilities. In general, put options on these high-volatility stocks should have relatively higher prices than put options written on lower-volatility stocks.

RELATIONSHIP TO TIME TO MATURITY Since put options, like call options, are depleting assets, the behavior of put options over time is similar to the behavior of call options. Put options written on the same stock with

Exhibit 2–4 Put Option Time Premium Decay

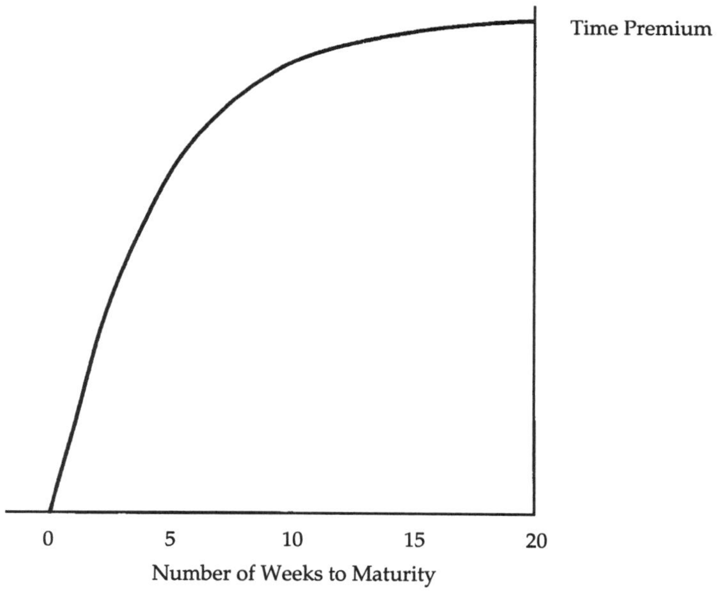

equivalent exercise prices will differ in price according to maturity. Longer-term put options will have higher prices. Furthermore, at-the-money put options will have the largest time premium, while far-from-the-money put options will have the smallest time premium. The put option's time premium will decay slowly until about forty-five days until maturity; after that, the decay process accelerates. Exhibit 2–4 graphically depicts this decay process for at-the-money and out-of-the-money put options, and Exhibit 2–5 illustrates the time premiums for IBM put options. The arrangement of Exhibit 2–5 is identical to that of Exhibit 2–3 and contains data for nine put options: three maturity months, October, January, and April, and three striking prices: $40, $45, and $50.

In Exhibit 2–5 it is easy to see the positive relationship between the put options' prices and time to maturity by examining the out-of-the-money options, the IBM 40 put options. Since all of the IBM 40 put options have no intrinsic value, their prices are composed totally of time

Exhibit 2–5 Put Option Price Quotations WSJ 9/20/93

Option & NY Close	Strike Price	Puts–Last Oct.	Jan.	Apr.
IBM				
43 3/8	40	3/8	1 7/16	2 1/8
43 3/8	45	2 5/16	3 3/4	4 1/2
43 3/8	50	6 3/4	7 1/2	7 3/4

premium. Observe how these put options increase in value with maturity. Since the IBM 45 puts all have 1 5/8 points of intrinsic value, 45 – 43 3/8, the time premiums for the October, January, and April put options are 11/16, 2 1/8, and 2 7/8 points respectively. Moreover, the 6 5/8 points of intrinsic value for the IBM 50 put options, 50 – 43 3/8, means that the time premiums for the October, January, and April put options are 1/8, 7/8, and 1 1/8 points. Notice that when the deep in-the-money IBM 50 put option time premiums and the out-of-the-money IBM 40 put option prices are compared to the prices of the near-the-money IBM 45 put options, it is clear that time value shrinks as the options go far-from-the-money.

Finally, there is a situation that all investors encounter at one time or another and deserves to be discussed. Theoretically, all options should be selling for at least their intrinsic value. However, suppose that the IBM October 50 put option was listed at 6 1/2 instead of its 6 5/8 intrinsic value. Since it is quoted at 1/8 point under parity, it appears that a sure profit of 1/8 point per share of IBM can be earned by purchasing the IBM October 50 for 6 1/2, purchasing IBM shares for 43 3/8, and then exercising the put option by selling the shares at 50; 1/8 = 50 – (6 1/2 + 43 3/8). Unfortunately, this will probably not be possible since it is not known whether or not IBM stock actually was trading at 43 3/8 when the October 50 put option traded at 6 1/2. It may be that the last IBM October 50 was traded long before IBM stock reached a price of 43 3/8. On the other hand, even if shares of IBM stock and the October 50 put option did trade simultaneously, professional traders and arbitragers would have capitalized on the mispricing situation, and theoretically consistent option prices would have been restored in a matter of minutes because of the trading strategy outlined above. Thus, when grossly mispriced options appear in the newspaper, rest assured that any available profits already have been captured by professional investors and speculators.

RELATIONSHIP TO EXERCISE PRICE The relationship between the fifth pricing factor—the exercise price—and the put option's price is positive and occurs because put options gain intrinsic value as exercise prices increase. Thus, put options written on a given stock with identical maturity dates will increase in value with their exercise prices. Conversely, put options with low exercise prices have low intrinsic values. This can be seen quite clearly in Exhibit 2–5 by reading down any of the maturity columns.

An inverse relationship exists between put option prices and unanticipated changes in interest rates. This relationship can be explained by focusing on put option buyers. One who owns a put option owns the right to the cash flow generated by the exercise price. An unanticipated increase in interest rates imposes an opportunity cost on the put option buyer since the buyer does not have the cash on hand to take advantage of these higher rates. Therefore, put options become less desirable and their premiums are bid down in the marketplace.

It is also possible to logically explain this inverse relationship using a present value argument. Specifically, the put option premium reflects the present value of the exercise price, where the present value is computed by discounting the put option's exercise price from maturity to the current time period. Lower interest rates increase the present value of the put option's exercise price and thus increase intrinsic value. Higher intrinsic values translate to higher put option prices. If interest rates increase, then the discounted present value of the exercise price drops which results in lower intrinsic values and lower put option prices.

Earlier it was emphasized that the relationship between interest rates and call options is predictable if stock prices remain unchanged. The same holds true for put options. One should not expect higher put option prices when interest rates decrease if the price of the underlying stock rises. The stock price must remain fixed for this relationship to be predictable.

This concludes the discussion of the relationships between the six key pricing factors and option prices. The following section focuses on a useful tool which is based on these relationships: the delta.

Option Deltas

DEFINITION OF DELTA An option's *delta* may be defined as a measure of how the option's price will change if the price of the underlying stock experiences a small change, assuming that the other pricing factors remain stable. The delta is simply the practical application of the relationship between the price of the underlying stock and the price of the option. Since call options have a positive relationship with the underlying stock's price, and put options have a negative relationship with the stock's price, call option deltas will be positive and put option deltas will be negative. Indeed, since the put option is the obverse of the call option, the put option delta will be computed by subtracting 1 from the call option's delta. Call option deltas will range in value from zero to 1, while put option deltas take values from zero to a –1. At-the-money call options and put options will have deltas of approximately ½ and –½ respectively. As options go deep in-the-money and gain intrinsic value, the absolute value of the delta will approach one. Thus, deep in-the-money call options will have deltas that approximate 1 and deep in-the-money put options will have deltas that are approximately –1. Both deep out-of-the-money put options and call options have deltas that are virtually zero.

These different delta values reflect the strength of the relationship between the option and the underlying stock. A deep in-the-money call option that has a delta of 1 has a strong positive relationship with the underlying stock and will experience a one-dollar price increase for each one-dollar gain in the price of the stock. Conversely, the value of a deep in-the-money put option, that has a strong inverse relationship with the stock and a delta of –1, will increase in value by one dollar for every one-dollar loss experienced by the underlying stock. This price behavior should not be surprising since the premiums for deep in-the-money options are composed almost entirely of intrinsic value. Moreover, these options are virtually perfect surrogates for positions in the underlying stock; with long call options mimicking long stock positions and long put options imitating short stock positions. Options that are deep out-of-the-money have no intrinsic value, a weak relationship with the underlying stock, extremely small deltas, and very little chance of being transformed into stock positions by the option owner. At-the-money options have no intrinsic value, but have the potential to become profitable surrogate stock positions for the option owner. Therefore, the delta values of ½, in absolute value, will reflect this profit potential.

DELTA NEUTRAL POSITIONS An option's delta is also important for its risk management capability. The delta provides the investor with the number of shares needed, in combination with the option, to construct a position that is insulated from the effects of small price movements in the underlying stock. When an investor combines options and stock to create such a position, the position is said to be *delta neutral*. The total value of the position will remain stable even though the values of the individual components will change. The following example will illustrate these concepts.

Assume that Nike's common stock is trading at 51 ½, and that the four-month put options and call options, with striking prices of 50, have values of 2 and 4 ¾ respectively. Assume also that the call option's delta is .63 and the put option's delta is –.37 (.63 – 1.00). These data imply that a $1 increase in the price of Nike stock will result in a $.63 increase in the price of the call option, and a $.37 decrease in the put option's price. Furthermore, a delta neutral call position can be created by purchasing sixty-three shares of Nike stock for every call option sold, while a delta neutral put position can be created by purchasing thirty-seven shares of stock for every put option that is purchased. Since stock price changes cause the call option prices to change in the same direction, one must take opposite positions in the call option and shares of stock to insulate the combined position from the underlying stock's price changes. The opposite directional change in the put option price that results from the stock price change dictates that similar positions be taken in the put option and the shares of stock to insure that this position is isolated from the effects of the stock price changes.

Exhibits 2–6 and 2–7 illustrate the behavior of these delta neutral positions. Exhibit 2–6 shows how the value of a total position, composed of a Nike call option and shares of Nike common stock, remains stable as stock and option prices change, while exhibit 2–7 presents the behavior of the Nike put option and stock position. Note that the values of the total positions remain stable because of each component's proportions. The

Exhibit 2–6 Delta Neutral Call Option Positions

Nike Common Stock	Nike 50 Calls	Component Values		Position Values
51 ½	Delta .63	Short 1 call @ 475		– 475.00
	Price 4.75	Long 63 shares @ 51 ½		+ 3244.50
			Net long	+ 2769.50
52 ½	Delta .63	Short 1 call @ 538		– 538.00
	Price 4.75 + .63 = 5.38	Long 63 shares @ 52 ½		+ 3307.50
			Net long	+ 2769.50
50 ½	Delta .63	Short 1 call @ 412		– 412.00
	Price 4.75 – .63 = 4.12	Long 63 shares @ 50 ½		+ 3181.50
			Net long	+ 2769.50

Exhibit 2–7 Delta Neutral Put Option Positions

Nike Common Stock	Nike 50 Puts	Component Values		Position Values
51 ½	Delta .37	Long 1 put @ 200		+ 200.00
	Price 2.00	Long 37 shares @ 51 ½		+ 1905.50
			Net long	+ 2105.50
52 ½	Delta .37	Long 1 put @ 163		+ 163.00
	Price 2.00 – .37 = 1.63	Long 37 shares @ 52 ½		+ 1942.50
			Net long	+ 2105.50
50 ½	Delta .37	Long 1 put @ 237		+ 237.00
	Price 2.00 + .37 = 2.37	Long 37 shares @ 50 ½		+ 1868.50
			Net long	+ 2105.50

key to understanding delta neutral positions is realizing that the effects of the stock price changes are neutralized by the relative proportions of the position's components.

Profit Graphs for Basic Investment Positions

The final section of this chapter is a discussion of the profit graphs for the six basic positions: long the stock, short the stock, long the call option, short the call option, long the put option, and short the put option. These graphs and the associated discussion serve two purposes: first, they should solidify one's understanding of the profit and loss potential of the various positions; and second, they provide a foundation for understanding more complex strategies that will be discussed in later chapters.

LONG STOCK POSITION Exhibit 2–8 depicts a long position in 100 shares of Apple Computer common stock where the purchase price is $30 per share, or $3000 for the total position. As the share price of Apple Computer stock rises, the position's profit accrues at a rate of $100 per dollar increase in the

Exhibit 2–8 Long Stock (Purchase Apple 30)

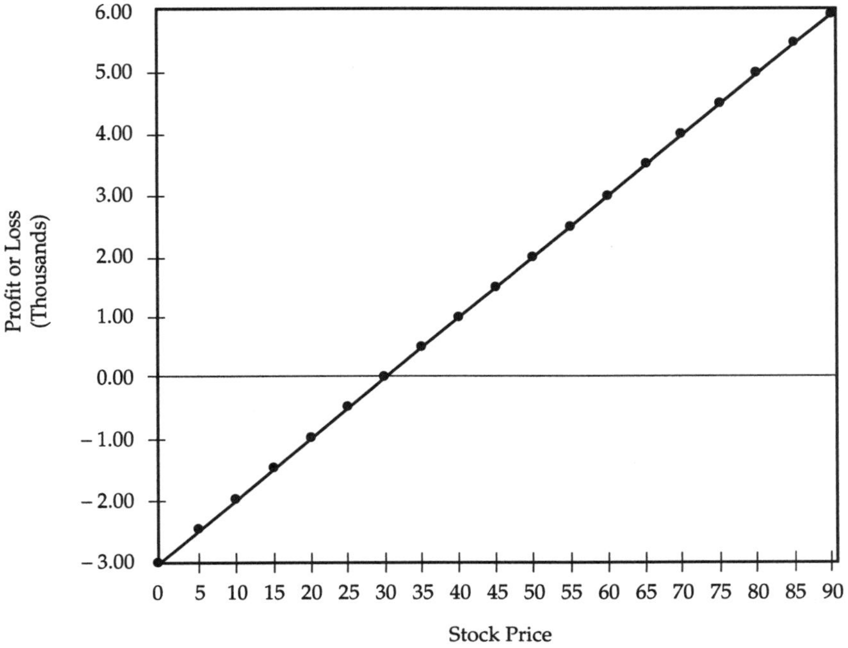

stock's price. Notice that if the price of Apple Computer stock drops to zero, then the maximum loss of $3000 is incurred. There is no maximum profit since there is no upper limit on the stock's price.

SHORT STOCK POSITION A short position in 100 shares of Apple Computer common stock is portrayed in Exhibit 2–9. Here the investor is attempting to capitalize on an anticipated share price decline from its current level of $30 per share. The rate of change in this short position's value is identical to the rate of change in the long position's value, $100 per dollar change in the price of Apple Computer common stock. The maximum profit that can be earned by the short seller is $3000 if Apple Computer stock becomes worthless. There is no maximum loss since there is no upper limit on the price of Apple Computer shares. Thus, it is theoretically possible for the short seller to suffer an infinite loss—an extremely risky position.

Exhibit 2–9 Short Stock (Sell Apple 30)

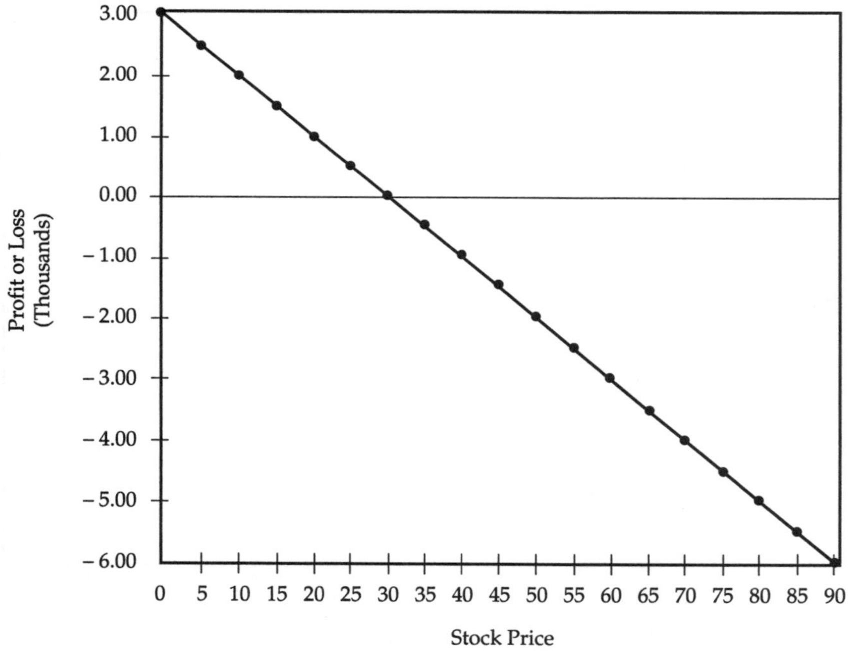

LONG CALL OPTION POSITION The third profit graph, Exhibit 2–10, illustrates the profit and loss potential of buying an Apple Computer call option and then holding it to maturity. In this example the call option has an exercise price of $35 and a premium of 3 points, or $300. If the call option expires at-the-money or out-of-the-money, then the maximum loss of $300 is incurred. The call option must be 3 points in-the-money, with a share price equal to $38, for the investor to break even. For share prices greater than $38, the long call option is profitable because by exercising the call option, shares can be purchased at a price of $35 and then sold at the higher market price. There is no upper limit on the call option's profit since there is no upper limit on the price of Apple Computer stock. Remember that if one hopes to earn unlimited profits and invests one's total wealth in a long call option position, one also runs the risk of total ruin within a short timespan.

Exhibit 2–10 Long Call (Apple 35 Call)

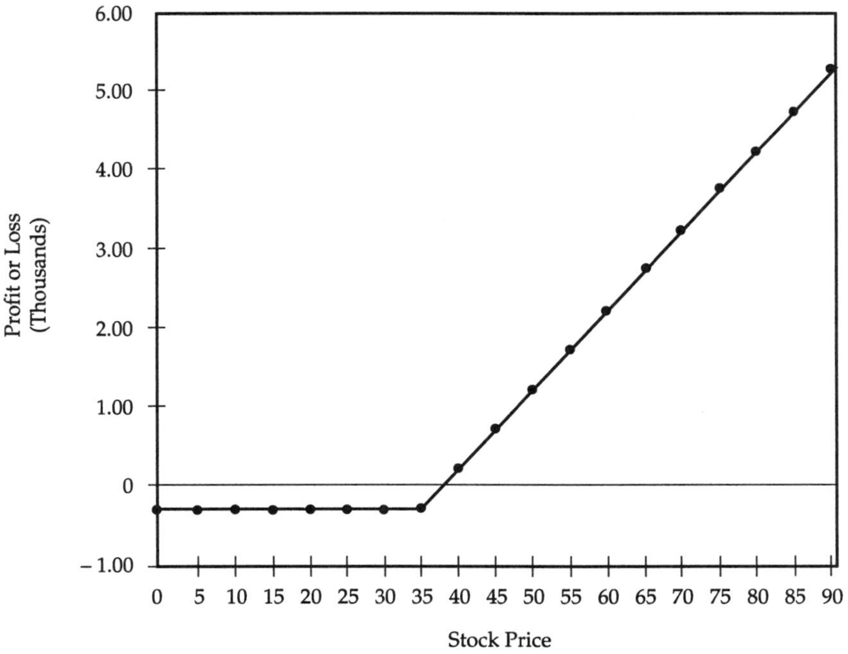

SHORT CALL OPTION POSITION Exhibit 2–11 represents the profit potential of writing *uncovered* or *naked* call options on General Motors stock. A short position is taken in a GM call option that controls 100 shares of General Motors stock, has a striking price of 50, and a premium of 5 points, or $500. If the call option is at-the-money or out-of-the-money at maturity, then the call option will expire worthless and the naked call option writer keeps the entire $500 premium as profit. However, if the price of General Motors stock rises, then the naked call option will experience large losses as the stock price moves past the break-even point of $55. At this point the in-the-money call option becomes worthwhile for its owner to exercise against the writer. Since the writer does not own shares of GM stock, they must be purchased in the market at the prevailing price. The greater the current market price, the more the writer must pay to acquire GM shares that will be delivered to the call option buyer at the striking price of $55 per share.

Exhibit 2–11 Short Call (GM 50 Call)

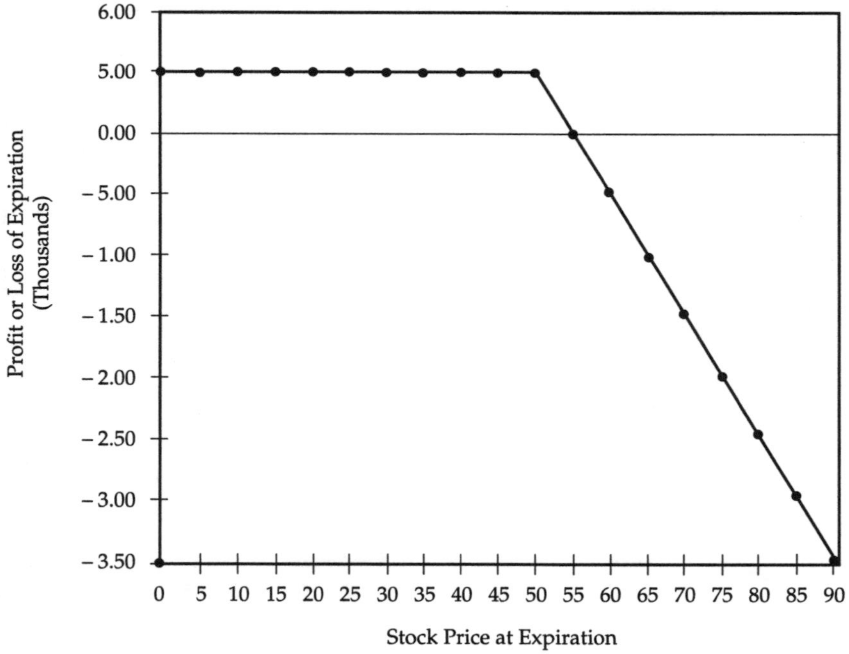

Since there is no upper limit on the stock price, there is no upper limit on the naked call option writer's potential loss. However, notice that the naked call writer's profit is limited to the amount of the premium taken in when the call option was sold. Again, a very risky position.

LONG PUT OPTION POSITION The profit potential of a long position in a General Motors put option is illustrated in Exhibit 2–12. The put option controls 100 shares of GM stock, has a striking price of $50, and can be purchased for 5 points, or $500. If the price of General Motors stock falls to zero, the put option owner will exercise the option and force the put option writer to pay $5000 for 100 shares of worthless GM stock. The put option owner will earn a profit of $4500 from this transaction, the $5000 exercise price minus the $500 put option premium. If the price of General Motors stock is greater than or equal to the put option's exercise price of

Exhibit 2–12 Long Put (GM 50 Put)

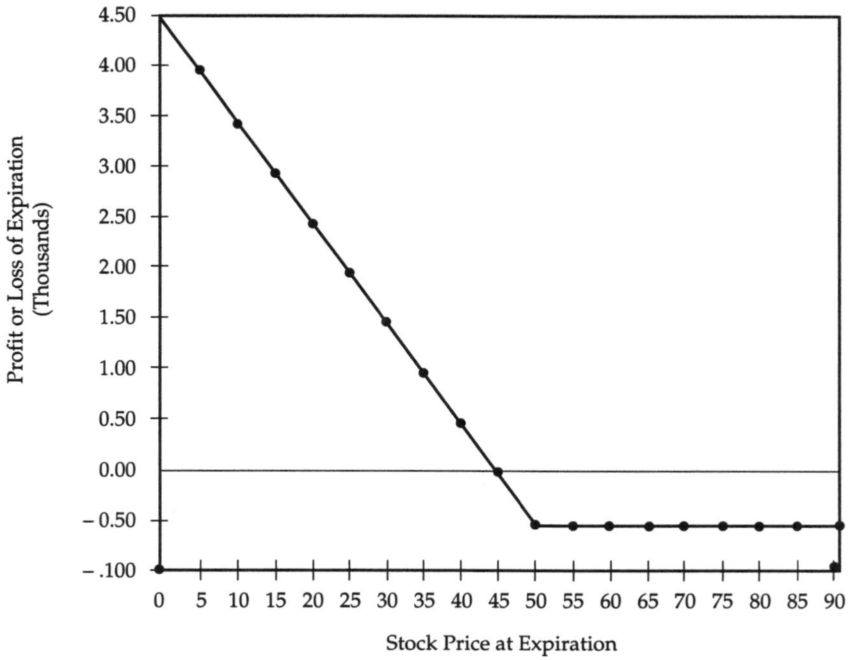

$50 at maturity, then the put option will expire worthless and the put option owner will forfeit the $500 premium. This position is less cumbersome and less risky than a short position in General Motors stock. However, even if one is positive that a large price decline in GM stock is imminent, one should be prudent and refrain from investing one's total wealth in these put options since there is the possibility of total ruin.

SHORT PUT OPTION POSITION The final profit graph is Exhibit 2–13, which portrays the profit potential for a General Motors put option writer. The parameters are identical to the long General Motors put option position: the put option controls 100 shares of General Motors stock, the striking price is $50, and the premium is $500. The put option writer collects the $500 premium and hopes that the stock price is greater than or equal to the striking price of $50 at the put option's expiration. Under these conditions

Exhibit 2–13 Short Put (GM 50 Put)

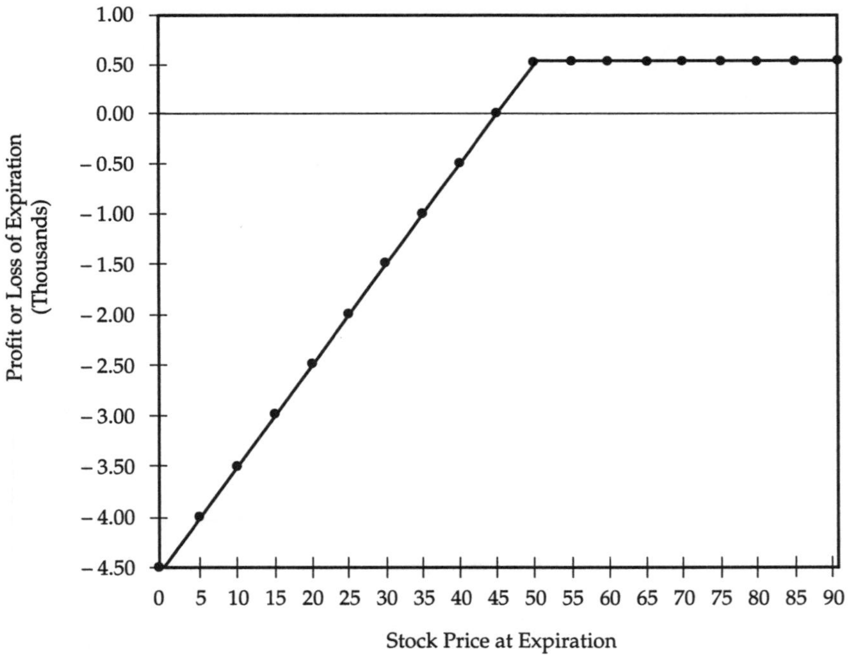

the put option will not have any value for its owner and the writer will profit by the $500 premium. However, at expiration if the stock price is less than $45, then the put option owner will profit and the put option writer will lose. The maximum loss that the put option writer can suffer is $4500, the value of the exercise price less the amount of the original premium. Notice that the writer runs the risk of losing $4500 for a maximum profit of $500, the amount paid to the writer when the put option was sold. Theoretically, the maximum loss for the put option writer is less than the naked call option writer's loss. However, practically speaking the consequences of an adverse movement in the stock price for both unsecured option writers are extremely severe: potential ruin.

Conclusion

This chapter has explored the relationships of call option prices and put option prices to the six basic option pricing factors: the underlying stock's price, the stock's dividends, the stock's price volatility, the time until the option expires, the option's exercise price, and interest rates. The discussion of these relationships was based upon the concepts of intrinsic value, parity, and time premium. The chapter ended with a graphical presentation of the six basic investment positions: long the stock, short the stock, long the call option, short the call option, long the put option, and short the put option. These graphs were used to reinforce the concepts of risk and return, and to prepare the reader for the more complex strategies that will be introduced in subsequent chapters.

Chapter Three

SIMPLE CALL OPTION STRATEGIES

Purchasing Call Options versus Purchasing Stock

Recall that call options give the purchaser the right to buy stock at a predetermined price (the striking price) between the date of purchase and the option's expiration date. A call option is usually purchased with the hope that the underlying security will increase in value. Usually the call option's price will increase as the underlying security's price goes up. The purchase of call options is considered a bullish strategy and is used to obtain greater leverage while limiting the investor's risk of loss. Purchasing call options alone is purely speculative, since options are a depleting asset—that is, their value diminishes over time if the underlying stock does nothing.

When an investor owns stock in a company—even a very small percentage—he or she in effect owns equity in that corporation. If the value of the stock decreases, the investor is under no time constraints to recoup losses. With a call option, on the other hand, the investor must hope that the underlying stock will move in his or her favor and increase in value by the time the call option expires.

Exhibit 3–1 compares the purchase of an at-the-money call option with a striking price of 45 and the purchase of a stock at $45 a share. (In the exhibits to follow, the thin line represents stock purchase or short sale, and the thick line represents option strategy.) As you can see, the loss on the call is limited to the call's purchase price of $250, which is significantly less than the potential loss on the stock at $4500. In addition, the call provides greater leverage since the call buyer has committed much less money than the stock purchaser. In order to fully understand this concept, let us consider a real-world situation.

Suppose that interest rates are declining and it appears that bank stocks will benefit from this trend. You want to speculate on improved earnings for Citicorp. You know that Citicorp common stock is trading at $35 a share and the call options are priced as follows:

Citicorp 6-month 30 call, 8 ½ points

Citicorp 6-month 35 call, 3 ½ points

Citicorp 6-month 40 call, 1 ½ points

For example, a 6-month at-the-money call is selling at 3 points, or $350 for the right to buy 100 shares of Citicorp stock at 35.

Now suppose your interest rate scenario proves to be correct and Citicorp stock goes up 5 points in just a few months to 40 for a 14.3 percent gain [5 points (profit)/35 (stock purchase price)]. At the same time, the call price increases from 3 ½ to 7 ½ (5 points intrinsic value and 2 ½ points time value) for a gain of 114 percent in the same time period [4-point increase in option/3 ½ (purchase price)]. As an investor in this call option, you could either sell it in the options market to realize your gain or exercise your right to buy 100 shares of Citicorp stock at $35 per share. Your decision will be based on whether you want to actually own the underlying stock or just take part in the quick move.

If your interest rate scenario was incorrect and you bought 100 shares of Citicorp stock, your downside risk theoretically would be 35 points. It is very unlikely that the shares of Citicorp stock would fall to zero. However, the point is that if you were speculating on a quick upturn

Exhibit 3–1 Buy At-the-Money Call with a Striking Price of 45 at 2 ½ or $250

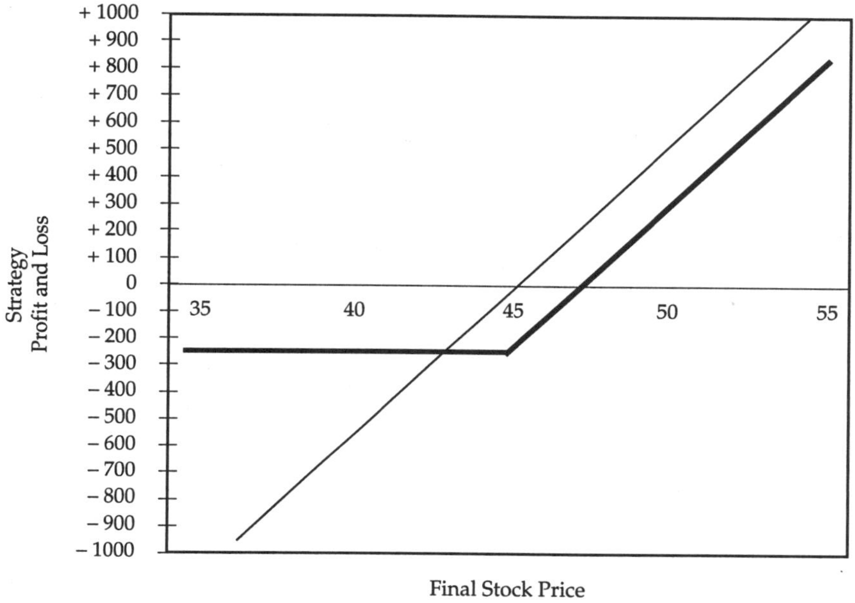

rather than investing for the long term, the purchase of the 6-month at-the-money call might meet your speculative objectives more directly and limit your downside risk by the amount of the option—in this case, $350 as opposed to $3500. It would also offer you potentially *greater leverage.*

If you wanted to be very speculative, you could buy 10 6-month at-the-money call options for 3 ½ points, or $3500. Then, if Citicorp moves up 5 points to 40, you will make $4000 (4-point increase in option × number of options, or 10) as compared to $500 had you only bought 100 shares of Citicorp stock in anticipation of a quick move in the stock price. However, if Citicorp stock remains flat or goes down, you will lose your entire $3500 investment.

Time Considerations

In the above investment situation, we compared purchasing a stock at 35 with buying a 6-month at-the-money call option. However, this situation rarely occurs in everyday life. Usually an investor must decide between the purchase of an out-of-the-money or in-the-money call option. Our next consideration is how much time value to buy—three, six, or nine months.

Typically, a speculator purchases the cheapest call option available, which, of course, would be the nearest-term out-of-the-money option. This might be the appropriate strategy if one were expecting a major move in the stock within a relatively short period. However, the dollar price alone should not be the determining factor in deciding whether or not to purchase a particular call option. Some people look at it from a purely economic perspective, namely that they may lose only a small amount of money but enjoy a potential for large gains. The point to keep in mind is that even though an out-of-the-money call option provides the greatest amount of leverage, the purchaser has a greater chance of losing all of his or her money. Also, if the stock rises only moderately, an in-the-money call option may outperform an out-of-the-money option.

Returning to the Citicorp example, it is clear that if you purchased the out-of-the-money 40 call option at 1, you would lose your entire investment unless Citicorp stock rose above 40 during the option's life. However, if you bought the in-the-money 30 call option at 6 ½, you would need only a rise in the stock price to above 36 ½ in order to make a profit. In this example, you would have more dollars at risk by purchasing the in-the-money call option than by buying the out-of-the-money call option, which is why you must assess the amount of dollar exposure you are willing to assume in any option purchase decision.

Let us return to the decision of whether to purchase a 3, 6, or 9 month call option. As mentioned earlier, investors often purchase the nearest-term call option simply because it is the cheapest. However, the decision should initially be based on how quickly the investor thinks the underlying stock will increase in value.

If the investor is not confident that the increase will take place in the very near term, he or she should attempt to purchase the next-furthest-out call option in order to minimize the risk. If the investor thinks that the underlying stock is going to move up immediately, the nearest-term call option may be the best choice. When making this decision, it is important to remember that if a stock stays stagnant, the call options will maintain their time value on a consistent basis up until the last six weeks prior to expiration. This is when the most rapid deterioration in the option's time value will occur.

Purchasing a Call Option with an Existing Profit in the Stock

Another situation in which the purchase of call options may meet the investor's objectives and limit risk occurs when the investor is faced with taking a profit on a stock. For example, suppose you purchased Cisco Systems stock at $25 a share and doubled your money one year later. You still like Cisco Systems, but you think the stock may pull back and you wouldn't mind taking a profit. At the same time, you feel that the stock has some more upside potential because some of Cisco's new products are about to be introduced, and if not delayed, could add substantially to its earnings. In this situation, you could sell your stock and use a small percentage of your profits to purchase a call option in the event there is additional upside potential. You would then be able to partake in any additional gains yet have much less money at risk if there is a substantial fall in the stock's price.

Option Deltas

In Chapter Two, we discussed how an option's delta measures how much the option will move relative to the near-term movement of the underlying stock. The deeper in-the-money a call option is, the closer to 1 the delta will be. Note too that as the option's time value erodes, so does its delta if the underlying stock price remains unchanged. However, for deep in-the-money options, the delta may increase as maturity approaches. The delta on a particular stock option can be obtained from a variety of services, including brokers.

Deltas clearly are an excellent tool to use when deciding which call option to purchase. For example, suppose that XYZ Corporation stock is trading at 25. The 3-month 25 call option might have a delta of .50 and

3-month 30 call option a delta of .25. If the stock rises by 1 point, the 25 call option will probably move up one-half of a point and the 30 call option one-quarter of a point. If you want to purchase a call option that will mimic the stock price movement, you should buy the one with the highest delta.

Naked Call Writing

Writing or selling call options without owning the underlying stock is a bearish strategy known as *naked call writing.* Here the seller or writer of a call option receives the option premium from the buyer and incurs an obligation to sell the stock at the striking price. If the stock is below the striking price at expiration, the call option will expire worthless and the writer will have earned the premium as profit. If the stock is above the striking price, the buyer may exercise the call option and force the writer to sell the stock to him or her at the striking price. The writer's loss will be the stock's market price less the striking price less the premium received. The uncovered writer may, however, cancel the obligation at any time prior to the assignment by purchasing a call option with the same striking price and expiration date in the market through a broker, thus closing out the short position.

For example, suppose that XYZ Corporation common stock is trading at $45 a share and the call options are priced as follows:

XYZ 3-month 40 call, 5 ¾ points

XYZ 3-month 45 call, 2 ½ points

XYZ 6-month 50 call, ¾ points

If you think the price of XYZ Corporation stock is going to fall and sell the 3-month at-the-money call option for the 2 ½ point premium, you will incur an obligation to sell 100 shares of XYZ at 45 a share within the next 3 months. If the stock is below 45 at expiration, the option will expire worthless. Thus, you will have earned 2 ½ points, or $250. However, your risk is unlimited, since you will still be obligated to sell the stock to the call option purchaser at $45 per share upon demand. This is shown in Exhibit 3–2. If the stock price ran up to 80 on takeover speculation and you did not own the underlying stock, you would have to go into the marketplace and purchase it at the current market price. In this case, you would buy XYZ Corporation stock at 80, or $8000 for 100 shares, and sell it to the person who exercised the call option at 45, or $4500 for 100 shares. In this example, you would have a loss of $3250: $8000 (market price) – $4500 (striking price) – $250 (option premium). The seller could take a little less risk for less premium by selling a further-out call option. In this scenario, you could have sold the 3-month 50 call option for a premium of ¾, which would obligate you to sell XYZ Corporation stock to the call option purchaser for $50.

These are not necessarily attractive strategies for the average investor, since one takes a very large risk for a relatively small reward (the premium). They are, however, important to understand when looking at our next strategy: covered call option writing.

Exhibit 3–2 Sell At-the-Money Call with a Striking Price of 45 at 2 ½ or $250

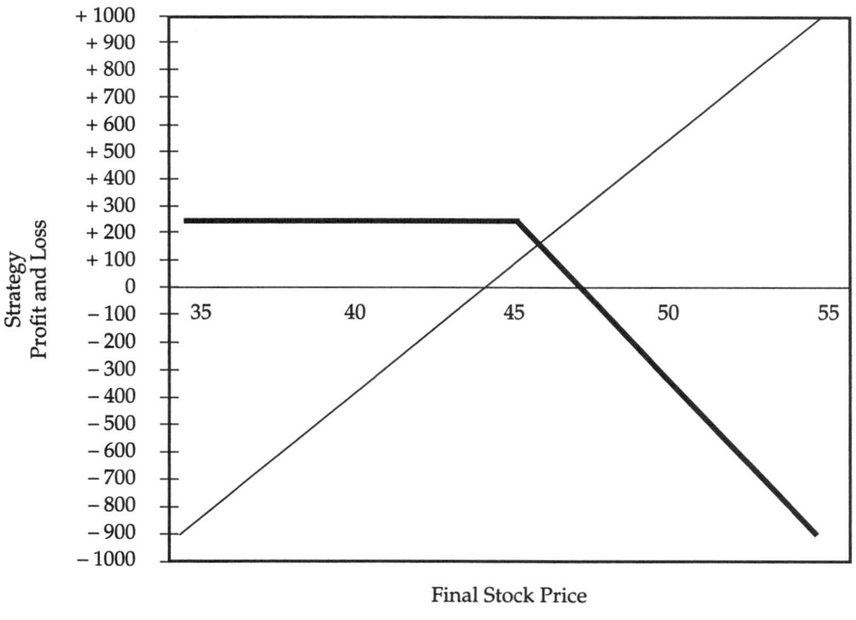

Exhibit 3–3 Sell In-the-Money Call with a Striking Price of 40 at 5 ¾ or $575

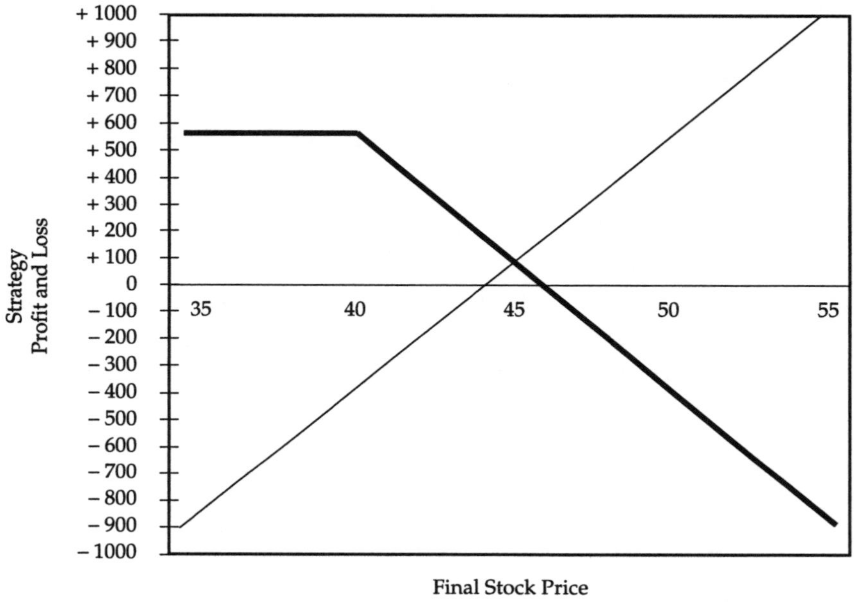

Covered Call Option Writing

In previous discussions, we noted that options are a depleting asset. If the underlying stock is stagnant over time, the out-of-the-money call option will expire worthless. When writing a covered call option, the investor buys a stock that he or she is comfortable owning and sells or writes a call option against that position.

We strongly recommend that you pick this stock based on its fundamental merits and not just because the returns promised by the strategy look attractive. The covered call option writing strategy reduces your downside risk by the amount of the premium that you received from the option's sale. At the same time, you will have limited your upside potential gain by the striking price at which you have agreed to sell the stock. This is a bullish strategy, which in fact is more conservative than the outright purchase of the stock because you will reduce your down-

Exhibit 3–4 Sell Out-of-the-Money Call with a Striking Price of 50 at ¾ or $75

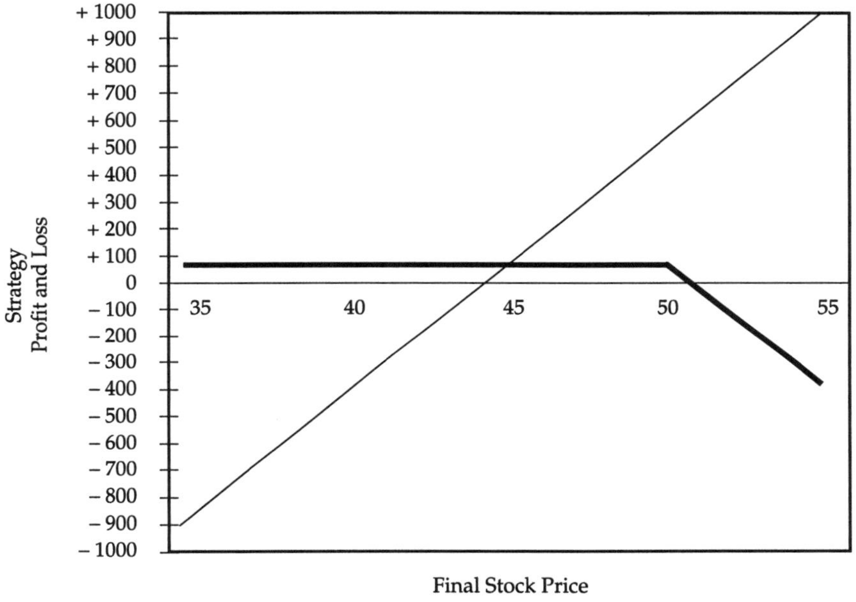

side risk by the amount of the premium. At the same time, you will realize additional income if the stock does nothing.

The covered call option writing strategy will outperform the outright stock purchase in three situations: If the stock (1) falls, (2) remains the same, or (3) rises slightly. The only time the outright purchase of the stock will outperform the covered call option writing strategy is when the stock price increases dramatically during the call option's life. When determining which call option to write, you should understand that writing in-the-money call options may offer more downside protection but may also fail to offer you the upside potential you are seeking. Conversely, an out-of-the-money covered write may offer you a higher potential yield but less downside protection than an in-the-money covered call write.

The following sections will help explain this point by presenting graphic depictions of three covered write situations on the same stock.

Exhibit 3–5 Buy Stock at 45 or $4500; Sell In-the-Money Call with a Striking Price of 40 at 5¾ or $575

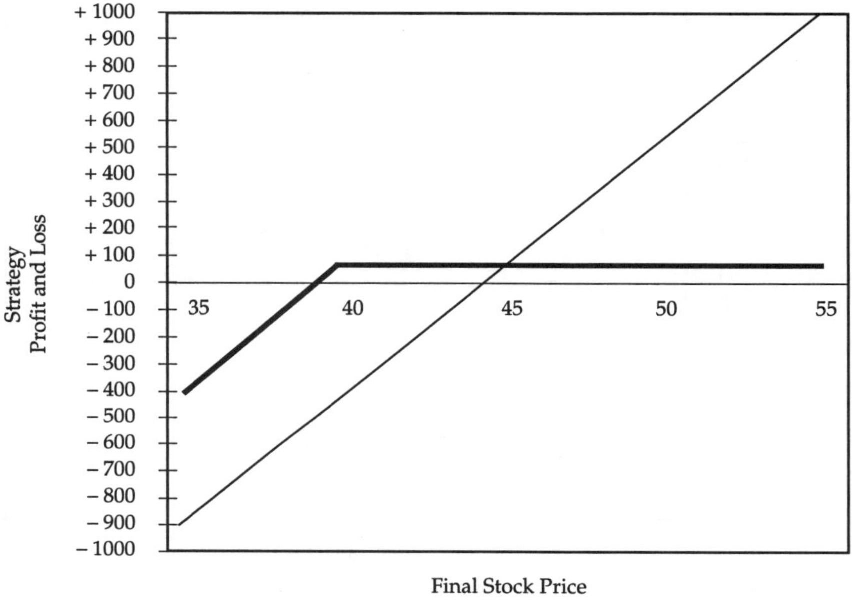

IN-THE-MONEY COVERED CALL WRITE In Exhibit 3–5, the investor has purchased 100 shares of a stock for $45 a share and sold an in-the-money call option with a striking price of 40 for 5 ¾ (5 points intrinsic value, ¾ point time value), or $575. From the graph, it is evident that the investor has 5 ¾ points of downside protection (striking price – current stock price + call option premium) but an upside potential of only ¾ point, which is the time value of the call option.

AT-THE-MONEY COVERED CALL WRITE In Exhibit 3–6, the investor has purchased 100 shares of the same stock for $45 a share and sold an at-the-money call option with a striking price of 45 for 2 ½ (all time value), or $250. The graph makes it clear that the investor has 2 ½ points of downside protection (striking price – current stock price + call option premium) and 2 ½ points of upside potential, which is the premium from the at-the-

Exhibit 3–6 Buy Stock at 45 or $4500; Sell At-the-Money Call with a Striking Price of 45 at 2 ½ or $250

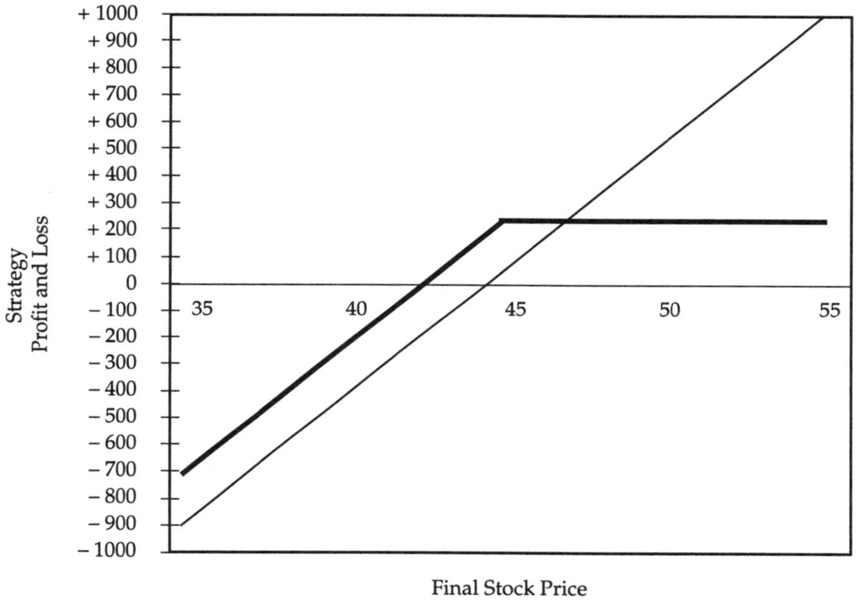

money call. This offers less downside protection but more upside potential than the in-the-money covered call option situation.

OUT-OF-THE-MONEY COVERED CALL WRITE In Exhibit 3–7, the investor has purchased 100 shares of the same stock for $45 a share and sold an out-of-the-money call option with a striking price of 50 for ¾ point (all time premium), or $75. From the graph, it is evident that the investor has ¾ point of downside protection and upside potential of 5 ¾ points (striking price – current stock price + call option premium). Clearly this offers more upside potential but less downside protection than the other two covered call option situations.

AN ILLUSTRATION Now that we have essentially defined covered call option writing, let's take a look at some realistic situations and their possible consequences.

Exhibit 3–7 Buy Stock at 45 or $4500; Sell Out-of-the-Money Call with a Striking Price of 50 at ¾ or $75

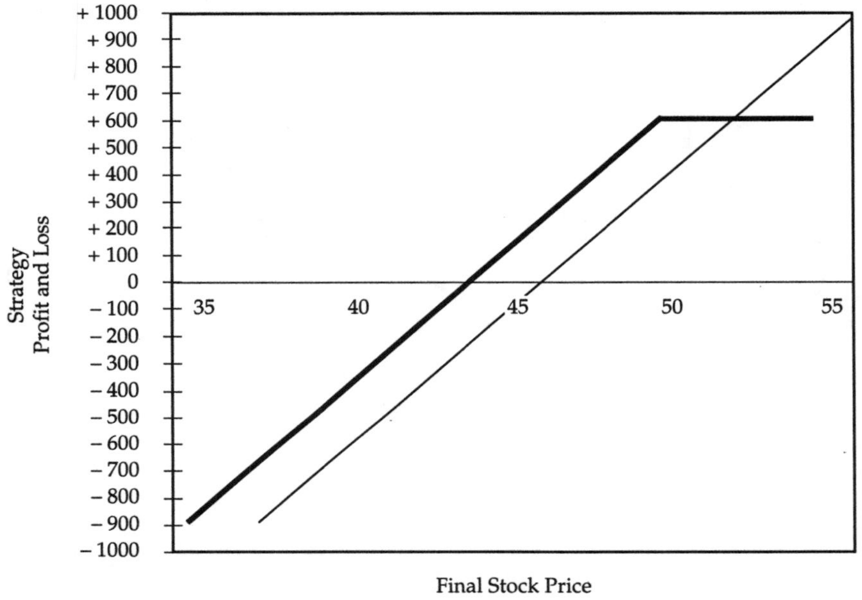

Phillip Morris (MO) looks like a very attractive investment. Its stock is currently selling for $45 a share and pays a $2.60 annual dividend for a yield of 5.78 percent ($2.60 dividend/$45 stock price). The call options are priced as follows:

MO 6-month 45 call, 4 points
MO 6-month 50 call, 2 points
MO 6-month 40 call, 7 points

If you thought the stock was going to move upward in a fairly short time, you would just purchase the stock or a call option. However, since you are not a good market or stock timer, an alternative to an outright purchase of Phillip Morris stock would be to buy the stock and sell a 6-month 50 call option for a premium of 2 points. This would give you 2 points of additional income or some downside protection, which would give you an effective cost basis of 43: $45 (market price) – $2 (call option premium). If the stock ran up and exceeded the striking price of 50 at expiration, it would be called away and your return would be 7 points (striking price – cost basis), or a 15 percent capital gain (7-point gain/$45 original cost). On an annualized basis, it would be a return of 30 percent 15[pc] × (12 months/6 months) plus any dividends you might have received in that six-month period.

In order to give you an even more accurate picture, we have provided an illustrative covered call writing worksheet for our example. This will allow you to accurately compute the cost basis, the return if the stock is called away, the return if the stock remains unchanged, and the breakeven or downside protection. Exhibit 3–8 is a standard worksheet format. Exhibit 3–9 shows the same worksheet with data supplied for our Phillip Morris example.

In our original example, we did not compute the returns including the dividends on MO. The worksheet in Exhibit 3–9 shows that if you include the dividends, your return increases by more than 7 percent, or 37.5 percent annualized. In this scenario, the largest risk you have taken for the locked-in return is the possibility that the stock will have a tremendous run-up and you will not take part in the profit above the $50 striking price.

It should be noted that although you made an obligation to sell Phillip Morris stock at 50, you may cancel that obligation by purchasing an identical call option in the market through a broker for a closing transaction. Let us look at a couple of scenarios in which you might want to consider this alternative.

ROLLING UP Suppose the stock ran up to 52 for a 15.5 percent increase over five months [(52 – 45)/45)] and the options were now priced as follows:

MO March 45 call, 7 ½ points
MO March 50 call, 3 points
MO March 55 call, 1½ points

The 50 call option that you originally sold for 2 is now worth 3 with one month until expiration. Two points of the premium are intrinsic value, and the remaining point is the option's time value. Further, the 4-month June call options are priced as follows:

MO June 45 call, 8 ½ points
MO June 50 call, 4 points
MO June 55 call, 2 points

Worksheet 3–8 Sample Covered Call Writing Worksheet

A. Initial Position Data

Underlying Stock	________					
Dividends Quarterly	________					________
Days until Option Expires	________					
1. Buy	________	________	at	_	for	________
2. Plus Commissions	# of shares	stock	at	_	for	________
3. Total Cost of Stock			at	_	for	________
4. Sell		________	at	_	for	________
5. Less Commissions		call	at	_	for	________
6. Net Call Options' Proceeds						________
7. Net Investment (3) – (6)						________

B. Return If Stock > Strike

8. Sell	________	________	at	_	for	________
9. Less Commissions	# of shares	stock	at	_	for	________
10. Plus Dividends Received	________		at	_	for	________
11. Total Balance			at	_	for	________
12. Net Profit (11) – (7)						________
13. Percentage Return (12)/(7)						________
14. Return Annualized (365)/Days until Expiration × (13)						________

C. Return If Stock is Unchanged

15. Net Option Income ________
16. Dividends Received ________
17. Total Income ________
18. Total Cost of Stock ________
19. Rate of Return (17)/(11) ________
20. Annualized Rate of Return (365)/Days until Expiration × (19) ________

D. Breakeven Point on Stock

21. Total Cost of Stock ________
22. Less Proceeds From Sale of Calls ________
23. Less Dividends Received ________
24. Subtotal ________
25. Breakeven Price per Share (24)/(# of shares) ________

Worksheet 3–9 Covered Call Writing Worksheet for Phillip Morris

A. Initial Position Data						
Underlying Stock	Phillip Morris					
Dividends Quarterly	0.65					$0.65
Days until Option Expires	182					
1. Buy	300	Phillip Morris	at	45	for	$13500.00
2. Plus Commissions			at	0	for	$0.00
3. Total Cost of Stock			at	0	for	$13500.00
4. Sell	3	March 50 Calls	at	2	for	$600.00
5. Less Commissions			at	0	for	$0.00
6. Net Call Options' Proceeds						$550.00
7. Net Investment (3) – (6)						$12900.00
B. Return If Stock > Strike						
8. Sell	300	Phillip Morris	at	50	for	$15000.00
9. Less Commissions			at	0	for	$0.00
10. Plus Dividends Received	0.65		at	2	for	$390.00
11. Total Balance			at	0	for	$15390.00
12. Net Profit (11) – (7)						$2490.00
13. Percentage Return (12)/(7)						19.30 %
14. Return Annualized (365)/(182) × (13)						38.71 %

C. Return If Stock is Unchanged	
15. Net Option Income	$600.00
16. Dividends Received	$390.00
17. Total Income	$990.00
18. Total Cost of Stock	$13500.00
19. Rate of Return (17)/(11)	7.33 %
20. Annualized Rate of Return (365)/(182) × (19)	14.71 %
D. Breakeven Point on Stock	
21. Total Cost of Stock	$13500.00
22. Less Proceeds From Sale of Calls	$600.00
23. Less Dividends Received	$390.00
24. Subtotal	$$12510.00
25. Breakeven Price per Share (24)/(# of shares)	$41.70

The MO June 55 call is selling for 2 points, which is composed entirely of time value.

At this point, you may elect to close the original position by purchasing an MO 50 call option for 3, which would result in a 1-point loss. However, you may now sell a 4-month 55 call option for 2 points. Now you will have increased your cost basis by one more point to 46 [45 (original cost) – 2 (original option sold) + 3 (repurchase of original option) – 1 (sell 55 call)] from 45 and made an obligation to sell the stock at 55. If the stock is called away when the option expires in four months, your capital gain will be 15.2 percent [(55 – 46)/46], or 30.4 percent annualized. By closing the position in the MO 50 and selling the XYZ 55, you will have rolled up to the call option with the next higher striking price. Note that we have not included dividends.

This follow-up strategy is known as *rolling up* and is defined as buying back the call option that you originally sold and simultaneously selling a call option with a higher striking price.

You may also sell an option that expires at a later date than the original, allowing you to take in additional time premium. If you thought that Phillip Morris had substantial upside, you may have decided not to sell the 55 call option and just hold the stock. Nevertheless, it is important to understand the rolling-up concept.

ROLLING DOWN There are also times when you may choose to roll down. *Rolling down* is defined as buying back the call option that you originally sold and simultaneously selling a call option with a lower striking price. Again you may opt to sell an option with a further-out expiration date than the original option's in order to take in additional time premium.

To illustrate, suppose that MO dropped from 45 to 40 over 5 months. Now the 50 call that originally was sold for 2 is trading at ¼ point, and the 4-month June call options are priced as follows:

MO June 40 call, 2 points
MO June 45 call, 1 ½ points
MO June 50 call, ¼ point

You could roll down by purchasing the MO 50 for ¼ and sell a 4-month MO June 45 call for 1 ½. Then the cost basis on the stock would be 41 ¾ [45 (original cost) – 2 (original option sold) + ¼ (repurchase of original option) – 1 ½ (sell 45 call)], with an obligation to sell it at 45. This would be an appropriate move if you thought the stock was going to stay flat or rise slightly. If you felt the stock was going to continue dropping, you should have just sold the stock. In this situation, your loss is less than it would be had you just purchased the stock because you sold the original call for 2 points, which gave you some downside protection.

Selling Call Options Against a Stock With an Existing Profit

There is yet another way to use calls in conjunction with stock as a tool for increasing your yield. For example, suppose you like ABC Corporation stock, which is currently at $30 a share. You have little interest in selling calls against it, because you think the next few quarters are going to be exceptionally strong from an earnings standpoint. Six months later, the stock indeed has reacted to favorable earnings: It has increased 40 percent in value to $42 a share, and the 3-month 45 call is trading at $3 a share.

At this point the market looks skittish, and you are not sure whether ABC stock can continue its upward momentum. You could either put in a stop-loss order or just sell the stock, but another alternative would be to sell the 45 call option for 3 points and thus reduce your cost basis to 27 from 30 [27 (stock price) – 3 (option premium)]. If the stock continued to rise and was above 45 at expiration, it would be called away, which would mean a 66 percent gain for your original investment [45 (strike price) – 27 (cost basis)/27 (cost basis)].

However, if the stock began to drop, your follow-up action would be to sell the stock and buy back the option for less than what you originally sold it for. For example, if ABC dropped approximately 10 percent (or 4 points) from 42 to 38 over a couple of months, some of the time value would have diminished from the 45 call option that you had sold. It may now be worth 1. At this point, you may be less optimistic about ABC Corporation. Because you had sold the 6-month call for 3 points and it is now worth 1 point, you have protected some of the profit. Had you done nothing, you would have lost 4 points of your profits and, by selling the 45 call, given yourself 3 points of downside protection. In this scenario, you gave up 2 points' profit as compared to 4 points had you taken no action.

Hedging a Short Sale

In Chapter One, we defined a *short sale* as a bearish strategy in which the investor has borrowed a stock to sell, with the hope of buying it back at a later date at a lower price. To hedge this position, the investor could purchase a call on the same underlying stock. The loss would then be limited only to the amount of an at-the-money call premium. At the same time, the investor's profit would come to the amount of decline in the stock less the cost of the call.

For example, suppose Intel stock is selling at $65 per share and a 3-month at-the-money call is selling for 5 points, or $500. The investor sells short Intel stock at $65 a share, anticipating that it may be purchased later at a considerably lower price. The investor's risk is that Intel may climb above $65 a share. To limit the potential loss, the investor could buy a call with a striking price of 65 for a premium of $500. Regardless of how high the stock rose, the investor would have the right to buy it back at $65 a share. If Intel rose 20 percent, or 13 points, the investor would incur a loss of $500—the call's premium—compared to a $1300 loss had the position not been hedged. Conversely, if Intel dropped in price 20 percent, or 13 points, the investor's profit would be $1300 less the cost of the option ($1300 – $500 = $800).

Conclusion

In this chapter, we have discussed a number of situations in which you may sell call options on a common stock. It may be a situation in which you are buying the stock and selling a call simultaneously or perhaps one in which you are selling a call option on stock that you have previously owned. In either case, you can take some follow-up action. If the stock drops, you can roll down, which will give you additional income. If the stock rises, you may elect to roll up, which will allow you to raise the price at which you had originally contracted to relinquish the stock. The point to keep in mind is that you may stick with your original objectives or modify them if there is any significant movement in the stock price.

Chapter Four

SIMPLE PUT OPTION STRATEGIES

Purchase of Put Options

Recall that a put option gives the purchaser the right to sell a stock at a predetermined price—the striking price—between the date of purchase and the option's expiration date. A put option is purchased with the hope that the underlying security will decrease in value. Usually the put option's price increases as the underlying security's price drops.

The purchase of put options is considered a bearish strategy and is used to obtain greater leverage while limiting the investor's loss. It is a purely speculative activity, because the put option is a depleting asset—that is, its value diminishes over time if the underlying stock increases in value or does nothing.

PUT OPTION PURCHASE VERSUS STOCK SHORT SALE The put option purchaser has the same objectives as the short seller. Recall that a *short sale* is defined as the sale of common stock not owned by the seller with the

Exhibit 4–1 Purchase of At-the-Money Put with a Striking Price of 35 at 3 Versus Stock Short Sale

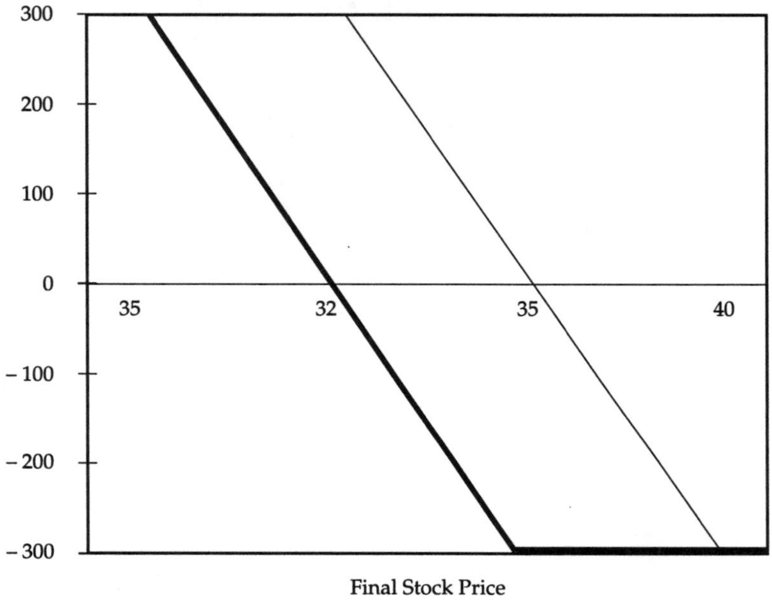

expectation that it may be purchased back at a lower price. Unlike the short seller, however, the put buyer can limit the extent of potential loss by the amount of the premium. Also, the put buyer is not subject to the margin requirements and rules by which the short seller must abide. On the other hand, the short seller is not under the same time constraints as the put option purchaser. For the put buyer, the stock must fall during the option's life.

Exhibit 4–1 compares the purchase of an at-the-money put option with a striking price of 35 and a short sale of the stock at 35. (In the exhibits that follow, the thin line represents stock purchase or short sale and the thick line represents option strategy.) As you can see, the loss on the put is limited to the put's purchase price of $300, which is significantly less than the unlimited potential loss to which the short seller is exposed. In addition, the put clearly provides greater leverage, since the purchaser has a large profit potential while committing much less money than the short seller.

Now let us look at a real-life situation. Suppose you think that retail sales will be sluggish. Thus, you want to speculate that Dayton Hudson (DH) is going to have lower than expected earnings for the quarter and, hence, that the stock price will decline in value. You observe that Dayton Hudson common stock is trading at $50 a share and the put options are priced as follows:

Dayton Hudson 6-month 45, 2 points

Dayton Hudson 6-month 50, 4 points

Dayton Hudson 6-month 55, 6 points

A 6-month at-the-money put is selling at 4 points, or $400 for the right to sell 100 shares of DH at 50.

Now suppose that your retail sales scenario proves correct and Dayton Hudson reports lower than expected earnings. In just a few months, Dayton Hudson stock has declined 5 points to 45, meaning a 10 percent gain (5 points profit/50 short stock) for the stock short seller. At the same time, the put price has increased from 4 to 7 (5 points intrinsic value + 2 points time value) for a gain of 75 percent over the same time period [3-point increase in option/4 (option purchase price)]. The reason the put option increased is that your right to sell Dayton Hudson at $50 a share must be worth at least 5 points if Dayton Hudson is now selling at $45 a share. However, there is still some time value remaining in the premium, which is why your 50 put option is worth 7 points. As an investor in this put option, you could sell it in the options market to realize your gain. Had you held 100 shares of Dayton Hudson, you could exercise your right to sell them at $50 per share. This is, however, a separate topic, which we will discuss later in the chapter.

If your retail sales scenario proves incorrect and you shorted 100 shares of Dayton Hudson at 50, your risk theoretically will be unlimited because Dayton Hudson could rise, possibly doubling or even tripling in value. The point to keep in mind is that if you want to speculate on a quick downturn, purchasing a put option may meet your objectives more directly and limit your downside risk by the amount of the put option—in this scenario, $400 versus an unlimited amount.

WHICH TYPE OF OPTION TO PURCHASE? In Chapter Three, we discussed the choice between the purchase of in-the-money, at-the-money, or out-of-the-money calls. The same type of analysis is needed when deciding which put option to purchase. For example, if you expect a major drop in the price of a stock within a relatively short time period, the purchase of the nearest-term at-the-money put option may best meet your objectives.

As in the case of call options, the dollar price should not be the sole factor in your choice of which put option to purchase. The chief consideration is that even though an out-of-the-money put option may provide you with the greatest amount of leverage, it also gives you a greater chance of losing all your money. In addition, if the stock drops only moderately, the in-the-money put option may out-perform the out-of-the-money option.

Returning to the Dayton Hudson example, it is clear that had you purchased the out-of-the-money 45 put option at 2, you would have lost the entire investment unless Dayton Hudson stock dropped to 43 during the option's life. In contrast, had you bought the in-the-money 55 put at 6, all you would need to make a profit is for the stock to drop below 49. In this example, you have more dollars at risk by purchasing the in-the-money put option versus the out-of-the-money put option, which is why you must assess the amount of dollar exposure you are willing to assume in any put option purchase decision.

TIME FACTORS The next decision to be made when buying a put option is whether to purchase a 3, 6, or 9 month option. Many people purchase the nearest-term out-of-the-money put option simply because it is the cheapest. However, if the stock does not drop within a relatively short period, you will lose the entire investment. Your decision should be based on how quickly you think the underlying stock will decrease in value.

If you are not confident that the decrease will take place in the very near term, you should attempt to purchase the next-furthest-out call option in order to minimize your risk. However, in making this decision it is important to remember that if the stock stays stagnant, the put option will maintain its time value on a consistent basis up until the last six weeks prior to expiration. This is when you will see the quickest deterioration in the option's time value.

PUT OPTION DELTAS In Chapter Two, we discussed how an option's delta measures how much the option will move relative to the near-term movement of the underlying stock. We also noted that calls have a positive and puts a negative relationship with the underlying stock's price. Hence, put option deltas will be negative.

The deeper in-the-money the put option is, the closer to –1 the delta will be. Note too that as time value erodes, so does the option's delta if the underlying stock price remains unchanged. As mentioned in Chapter Three, a delta on a particular stock option can be obtained from a variety of services, including brokers.

As in the case of calls, deltas are an excellent tool to use when deciding which put option to purchase. For example, suppose XYZ stock is trading at 25. The 3-month 25 put option might have a delta of –.50 and the 3-month 20 put option a delta of –.25. If the stock drops 1 point, the 25 put option will probably increase by one-half of a point and the 20 put option by one-quarter of a point. If you want to purchase a put option that will mimic the stock price movement, you should choose the option that is closest to –1.

Put Options as Insurance

PURCHASE OF STOCK AND PUT OPTION SIMULTANEOUSLY A put option may be seen as a type of insurance when it is purchased simultaneously with a stock. By purchasing the put in conjunction with the stock, you establish a minimum selling price for the stock. Remember that the put purchaser owns the right to sell a stock at a predetermined price. Thus, by purchasing a put and a stock simultaneously, you will limit your loss to the stock price minus the put option's striking price plus the option's premium. If the stock rises, your profit will decrease only by the cost of the put.

In order to fully understand this concept, let us take a look at a realistic scenario. You are bullish on Home Depot. Home Depot common stock is trading at $35 a share, and the put options are priced as follows:

Home Depot 6-month 30 put, 1 point

Home Depot 6-month 35 put, 3 points

Home Depot 6-month 40 put, 7 points

Since you are bullish on Home Depot, you purchase 100 shares at $35. On the same day, you buy a 6-month at-the-money put for 3 points, or $300. Now your cost basis is $38 [35 (stock price) + 3 (put option price)] a share, but the most you can lose is 3 points because you own the right to sell your stock at $35 a share. If Home Depot rises 20 percent and is trading at 42 at expiration, the 35 put option will expire worthless. The right to sell Home Depot at 35 cannot be worth much if Home Depot is trading at 42 in the marketplace. At this point, you will have realized a $300 loss on the put but also a $700 gain on your stock position for a net gain of $400. If the stock had risen to 42 before expiration, you might have been able to sell the put in the option market for some time value. If Home Depot had declined 20 percent and was trading at 28 at expiration, you could exercise your put option and sell your 100 shares of Home Depot for $35 a share. Your net loss would be the $300 you paid for the option as opposed to $700 had you done nothing.

In this scenario, another alternative would be to sell the put for a profit and hold your stock if you still remain bullish on Home Depot. Here the 6-month 35 put will be worth at least $700 if the underlying stock is trading at 28. Thus, you will have a profit on the put option of at least $400 [700 (current put option price) 300 (purchase price on put option)]. If Home Depot is unchanged at expiration, the put will expire worthless. However, the put will have acted as term insurance against a decline in the value of Home Depot common stock.

Exhibits 4–2, 4–3, and 4–4 compare the purchase of at-the-money, out-of-the-money, and in-the-money put options, respectively, in conjunction with the purchase of the common stock. As you can see, the put options that are further in-the-money offer you the most protection against a drop in the stock, but they also cost the most.

PURCHASE OF A PUT OPTION WITH AN EXISTING PROFIT ON THE STOCK Purchasing put options on a stock with an existing profit is another way of using put options as insurance. Suppose you have bought 100 shares of Bombay at $30 a share. Over the following year, housing sales improve and Bombay records better than expected earnings. As a result, the stock runs up 50 percent (15/30) to $45 a share. As an investor in Bombay, you are concerned that declining housing starts may negatively impact home furnishing stocks. At this point, you may elect to buy a put on Bombay to

Exhibit 4–2 Buy Stock at 35 or $3500; Buy At-the-Money Put with a Striking Price of 35 at 3 or $300

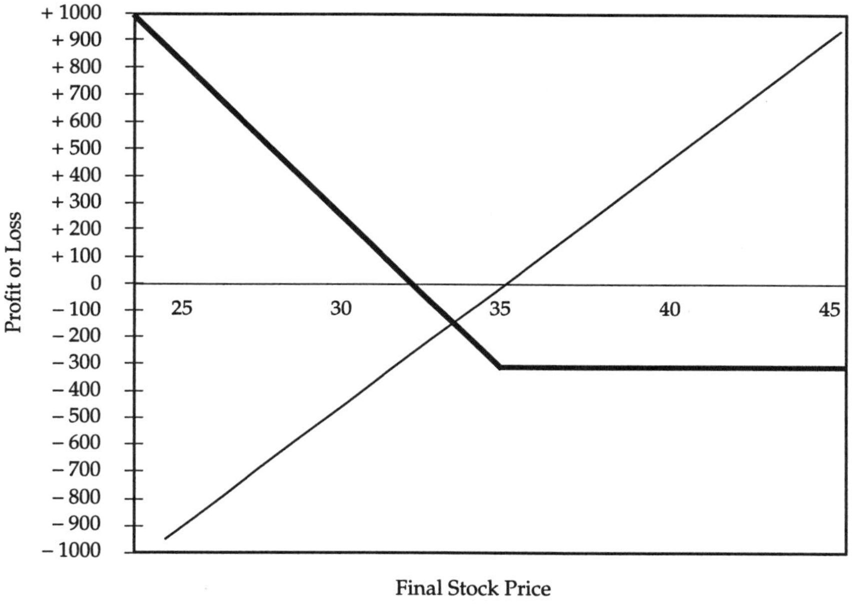

protect your gain in the long stock position. Remember that the put purchaser owns the right to sell his or her shares of stock at a predetermined price up to and including the expiration date.

In this scenario, Bombay is at 45 and the 6-month put options are priced as follows:

Bombay 6-month 40 put, 1 point

Bombay 6-month 45 put, 3 points

Bombay 6-month 50 put, 7 points

Although you continue to be bullish on Bombay's long-term prospects, you want to protect your capital gains. The purchase of the 6-month at-the-money put with a striking price of 45 for a premium of 3 points, or $300, will give you the right to sell Bombay at $45 a share. Thus, your loss will be limited to the option's cost. You may continue to realize

Exhibit 4–3 Buy Stock at 35 or $3500; buy Out-of-the-Money Put with a Striking Price of 30 at 1 or $100

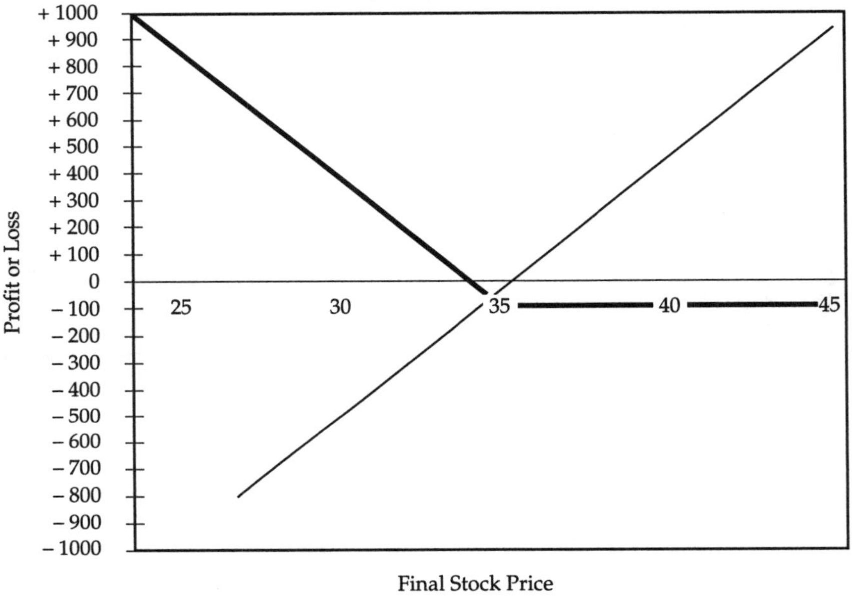

gains if the stock keeps rising; however, any such gains will be reduced by the purchase price of the put.

Given this Bombay example, let us see what the net result on the position will be when the stock rises, declines, and remains unchanged.

If Bombay rises to 56.25, or 25 percent, you will have participated in the additional gain in your long stock position. The put will drop in value as the stock continues to rise and finally expire worthless, but it will have fulfilled the role of term insurance. You could have limited your loss on the put by selling it in the options market prior to expiration for whatever time value remained.

If Bombay declines 25 percent, or 11.25 points, to 33.75, you can exercise your put and thus sell your stock for the striking price of $45 a share. Your profit will be the striking price (45) minus the original cost (30) plus the option premium (3). If you continue to remain bullish on

Exhibit 4–4 Buy Stock at 35 or $3500; Buy In-the-Money Put with a Striking Price of 40 at 7 or $700

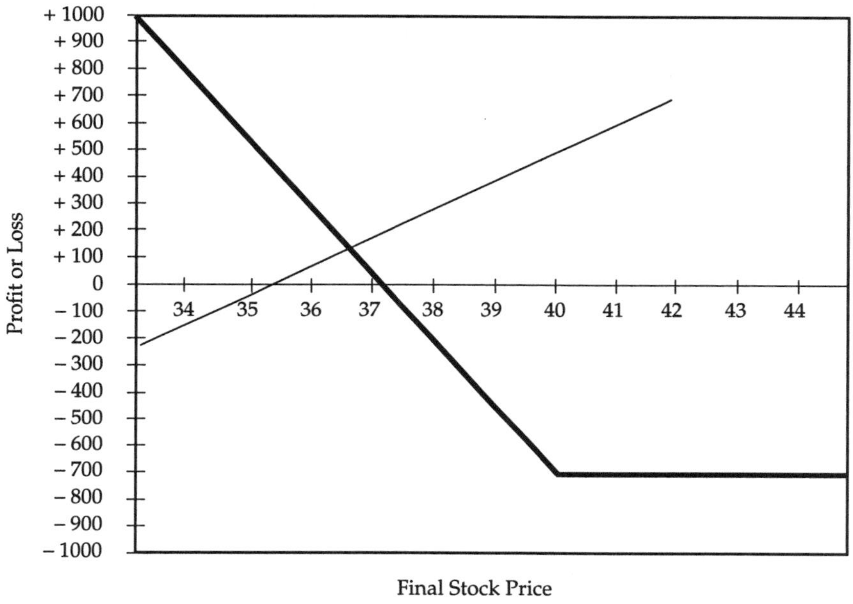

Bombay, you can sell the put option for a profit and continue to hold the common stock. In this scenario the put will be worth at least 11.25 points, or the difference between the current market price and the option's striking price.

If Bombay remains unchanged and is $45 at expiration, the put will expire worthless. Again the put will have acted as insurance.

PUT PURCHASE VERSUS STOP-LOSS ORDER In the Bombay example, you may have also considered entering a stop-loss order on the 100 shares of stock. When you enter a stop-loss order, your broker will attempt to sell the stock as soon as it reaches a predetermined price. The advantage of this strategy versus a put purchase is that a stop-loss order has no expiration date; it can be maintained indefinitely. It may also be used on positions of fewer than 100 shares.

A stop-loss order also has disadvantages relative to a put option purchase. In a sharply declining market, the stock may not be sold at all or be sold for less than the desired price. In addition, a stop-loss order does not offer the gains that a put option provides. The put purchaser may exercise the option or sell it for a profit if the underlying stock declines.

USING A PUT OPTION AT YEAR END TO PROTECT GAINS Another situation in which the purchase of a put on an existing stock may come in handy occurs when you have realized a profit on the stock at year end. In this case, you may want to take the capital gains in the following year. By purchasing a put on the stock with an expiration date in the following year, you will guarantee a selling price. However, the purchase of puts on a stock held short term will wipe out the holding period for tax purposes. The holding period will re-start upon the options expiration. The purchase of a put will not affect the holding period on stock held long term. Please consult with your tax advisor when considering this strategy.

Selling Puts

So far, our discussion has focused on the purchase of puts. Now we will look at the other side of the transaction—selling, or writing, puts.

SELLING PUTS AS A WAY OF ACQUIRING STOCK Recall that the buyer of a put profits when the underlying stock drops in price. Conversely, the seller of a put profits when the underlying stock increases in value. The seller, or writer, of a put option receives the option premium from the buyer and makes an obligation to buy the stock at the striking price. The seller may, however, cancel the obligation by purchasing a put option in the marketplace with the same striking price and expiration. If the stock is above the striking price at expiration, the put option will expire worthless and the seller will have earned the premium as profit. If the stock is below the striking price, the buyer may exercise the put option and force the seller to purchase the stock at the striking price.

The put writer's objective is to earn premium income or a means of acquiring a common stock at a price lower than the current market price. The writer's cost would be the striking price minus the premium received. Although the put writer may expect the underlying stock to increase in value, he or she should be prepared to acquire the stock at the predetermined striking price. Thus, one should sell puts only on stock on which one is fundamentally bullish.

MARGIN REQUIREMENTS Before examining some specific examples of put writing, let us look at the margin requirements involved.

Under the current requirements, an investor who is short a put must post 20 percent of the value of the underlying stock plus the put's premium less the amount out-of-the-money, with a minmum of $2000. This may be in the form of cash or double the margin requirement in the case of marginable stock, Treasury securities, and municipal bonds. These margin requirements insure that there will be funds available in the event the stock is put to the investor.

The stringency of margin requirements may vary among brokerage firms. In all cases, however, the requirements must meet the minimum standards set by the Securities and Exchange Commission. For example, if you sold 5 out-of-the-money puts on Autozone and Autozone stock was trading at $50 a share and the out-of-the-money 45 put was trading at 2 points, or $200, the margin requirements would be as follows:

20% of Autozone ($50 × 500 = 25,000)	$5000
Minus out-of-the-money ($500 × 5 options)	(2500)
Plus premium	1000
Margin deposit required	$3500

An alternative would be to deposit double this amount, or $7000, in marginable securities. This probably would be a more desirable alternative, since you would be able to keep any interest or dividends accrued by these securities and the cash in a margin account earns no interest. (Note: This situation is given for illustrative purposes only. Be sure to consult your broker for specific margin requirements.)

CHOICE OF PUT OPTION TO WRITE In order to better understand the put writing strategy, let us look at a realistic situation. Suppose the Walgreen Co. is trading at $40 a share and the put options are priced as follows:

Walgreens 6-month 35 call, 1 point
Walgreens 6-month 40 call, 3 points
Walgreens 6-month 45 call, 7 points

If you are bullish on Walgreens, you may want to consider selling a 6-month at-the-money put for $3 premium. This will obligate you to purchase 100 shares of Walgreens at $40 a share within the next 6 months. If the stock is above 40 at expiration, the option will expire worthless. Thus, you will have earned 3 points, or $300. If Walgreens is trading below $40 per share at expiration, the put option will most likely be exercised and you will have to purchase 100 shares at $40 per share. Thus, your cost basis will be $37 [40 (striking price) – 3 (option premium)]. If Walgreens is below $37 a share, you will have realized a paper loss. If Walgreens is unchanged at expiration, the put option will most likely expire worthless. Thus, you will realize a gain of 3 points, or $300.

Exhibit 4–5 Sell At-the-Money Put with a Striking Price of 40 at 3 or $300

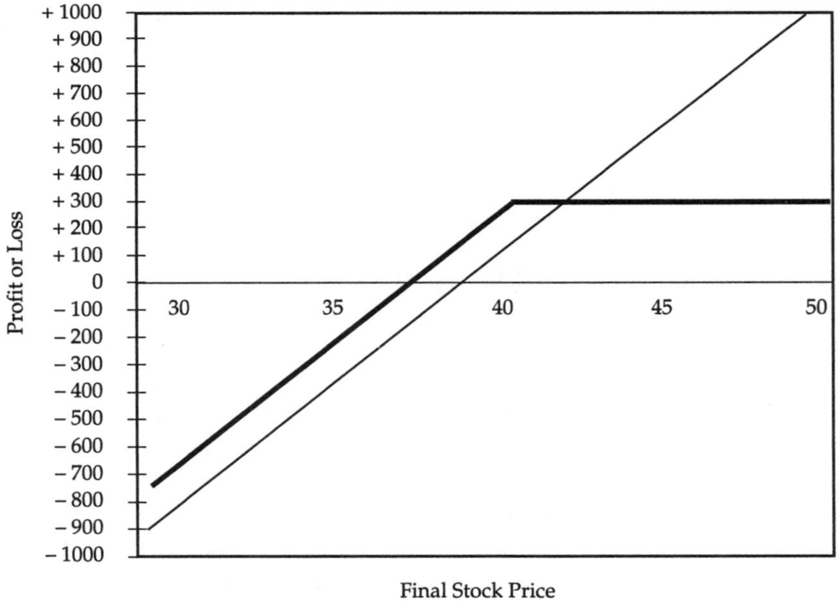

If you sell an out-of-the-money 35 put, you will receive 1 point. However, you will be taking less risk than an at-the-money or in-the-money put writer. The only time you would sell a deep-in-the-money put would be when the time value was greater than the at-the-money put or you thought there was going to be a substantial rise in the price of the stock.

Exhibits 4–5, 4–6, and 4–7 (pages 75–77) illustrate the selling of an at-the-money put, an out-of-the-money put, and an in-the-money put, respectively. Worksheet 4–1 (page 78) is a sample worksheet for use in establishing and following your put option writing. Worksheet 4–2 (page 79) incorporates data from our Walgreens example.

In summary, selling puts can be an excellent way to buy stock below current market prices and get paid for it. You can compare this strategy to putting in a good-till-cancelled order below the market and receiving cash up front.

PUT WRITING VERSUS COVERED CALL WRITING In order to better understand the philosophy of selling puts, let us compare it to a covered call write on the same underlying stock. Assume the following information:

Walgreens = 40	April 40 call = 5	
	April 40 put = 4	
Put Seller	*Covered Call Writer*	
Sell 1 Apr 40 @ + 400	Buy 100 S @ 40	$4000
+ ($2000 cash or	Sell 1 Apr 40 call @ 5	(500)
marginable securities)	Cash required	$3500

Remember that a covered call writer purchases stock and sells calls against it, thus making an obligation to sell the stock at the striking price. In this example, the covered call writer buys 100 shares of Walgreens at $40 a share and sells 1 call option with a striking price of 40 for a premium of 5 points, or $500; this provides 5 points of downside protection and 5 points of upside potential. The put seller sells 1 put with a striking price of 40 for 4 points, or $400; this creates the obligation to purchase 100 shares of Walgreens if it is below $40 a share at expiration. The cost to the covered writer is $3500 [100 shares of Walgreens @ 40 – 5 (call option premium)], while the put seller needs only collateral. The put seller may invest the difference in some other fixed-income instrument, while the covered call writer will receive dividends from the stock.

Exhibit 4–6 Sell Out-of-the-Money Put with a Striking Price of 35 at 1 or $100

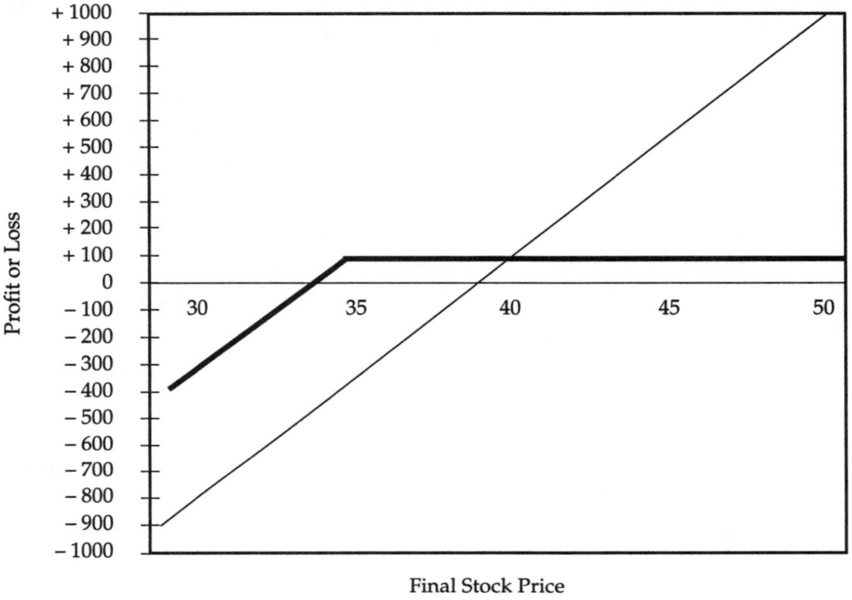

Stock Increases 20% to $48 at Expiration:

Short put expires	+ 400	Stock called @ 40	$4000
		Original investment	3500
Gain	$400	Gain	$ 500

With the stock up 20 percent or at $48 at expiration, the covered writer delivers the 100 shares of Walgreens at 40 for a gain of $500. The short put expires worthless, and the put writer keeps the $400 premium as profit.

Stock Decreases 20% to $32 at Expiration:

Purchase short put	@ 8	Stock down 8 points	$(800)
Originally sold	@ 4	Call premium received	500
Loss	(400)	Loss	$(300)

Exhibit 4–7 Sell In-the-Money Put with a Striking Price of 45 at 7 or $700

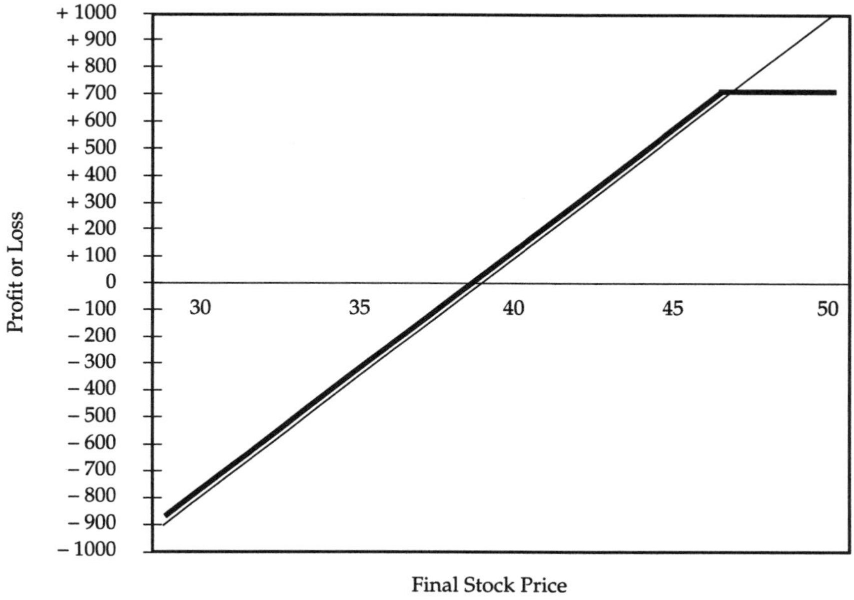

On the downside, the put writer has a breakeven at 36 (40 strike price – 4 put option premium) and the covered call writer a breakeven at 35 (40 stock purchase price – 5 call option premium). The covered call writer however, has the luxury of being able to hold on to the stock to recoup some or all of the loss if the stock rallies.

In summary, these are both bullish positions. The main difference is that the covered call writer must come up with cash to carry out the strategy, while the uncovered put writer may use his or her portfolio as collateral to establish the position.

Worksheet 4–1 Sample Selling (Writing) Put Option Worksheet

A. Initial Position Data

Underlying Stock ________

Current Stock Price ________

Put Options' Maturity Month ________

Put Options' Striking Price ________

Put Options' Premium ________

Days until Option Expires ________

1. Sell ________ (#) ________ (puts) at — for ________
2. Less Commissions at — for ________
3. Net Proceeds at — for ________
4. Collateral Required ________

B. Result of Position If Put Expires (occurs if stock is above strike price)

5. Profit is Equal to (3) at — for ________

C. Result of Cost Basis of Stock If Puts are Exercised (occurs if stock is below strike price)

6. Buy ________ (#) ________ (shares) at — for ________
7. Plus Commissions at — for ________
8. Gross Cost of Shares ________
9. Net Cost of Shares (8) – (3) ________
10. Net Cost per Share (9)/(# of shares) ________

Worksheet 4–2 Selling (Writing) Put Option Worksheet for Walgreens

A. Initial Position Data						
Underlying Stock	Walgreens					
Current Stock Price	40					$40.00
Put Options' Maturity Month	June					
Put Options' Striking Price	40					
Put Options' Premium	3					
Days until Option Expires	182					
1. Sell	1	Put	at	3	for	$300.00
2. Less Commissions			at	0	for	$0.00
3. Net Proceeds			at	0	for	$300.00
4. Collateral Required	$2000.00					
B. Result of Position If Put Expires (occurs if stock is above strike price)						
5. Profit is Equal to (3)			at	0	for	$300.00
C. Result of Cost Basis of Stock If Put is Exercised (occurs if stock is above strike price)						
6. Buy	100	Walgreens	at	40	for	$4000.00
7. Plus Commissions			at	0	for	$0.00
8. Gross Cost of Shares						$4000.00
9. Net Cost of Shares (8) – (3)						$3700.00
10. Net Cost per Share (9)/(# of shares)						$37.00

Conclusion

In this chapter, we discussed some basic put strategies that can help you achieve some bullish and some bearish objectives. These fundamental strategies, along with the basic call strategies that we explored in Chapter Three, will serve as a foundation for the more advanced strategies to be discussed in the following chapters.

Chapter Five

BASIC SPREADS

Spread Definition

The option strategies that were discussed in the preceding chapters were quite simple and used either long or short positions in options to achieve the desired objective. One problem associated with these positions is that their risk can be quite high. This chapter's purpose is to introduce the concept of creating an overall option position where long and short option positions are combined in such a way that the overall position's risk is limited. These limited risk positions are called spreads.

In general, a *spread* may be defined as the simultaneous purchase and sale of options that have the same underlying security and are of the same class, but which are of different series. It is clear from this definition that spreads are composed of either puts or calls which differ in either striking price or time to maturity. Positions that employ call options with put options are known as *combinations,* and will be discussed in the following chapter. This chapter will explain three types of spreads: the bull spread, the bear spread, and the time spread.

Bull Spread

The *bull spread* is used when one wants to profit from a generally rising market while maintaining a relatively low level of risk. The simplest way to accomplish this is by purchasing an at-the-money call option and by selling an out-of-the-money call option. In a bull spread, both of the call options have the same time to maturity but differ in their striking prices. The logic of the spread is for the investor to take a long position in the option that will have the greater price appreciation if the market rises. The cost of the long position is reduced by the amount received from the sale of the call option when the short position is established. If the investor was absolutely certain that the market was going to rise dramatically, then call options should be purchased. A simple long position in call options has unlimited profit potential but runs the risk of losing the entire amount paid for the call option if the market fails to rise as anticipated. A bull spread is less risky than a simple long call option position because the cost of the bull spread's long position is reduced by the amount of revenue generated by the spread's short option position. However, the spread's profit potential is much less than the profit potential of the long call option's position. In general, the bull spread's maximum profit potential is equal to the difference between the call options' striking prices less the total cost of the spread.

Exhibit 5–1 shows the behavior of a Motorola October 90–100 bull spread over time. The spread is established by purchasing the October 90 call option for 6 ¼ points, or $625, and selling the October 100 call option for 2 ¼ points, $225, for a net cost of 4 points or $400. The line labeled "T = 0" shows the spread's profit or loss at maturity for Motorola stock prices ranging from $80 per share to $120 per share. The line labeled "T > 0" shows the bull spread's profit or loss prior to the call options' expiration. Note that when the spread is showing a profit prior to maturity time becomes an ally for the investor since the profit increases as maturity, T = 0, approaches. Conversely, if the spread is posting a loss prior to expiration, then time is working against the investor. However, as the graph shows, the greatest loss that the investor can incur is equal to the cost of the spread—in this case $400.

Exhibit 5–1 Motorola Bull Spread
Buy October 90 Call, Sell October 100 Call

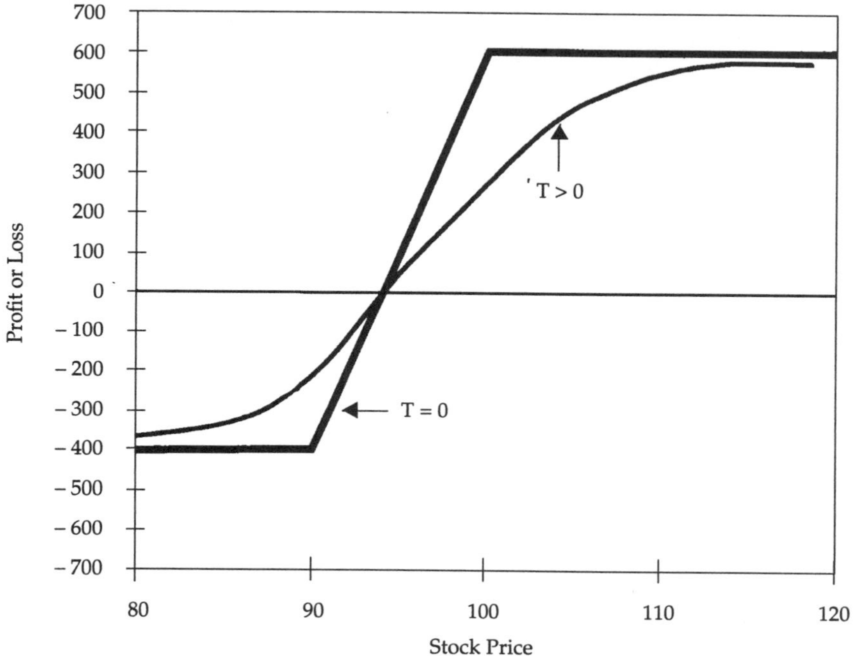

ILLUSTRATIVE BULL SPREAD: MOTOROLA The behavior of Motorola's common stock and call option prices between October 1992 and January 1993 provides a good example of conditions favorable for a bull spread. In 1992 Motorola began to experience extremely strong sales for its cellular phones and semiconductors. The long-term commitment that Motorola had made to cellular phone technology was being rewarded. Market share was expanding rapidly and Motorola had become the dominant player in the cellular phone market. The success in the cellular phone and semiconductor markets was manifested by increasing quarterly earnings and profits.

The stock market began to anticipate a strong performance for Motorola in the latter months of 1992. On October 21, Motorola's share price stood at 97 ¼ with the December 90 call option trading at 8 ½, and the December 100 call option trading at 1 ⅞. Given the recent increases in market share and quarterly profits, the company's future seemed to be quite bright. Thus, the situation was ideal for the creation of a bull spread that would allow a conservative investor to take part in the anticipated increase in Motorola's price, while limiting the riskiness of the position. On October 21, 1992, an investor could have created a bull spread in Motorola call options by purchasing a December 90 call option for 8 ½, or $850, and by selling a December 100 call option for 1 ⅞, or $187.50, for a net cost of 6 ⅝, or $662.50.

In the following weeks, the prices of Motorola's shares and call options began to rise. Much of the increase can be attributed to the November 4 announcement that Motorola's board of directors were declaring a two-for-one stock split and an increase in the quarterly dividend as of January 15, 1993. The market responded by bidding up the price of Motorola shares to 100, the price of the December 90 call option to 10 ½, and the price of the December 100 call to 3 ¼ on November 11. These call option prices translated to a value of 7 ¼, or $725, for the Motorola December 90–100 Bull spread; computed by taking the value of the long position, 10 ½ for the December 90 call option, and subtracting the value of the short position, 3 ¼ for the December 100 call option. Thus, with approximately one month remaining until expiration, the Motorola December 90–100 bull spread had increased in value by ⅝ of a point, or $62.50.

Motorola's share price and call option prices remained strong for the next month, so that on December 15, the Wednesday of expiration week, Motorola's shares were at 100 ¼, the December 90 call option settled at 11 ¼, and the December 100 call option settled at 1 ¼. Given these prices, the value of the December 90–100 bull spread was 10, 11 ¼ minus 1 ¼, or $1,000.00. With Motorola doing so well and the spread at its maximum value, the investor had to make a decision. There were two alternatives. In the first alternative, the investor could have closed out the position and simply pocketed the profit by liquidating the position for 10 points by selling the long position in the December 100 call option for 11 ¼, and by purchasing a December 100 call for 1 ¼ to obtain a cash inflow of $1,000 for a profit of 3 ⅜ points (10 – 6 ⅝) or $337.50. The investor's second alternative was to take the spread's profit and use it to create another spread by rolling up. An investor *rolls up* from one call option position to another by closing out the position with the lower striking price and opening a position with a higher striking price.

In this situation the investor could have accomplished the roll up from the Motorola December 90–100 spread to the Motorola January 100–105 spread via the following steps. First, the December 90–100 bull spread had to be closed out by selling the December 90 call option for 11 ¼ points and purchasing a December 100 call option for 1 ¼ points, for a cash inflow of 10 points or $1,000 and a profit of $337.50, the difference between the $1000 cash inflow and the December 90–100 spread's original cost of $662.50. Second, since the January 100 call option was at 3 ¼ and the January 105 call option was at 1 5⁄16, the January 100–105 spread could be established by using $193.75 of the December bull spread's profit to purchase a January 100 call option for 3 ¼ points and to sell a January 105 call option for 1 5⁄16 points (3 ¼ – 1 5⁄16). Note that the cost of the January 100–105 spread is more than covered by the profits generated by the December 90–100 spread. Thus, after rolling up, the investor was able to pocket the $143.75 difference between the profits of the December 90–100 spread and the cost of the January 100–105 spread, $337.50 minus $193.75, while maintaining a position in the market that would permit profiting from any further increases in the price of Motorola common stock.

The only disturbing aspect of this strategy is that the investor was unable to pocket an amount equal to the cost of the December 90–100 spread, $662.50, when rolling up. Ideally, one would prefer to have enough profit available to cover the cost of the new spread as well as the cost of the original spread. In this case, the $143.75 that remained after rolling up into the March 60–65 spread was $518.75 less than the cost of the original December 90–100 bull spread. Thus, if the price of Motorola stock droppped below 100 by the January options' expiration, the investor stood to lose a total of $518.75 plus commissions.

During the next four weeks Motorola's share price rose steadily. This rise in share price was accompanied by an increase in the option values so that on January 11, four days before expiration and the two-for-one stock split, Motorola's common stock had reached a level of 112 ¾, the January 100 call option was at 13, and the January 105 call option's value was 8 ⅛. Given these prices, the value of the January 100–105 bull spread was 4 ⅞, or $487.50. Since this was Monday of expiration week, it was time for conservative investors to close out their positions.

The January 11 prices for Motorola's common stock and call options translate to a value of 4 ⅞ points, or $487.50, for the January 100–105 bull spread; 13 points for the long position in the January 100 call option, minus 8 ⅛ points for the short position in the January 105 call option. The investor who had rolled up from the December 90–100 bull spread to the January 100–105 bull spread could have closed the January spread and captured the entire $487.50 since the January 100–105 bull spread was funded by the profits of the December 90–100 bull spread. However, this is only part of the total profit generated by the rolling up strategy. Recall that the investor was able to pocket $143.75 when the December 90–100 bull spread was created. Thus, the total profit for this strategy was $631.35, or approximately 6 5⁄16 points—$487.60 profit at liquidation of the March 60–65 spread, plus $143.75 profit from the December 90–100 spread.

SAMPLE WORKSHEETS Worksheets 5–1 and 5–2 (see pages 88 – 91) present the computations for the Motorola bull spread and subsequent roll up. Both worksheets begin with sections that organize the stock and call option data in terms of current market prices, maturities, and striking prices. On both worksheets, lines 1 through 5 are identical and provide the investor with the net cost of the initial position. Worksheet 5–1 is completed by the liquidation data and by the profit or loss computations. In Worksheet 5–2 the roll up section documents the transition from the Motorola December 90–100 bull spread to the Motorola January 100–105 bull spread. The value for the roll up cash flow is derived by adding all the revenues generated via the option sales, lines 6 and 10, to obtain the cash inflow, and then subtracting the total cost of all option purchases, lines 8 and 14, from the total cash inflow. Finally, recall that the examples in the book do not include commissions. Be sure that applicable commissions are included when computing the net profit or loss for any positions that might be held.

Bear Spread

The *bear spread* is used when one wants to profit from a declining market, while maintaining a relatively low level of risk. The easiest way to accomplish this is by purchasing an at-the-money put option, and selling an out-of-the-money put option. In a bear spread, both of the put options have the same time to maturity but differ in their striking prices. Again, the investor wants to establish a long position in the option that will achieve the greatest gain if the stock moves as anticipated.

As in the bull spread, the revenue generated by the short position is used to offset part of the long position's cost. If the investor is positive that the market is going to fall, then put options should be purchased.

While a simple long position in put options has a large profit potential, equal to the striking price minus the position's total cost, it runs the risk of losing the entire amount paid for the put option if the market fails to fall as anticipated. A bear spread is less risky than a simple long put option position because the cost of the spread's long position is reduced by the amount of revenue generated by the spread's short option position. However, the spread's profit potential is much less than the profit potential of the long put option's position. In general, the Bear spread's maximum profit potential is equal to the differ-ence between the put options' striking prices less the total cost of the spread.

Exhibit 5–2 shows the behavior of an IBM September 45–50 bear spread over time. The line labeled "T = 0" shows the spread's profit or loss at maturity for IBM's stock prices ranging from $35 to $60 per share. The line labeled "T > 0" shows the Bear spread's profit or loss prior to the put options' expiration. When the spread is showing a profit prior to maturity, time becomes an ally for the investor since the profit increases as maturity, T = 0, approaches. On the other hand, if the spread is showing a loss prior to expiration, then time is working against the investor. The greatest loss that the investor can suffer is equal to the $200 cost of the spread.

ILLUSTRATIVE BEAR SPREAD: IBM The situation that prevailed in the computer hardware market between the summer of 1992 and the winter of 1993 created conditions that were perfect for creating bear spreads in IBM stock. At this time it appeared that the demand for large mainframe computers was disintigrating. IBM's large and expensive mainframe computers faced extremely stiff competition from increasingly powerful personal computers, workstations, and parallel processing software systems that were able to accomplish virtually all the tasks required of the

Worksheet 5–1 Bull Spread Purchase Worksheet

A. Position Data						
Underlying Stock	Motorola					
Current Stock Price	97 ¼					$97.25
Days until Option Expiration	60					
Options' Maturity Month	December					
Low Strike Price	90					
Low Strike Option Intrinsic Value	7 ¼					
Low Strike Option Time Value	1 ¼					
Low Strike Option Premium	8 ½					$8.50
High Strike Price	100					
High Strike Option Intrinsic Value	0					
High Strike Option Time Value	1 ⅞					
High Strike Option Premium	1 ⅞					$1.88
Spread Value	6 ⅝					$662.50
B. Initial Position						
1. Sell	1	high strike options	at	1 ⅞	for	$187.50
2. Less Commissions			at	0	for	$0.00
3. Buy	1	low strike options	at	8 ½	for	$850.00
4. Plus Commissions			at	0	for	$0.00
5. Net Cost						$662.50

C. Position Profit or Loss						
Stock Price at liquidation	100 ¼					$100.25
Days until Option Expiration	3					
Options' Maturity Month	December					
Low Strike Price	90					
Low Strike Option Intrinsic Value	10 ¼					
Low Strike Option Time Value	1					
Low Strike Option Premium	11 ¼					$1,125.00
High Strike Price	100					
High Strike Option Intrinsic Value	1					
High Strike Option Time Value	¼					
High Strike Option Premium	1 ¼					$125.00
Spread Value	10					$1,000.00
6. Sell	1	low strike options	at	11 ¼	for	$1,125.00
7. Less Commissions						
8. Buy	1	high strike options	at	1 ¼	for	$125.00
9. Plus Commissions						
10. Net Revenues						$1,000.00
Net Profit or Loss (10) – (5)						$337.50

Worksheet 5–2 Motorola Bull Spread Roll-Up Worksheet

A. Initial Position Data								
Underlying Stock	Motorola							
Current Stock Price	97 ¼							$97.25
Days until Option Expiration	60							
Options' Maturity Month	December							
Low Strike Price	90							
Low Strike Option Intrinsic Value	7 ¼							
Low Strike Option Time Value	1 ¼							
Low Strike Option Premium	8 ½							$8.50
High Strike Price	100							
High Strike Option Intrinsic Value	0							
High Strike Option Time Value	1 ⅞							
High Strike Option Premium	1 ⅞							$1.88
Spread Value	6 ⅝							$662.50
1. Sell	1	December	high strike options		at	1 ⅞	for	$187.50
2. Less Commissions					at	0	for	$0.00
3. Buy	1	December	low strike options		at	8 ½	for	$850.00
4. Plus Commissions					at	0	for	$0.00
5. Net Cost								$662.50
B. Roll-Up Position Data								
Underlying Stock	Motorola							
Current Stock Price	100 ¼							$100.25
Days until Option Expiration	3							
Options' Maturity Month		December						
Option Premium	11 ¼		at striking price	90				
Option Premium	1 ¼		at striking price	100				
Option Premium			at striking price					
Days until Option Expiration	31							
Options' Maturity Month		January						
Option Premium	3 ¼		at striking price	100				
Option Premium	1 5/16		at striking price	105				
Option Premium			at striking price					

6. Sell	1	December	at striking price	90	at	11 ¼	for	$1,125.00
7. Less Commissions								
8. Buy	1	December	at striking price	100	at	1 ¼	for	$125.00
9. Plus Commissions					at	0	for	$0.00
10. Sell			at striking price		at	0	for	$0.00
11. Less Commissions					at	0	for	$0.00
12. Sell	1	January	at striking price	105	at	1 5/16	for	$131.25
13. Less Commissions					at	0	for	$0.00
14. Buy	1	January	at striking price	100	at	3 ¼	for	$325.00
15. Plus Commissions					at	0	for	$0.00
16. Sell			at striking price		at	0	for	$0.00
17. Less Commission			at striking price		at	0	for	$0.00
18. Roll-Up Cash Flow								$806.25
19. Net Cash flow (18 – 5)								$143.75
C. Total Position Profit or Loss								
Stock Price at Liquidation	112 ¾							$112.75
Days until Option Expiration	4							
Options' Maturity Month		January						
Low Strike Price	100							
Low Strike Option Intrinsic Value	12 ¼							
Low Strike Option Time Value	¾							
Low Strike Option Premium	13							$13.00
High Strike Price	105							
High Strike Option Intrinsic Value	7 ¾							
High Strike Option Time Value	⅜							
High Strike Option Premium	8 ⅛							$813.00
20. Buy	1	January	at striking price	105	at	8 ⅛	for	$812.50
21. Plus Commissions					at	0	for	$0.00
22. Sell	1	January	at striking price	100	at	13	for	$1,300.00
23. Less Commissions					at	0	for	$0.00
24. Net Revenues								$487.50
Net Profit or Loss (24) + (19)								$631.25

Exhibit 5–2 IBM Bear Spread
Buy September 50 Put, Sell September 45 Put

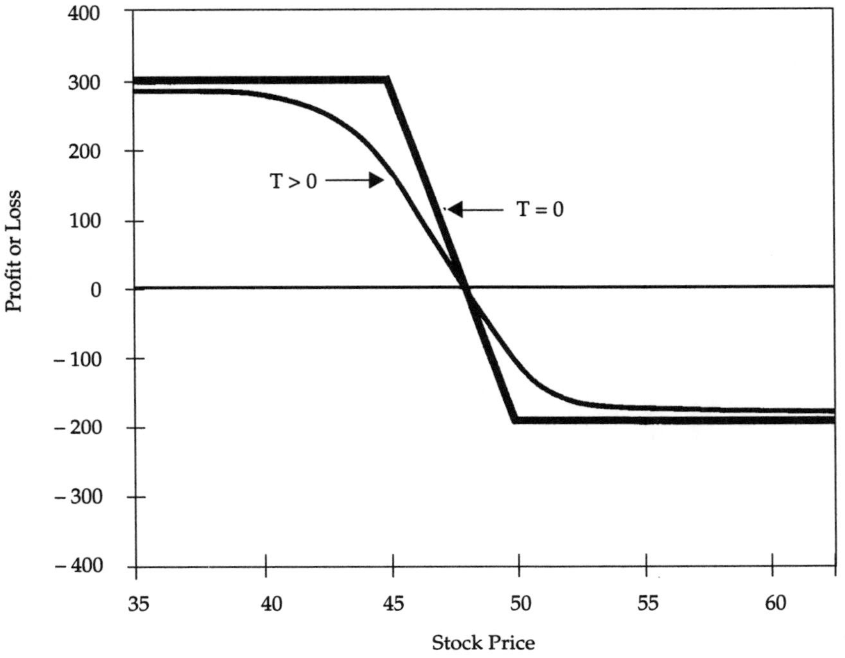

large mainframe computers, but at a much smaller cost. IBM also had to deal with extreme competitive pressures in the personal computer market due to the many IBM compatible PCs. These competitive pressures translated to a steep decline in its worldwide computer industry market share; a drop from approximately 30% market share in 1985 to only about 20% market share in 1991. These overwhelming market forces culminated in a $2.8 billion loss in 1991 and intense pressure on IBM's chairman, John Akers, to turn the firm around. Akers responded with a massive restructuring of the firm into fourteen autonomous divisions and the elimination of 40,000 jobs to reduce its worldwide workforce to 300,000. These measures seemed to work during the first half of 1992. IBM began the year trading at about $90 per share and climbed to a level of approximately $100 per share by the middle of July. However, poorer than expected earnings for the second quarter and a continuing lack of demand for mainframe computers ignited a slide in share value that resulted in a $49 share value on the day John Akers announced that he was leaving IBM, January 26, 1993.

On October 14, 1992, the price of IBM's common stock was 78, down by more than sixteen points from its value of 94 5⁄8 in late July. The IBM January 70 put option was at 1 3⁄8, and the IBM January 75 put option had a value of 2 13⁄16. Given the situation with IBM's most recent quarterly performance, it did not appear that IBM's share price would recover. Indeed, it seemed more likely that it would continue to drop in the near future. However, one could not be certain that IBM's share price would fall as rapidly as some analysts were predicting. A bear spread in IBM put options was a relatively low risk strategy that offered the conservative investor an opportunity to profit from this situation.

Thus, on October 14 an IBM January 70–75 bear spread could have been formed by purchasing the January 75 put option for 2 13⁄16 points and by selling the January 70 put option for 1 3⁄8 points. The net cost of the spread, $143.75, or 1 7⁄16 points, was the difference between the amount paid for the January 75 put option, $281.25, and the amount received for the sale of the January 70 put option, $137.50.

There are two things worth noting about this bear spread. First, there is only a five-point difference between the striking prices. Usually it is best to form bear spreads with put options that are one striking price apart because of liquidity considerations. Bear spreads that are formed with put options that are more than one striking price apart run the risk of having the spread's long put option position go deep in-the-money, which means the long put option position may be worth exercising. Since market makers will be unwilling to trade this put option if exercise is imminent, there will be virtually no market volume, or liquidity, for the option. Thus, the investor will find it virtually impossible to liquidate the spread at a fair price. The second noteworthy feature of this spread is that it was established for less than two points, or $200. This is important when one considers commissions, since the spread's maximum profit is equal to the difference between the striking prices minus its total cost. If the difference between the spread's long position and short position is too great, there will be very little profit available to the investor after commissions are paid.

In the following weeks, the bear spread's value rose while IBM's share price continued to fall. On November 18, 1992, IBM's common stock had a value of 63 ⅛, the January 65 put option had a price of 3 ⅝, the January 70 put option was at 7 ⅜, and the value of the January 75 put option was 12. These put option prices implied a value of 4 ⅝, or $462.50 for the IBM January 70–75 bear spread, the 12 point value of the January 75 put option long position, minus the 7 ⅜ point value of the short position's January 70 put option. With nine weeks left until the spread's expiration, the investor had to make a decision. There were three alternatives. First, the investor could have done nothing and left the spread intact. Second, the investor could have closed out the position and taken a $318.75 profit, $462.50 current value less the $143.75 original cost. Third, the investor could have used the existing spread's profits to create another spread by rolling down. An investor *rolls down* from one put option position to another by closing out the position with the higher striking price, and opening a position at a lower striking price.

If the investor had chosen the first alternative, then the spread's profit of 3 3/16 points, or $318.75, was being jeopardized by exposing the position's value to an accelerating time decay during the remainder of the spread's life. Thus, the first alternative seemed to be unnecessarily risky for the prudent and conservative investor. The second alternative of closing the position and taking the profits would not have exposed the position's profits to the rapid time decay. However, the investor would have forfeited any profits generated by further decreases in IBM's stock price. With nine weeks remaining in the spread's life, the investor's goal should have been to profit from any further decreases in the price of IBM stock while minimizing the effects of time decay. The third alternative, rolling down, provided the investor with a strategy that was able to accomplish this goal.

In this situation the investor would have rolled down from the IBM January 70–75 bear spread to the IBM January 65–70 bear spread via the following steps. First, the investor would have closed out the January 70–75 spread by selling the January 75 put option for 12 points, and purchasing a January 70 put option at 7 ⅜ points for a 3 3/16 points, or $318.75 profit. Second, the January 65–70 bear spread would have been created by purchasing a January 70 put option for 7 ⅜ points and selling a January 65 put option for 3 ⅝ points, for a net cost of 3 ¾ points, or $375.

Note that the cost of the January 65–70 spread is not covered by the profits generated by the January 70–75 spread. As with the bull spread, it is disturbing that the investor was unable to keep an amount equal to the cost of the January 65–70 spread, $375, when rolling down. Here, the $318.75 profit generated by the January 70–75 spread was $56.25 short of the $375 needed to create the January 65–70 bear spread. Thus, if the price of IBM's stock had risen to more than 70 by expiration, then the investor stood to lose a total of $56.25 plus commissions.

Between November 18 and December 18, IBM's share price fell steadily to a value of 51 ⅜. This drop in price was accompanied by an increase in the prices of the January put options. Thus, on December 18 the IBM January 70 put option was at 18 ⅝, the January 65 put option had a price of 13 ¾, the January 55 put option had a price of 4 ½, and the January 50 put option had a price of 1 15⁄16. At these prices, the value of the January 65–70 bear spread was 4 ⅞ points, the difference between the 18 ⅝ value of the long position in the January 70 put option and the 13 ¾ value of the short position in the January 65 put option; while the January 50–55 bear spread had a value of 2 9⁄16, the 4 ½ value of the long position in the January 55 put option minus the 1 15⁄16 value of the short position in the January 50 put option. Since it was approximately five weeks until the January options expired, the investor could roll down again from the January 65–70 spread to the January 50–55 spread. This would position the investor to take advantage of any further price declines in IBM stock while maintaining a position in the January options and protecting the overall strategy from time decay.

The investor would have rolled down from the IBM January 65–70 bear spread to the IBM January 50–55 bear spread by: First, closing out the January 65–70 spread by selling the January 70 put option for 18 ⅝ points, and purchasing a January 75 put option at 13 ¾ points for a 4 ⅞ points, or $487.50 profit. Second, the January 50–55 bear spread would have been created by purchasing a January 55 put option for 4 ½ points and selling a January 50 put option for 1 5⁄16 points, for a net cost of 2 9⁄16 points, or $256.25. Note that the 4 ⅞ points or $487.50 revenues generated by the January 65–70 spread are sufficient to pay for the 2 9⁄16 points or $256.25 cost of the January 50–55 spread and to cover the $56.25 net cost of the January bear spread strategy. Moreover, by rolling down again, the investor is able to pocket the remaining $175.00 in revenue from the

January 65–70 bear spread. Thus, since the January 50–55 IBM bear spread did not require any cash outflow there was no risk attached to the position. Indeed if IBM should rise above 55 by expiration and the spread expires worthless, the investor still keeps the $175.

During the next month IBM's share price experienced a further decline so that on January 11 it was trading at 47 ¾. Since the January 55 put option was trading at 7 ⅜ and the January 50 put option was at 2 9/16 the spread was trading at 4 13/16, or $481.25. With four days until expiration it was time for the prudent investor to close the position and take the profits. The spread's liquidation value of 4 13/16 points is only part of the total profit generated by the rolling down strategy. Recall that the investor was able to keep 1 ¾ points when the January 50–55 spread was created. Therefore, the total profit for this strategy was 6 9/16 points, or $656.25 (4 13/16 points, or $481.25 profit at liquidation of the January 50–55 spread, plus the 1 ¾ points or $175 profit from the earlier rolling down activities). A much better outcome than simply leaving the original spread intact.

SAMPLE WORKSHEETS Worksheets 5–3 and 5–4 (See pages 100–104) present the computations for the IBM Bear spread and roll down, respectively. These worksheets are basically the same as the bull spread worksheets, 5–1 and 5–2. As before, both worksheets begin with sections that organize the stock and option data in terms of current market prices, maturities, and striking prices. On both worksheets, lines 1 through 5 are identical and provide the investor with the net cost of the initial position. Worksheet 5–3 is completed by the liquidation data and by the profit or loss computations. In Worksheet 5–4 the roll down sections document the transition from the IBM January 70–75 bear spread to the January 65–70 bear spread, and then to the January 50–55 bear spread. The net cash flow and net profit or loss values are derived as indicated by the line numbers that follow the line entry. Finally, notice that on line 8 the investor is buying both January 70 put options in one transaction to save commissions. Always trade in the most efficient manner possible.

Time Spread

The time spread is used by an investor who is neither bullish nor bearish. The *time spread,* or *calender spread,* is profitable in flat or unchanging markets. This spread's profitability results from the accelerating time decay of an option's premium as maturity approaches. The Time spread's components are at-the-money options that have identical striking prices, but differ in the length of time until maturity. Since the options are at-the-money, they have no intrinsic value. Their prices are composed entirely of time value. Theoretically, an investor can create a time spread from either call options or put options. In the following examples only call options will be used since call options have several advantages over put options. Among these advantages are the call options' greater liquidity and larger time value.

When creating a time spread the investor purchases the longer maturity at-the-money call option and sells the nearby at-the-money call option. The spread's cost is the difference between the amount paid for the longer-term call option and the amount received for the shorter term option. Since the underlying stock's price is expected to remain stable, the logic is for the investor is to be long the option that will retain the greatest amount of value as time passes, and to be short the option that will lose the greatest amount of value as maturity approaches. Ideally, the investor wants both call options to be at-the-money when the nearby call option matures because this is where the time spread's maximum profit is earned. In this situation neither the long call option position nor the short call option will have any intrinsic value. Thus, the spread's short position will expire worthless. However, the long position will have retained most of its original value. Therefore, the difference between the long position's value and the short position's value will have increased during the time spread's existence, which means a profit for the investor. The time spread's risk is relatively low since the maximum amount that can be lost is the cost of the spread. This will occur if the underlying stock makes a large move so that both call options are either deep in-the-money or deep out-of-the-money at the nearby call option's expiration. In general, when options are far-from-the-money, they have virtually no time premium. Thus, the difference between the value of the long call option position and the short call option position will be virtually zero.

If flat, or unchanging, share prices are anticipated, then the time spread is a much better strategy for the conservative investor than either the call writing or put writing strategies. These simple writing strategies carry enormous amounts of risk for very little profit. Conversely, the time spread has a limited level of risk and almost as much profit potential as the simple option writing strategies in flat markets. In spite of this favorable risk-return relationship, some investors would rather receive a cash inflow from writing options than pay a cash outflow from creating a time spread. We feel that these writing strategies are too risk, and strongly recommend that the time spread be used when flat markets are anticipated.

Exhibit 5–3 shows the behavior of an MCI Communications September–January time spread. The line labeled "T = 0" shows the spread's profit or loss at maturity for MCI stock prices ranging in value from $20 per share to $40 per share. The line labeled "T > 0" shows the time spread's profit or loss prior to the September call option's expiration. Like the bull and bear spreads, time becomes an ally for the investor since the profit increases as maturity, T = 0, approaches. Conversely, if the spread is exhibiting a loss prior to expiration, time is working against the investor. Here, the greatest loss that the investor can incur is equal to the cost of the spread, $60.

ILLUSTRATIVE TIME SPREAD: THE GAP In the first half of 1992, The Gap's share price declined from 58 in January to 34 in June. Among the reasons for this decline were: the overall economic recession in the United States that had hit retailers extremely hard, and the Gap began to feel the ill effects of shopper polarization where consumers purchase expensive wardrobe items, such as fashion sweaters, from high-end retailers and then purchase basic wardrobe items such as denim jeans and shirts from low-end large volume retailers or outlet malls. This cross-shopping behavior caused a deterioration in Gap's market share for basic wardrobe items and contributed to rising inventory levels. Gap responded by cutting prices and vigorously promoting their basic denim clothes through back-to-school sales. This response halted the decline in market share but the competitive pricing pressure resulted in lower profit margins and earnings. Gap's shares responded by sliding to 30 ⅝ in mid-October but rose to 34 by mid-November. Given this situation, many analysts did not

Exhibit 5–3 MCI Time Spread
Sell September 30 Call, Buy January 30 Call

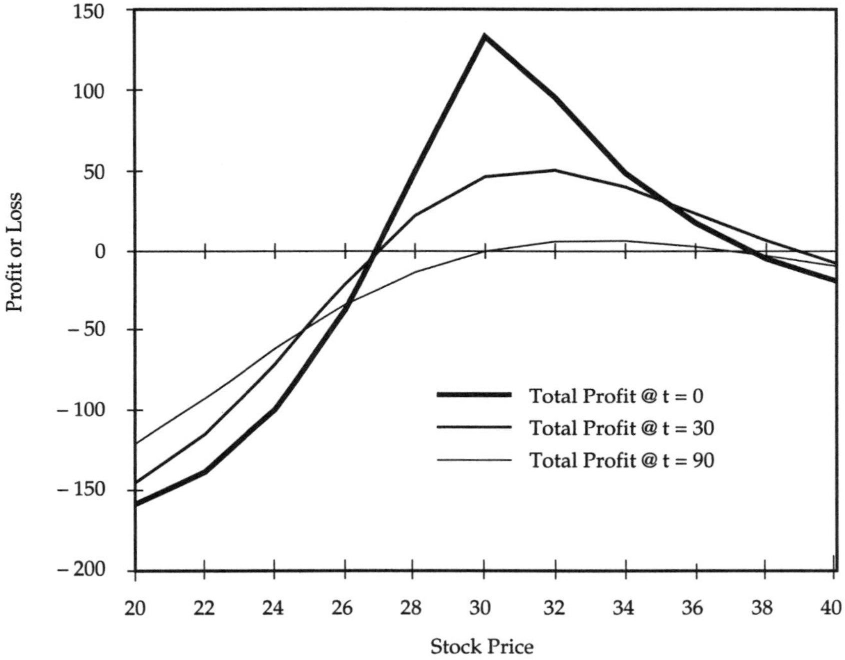

expect Gap's share price to make any major moves away from the mid-30s in the near future. An investor wishing to take advantage of this situation via a low risk position would have been wise to construct a Time spread using Gap call options.

On November 13, 1992, the share price of the Gap's stock stood at 34 ½, the December 35 call option's price was 1 ⅜, the January 35 call option's price was 2 $^{3}/_{16}$, and the price of the March 35 call option was 3. At this time an investor could have created a two-month time spread in Gap call options by purchasing a March 35 call option for 3 points, or $300, and by selling a January 35 call option for 2 $^{3}/_{16}$, or $218.75, for a net cost of $^{13}/_{16}$, or $81.25. Alternatively, the investor could have constructed a one-month time spread by purchasing the March 35 call option for $300,

Worksheet 5–3 Bear Spread Purchase Worksheet

A. Position Data							
Underlying Stock	IBM						
Current Stock Price	78						$78.00
Days until Option Expiration	94						
Options' Maturity Month	January						
Low Strike Price	70						
Low Strike Option Intrinsic Value	0						
Low Strike Option Time Value	1 3/8						
Low Strike Option Premium	1 3/8						$137.50
High Strike Price	75						
High Strike Option Intrinsic Value	0						
High Strike Option Time Value	2 13/16						
High Strike Option Premium	2 13/16						$281.25
Spread Value	1 7/16						$143.75
B. Initial Position							
1. Sell	1	January	low strike options	at	1 3/8	for	$137.50
2. Less Commissions				at	0	for	$0.00
3. Buy	1	January	high strike options	at	2 13/16	for	$281.25
4. Plus Commissions				at	0	for	$0.00
5. Net Cost							$143.75

C. Position Profit or Loss

Stock Price at Liquidation	63 ⅛						$63.13
Days until Option Expiration	63						
Options' Maturity Month	January						
Low Strike Price	70						
Low Strike Option Intrinsic Value	6 ⅞						
Low Strike Option Time Value	½						
Low Strike Option Premium	7 ⅜						$737.50
High Strike Price	75						
High Strike Option Intrinsic Value	11 ⅞						
High Strike Option Time Value	⅛						
High Strike Option Premium	12						$1200.00
Spread Value	4 ⅝						$462.50
6. Buy	1	January	low strike options	at	7 ⅜	for	$737.50
7. Plus Commissions				at	0	for	$0.00
8. Sell	1	January	high strike options	at	12	for	$1200.00
9. Less Commissions				at	0	for	$0.00
10. Net Revenues							$462.50
Net Profit or Loss (10) – (5)							$318.75

Worksheet 5–4 Bear Spread Roll-Down Worksheet

A. Initial Position Data								
Underlying Stock	IBM							
Current Stock Price	78							$78.00
Days until Option Expiration	94							
Options' Maturity Month	January							
Low Strike Price	70							
Low Strike Option Intrinsic Value	0							
Low Strike Option Time Value	1 3/8							
Low Strike Option Premium	1 3/8							$137.50
High Strike Price	75							
High Strike Option Intrinsic Value	0							
High Strike Option Time Value	2 13/16							
High Strike Option Premium	2 13/16							$281.25
Spread Value	1 7/16							$143.75
1. Sell	1	January	low strike options		at	1 3/8	for	$137.50
2. Less Commissions					at	0	for	$0.00
3. Buy	1	January	high strike options		at	2 13/16	for	$281.25
4. Plus Commissions					at	0	for	$0.00
5. Net Cost								$143.75
B. Roll-Down Position Data								
Underlying Stock	IBM							
Current Stock Price	63 1/8							$63.13
Days until Option Expiration	63							
Options' Maturity Month		January						
Option Premium	3 5/8	January	at striking price	65				

Option Premium	7 3/8	January	at striking price	70				
Option Premium	12	January	at striking price	75				
Days until Option Expiration	31							
Options' Maturity Month		January						
Option Premium	3 1/4		at striking price	100				
Option Premium	1 5/16		at striking price	105				
Option Premium			at striking price					
6. Sell	1	January	at striking price	75	at	12	for	$1200.00
7. Less Commissions					at	0	for	$0.00
8. Buy	2	January	at striking price	70	at	7 3/8	for	$1475.00
9. Plus Commissions					at	0	for	$0.00
10. Sell	1	January	at striking price	65	at	3 5/8	for	$362.50
11. Less Commissions					at	0	for	$0.00
12. Buy			at striking price		at		for	$0.00
13. Plus Commissions					at	0	for	$0.00
14. Roll-Down Cash Flow								$87.50
15. Net Cash Flow								($56.25)
Underlying Stock	IBM							
Current Stock Price	51 3/8							$51.38
Days until Option Expiration	36							
Options' Maturity Month		January						
Option Premium	1 15/16	January	at striking price	50				
Option Premium	4 1/2	January	at striking price	55				
Option Premium	13 3/4	January	at striking price	65				
Option Premium	18 5/8	January	at striking price	70				
16. Sell	1	January	at striking price	70	at	18 5/8	for	$1862.50
17. Less Commissions					at	0	for	$0.00
18. Buy	1	January	at striking price	65	at	13 3/4	for	$1375.00
19. Plus Commissions					at	0	for	$0.00

20. Buy	1	January	at striking price	55	at	4 ½	for	$450.00
21. Plus Commissions					at	0	for	$0.00
22. Sell	1	January	at striking price	50	at	1 15/16	for	$193.75
23. Less Commissions					at	0	for	$0.00
24. Roll-Down Cash Flow								$231.25
25. Net Cash Flow (24) + (15)								$175.00
C. Total Position Profit or Loss								
Stock Price at Liquidation	47 ¾							$47.75
Days until Option Expiration	6							
Options' Maturity Month	January							
Low Strike Price	50							
Low Strike Option Intrinsic Value	2 ¼							
Low Strike Option Time Value	5/16							
Low Strike Option Premium	2 9/16							$256.25
High Strike Price	55							
High Strike Option Intrinsic Value	7 ¼							
High Strike Option Time Value	⅛							
High Strike Option Premium	7 ⅜							$737.50
Spread Value	4 13/16							$481.25
26. Buy	1	January	at striking price	50	at	2 9/16	for	$256.25
27. Plus Commissions					at	0	for	$0.00
28. Sell	1	January	at striking price	55	at	7 ⅜	for	$737.50
29. Less Commissions					at	0	for	$0.00
30. Net Revenues								$481.25
Net Profit or Loss (30) + (25)								$656.25

and by selling a December 35 call option for 1 3/8, or $137.50, for a net cost of 1 5/8, or $162.50. Note that all three call options are out-of-the-money and that the difference in their values is composed entirely of the difference between their time premiums. Furthermore, the maximum amount that the investor can lose is the spread's cost, $81.25, for the two month spread and $162.50 for the one month spread plus any commissions paid.

At this point it is fair to ask which of the two spreads is better. The answer is not obvious. Although the January–March spread is cheaper, it has a longer exposure to a fluctuating share price. If the Gap call options are away-from-the-money at January expiration then the spread will be almost worthless. On the other hand, if the options are at-the-money in January then the spread should widen appreciably. Thus, if one truly believes that the Gap will remain stable for two months, then the January–March time spread is a sound strategy. If the investor is skeptical about the stability of Gap's stock for the next few months, then the December–March spread should be established.

Suppose an investor felt that Gap's stock was going to remain stable for the next few months and decided to set up the January–March 35 time spread for $81.25 on November 13. During the next two months Gap's share price remained quite stable so that on the last day of trading for the January 35 call option, January 15, Gap's share price was 34, the January 35 call option price was 1/16 or $6.25, and the March 35 call option was trading at 1 9/16, or $156.25. These call option prices imply a spread value of 1 ½ or $150.00, the 1 9/16 value of the March 35 call option less the 1/16 value of the January 35 call option. Given these prices, the spread's profit is 11/16 of a point, or $68.75 (the spread's 1 ½ point maturity value, $150.00, less the 13/16 point cost, $81.25). The spread's value had risen from 13/16 to 1 ½ because the difference between the prices of the January 35 and March 35 call options had increased. The principal reason for this increase was the time decay's relatively greater effect on the nearby call option's price than on the deferred option's price. Note that the January 35 call option had lost 2 1/8 points of its November 15 value while the March 35 call option lost only 1 7/16 of a point of value in the same timespan.

Now assume that an investor believes the Gap stock will be stable for only the next month and chooses to create the December–March 35 time spread on November 13 for 1 5/8 points, or $162.50. In the ensuing weeks, Gap's share price made a series of small, erratic moves until it dropped to a level of $33\frac{7}{8}$ on December 18, the last trading day for the December 35 call option. The value of the December 35 call option had declined to $\frac{1}{16}$ of a point from its November 13 value of $1\frac{3}{8}$, the January 35 call option had dropped to $1\frac{1}{8}$ from its earlier value of $2\frac{3}{16}$, and the March 35 call option had fallen to a value of $2\frac{1}{4}$ points from its value of 3 points one month earlier. These call option prices translated to a value of $2\frac{3}{16}$ points, or $218.75 for the Gap 35 December–March time spread: the value of the long position ($2\frac{1}{4}$ for the March 35 call option) minus the value of the short position ($\frac{1}{16}$ for the December 35 call option). These call option values also meant that the spread had generated a profit of $\frac{9}{16}$ of a point, or $56.25 (the $218.75 December 18 value minus the $162.50 cost).

The spread's value had risen from $1\frac{5}{8}$ to $2\frac{3}{16}$ because the difference between the prices of the December 35 and March 35 call options had increased. Once again, the principal reason for this increase was the relatively greater time decay for the nearby call option versus the deferred call option.

With approximately three months left until the March option's expiration and no indication that the Gap's share price was going to make any kind of large move, the investor had to make a decision and choose one of two possible courses of action. First, the investor could have closed out the position and taken the $56.25 profit. Second, the investor could have used the existing' spread's profits to create another spread by rolling forward. An investor rolls forward from one time spread to another by closing out the spread with the closer maturity and then creating a spread with a more distant maturity.

The first alternative of closing the position and taking the profits would not have exposed the spread's profits to the effects of share price movement. However, the investor would have forfeited any profits generated by an unchanging Gap share price and a rapidly decaying January 35 call option price. At this point, the investor's goal should have been to create a position that would profit from a relatively stable Gap share price by capitalizing on the effects of time decay. The second alternative, rolling forward, was a strategy that could accomplish this goal.

In this situation the investor could have rolled forward from the Gap December–March 35 time spread to the Gap January–March 35 time spread by closing out the December–March spread via buying the December 35 call option for $\frac{1}{16}$ of a point and selling a January 35 call option for 1 ⅛ of a point, yielding a cash inflow of 1 1⁄16 points, or $106.25. The difference between this cash inflow and the December–March 35 spread's original cost of $162.50 reduces the overall strategy's cost to 9⁄16 of a point, or $56.25. Thus, after rolling forward, the investor was able to lower the the time spread's cost while maintaining a position in the market that was able to profit from a stable Gap common stock price.

During the next month, Gap's share price remained quite stable, and the value of the January–March time spread appreciated. Recall from above that on January 15, Gap's common stock was at 34, the January 35 call option price was 1⁄16 or $6.25, the March 35 call option was trading at 1 9⁄16, or $156.25, and the spread was valued at 1 ½ or $150. Since many analysts were predicting that Gap's earnings would decline further and its share value would probably decrease in the near future, it was time for the investor to close out the January–March time spread.

The January 15 prices for Gap's common stock and call options imply a total profit of 15⁄16 point, or $93.75, for the investor who had rolled forward from the December–March 35 spread to the January–March 35 spread. This investor could have closed the January–March spread for 15⁄16 of a point, or $93.75, profit since it was funded in part by the 9⁄16 point gain of the December–March 35 spread. A much better outcome than simply allowing the December–March 35 spread to expire.

SAMPLE WORKSHEETS Worksheets 5–5 and 5–6 (see pages 108–111) present the computations for the Gap time spread and subsequent roll forward. Each worksheet begins with a section that organizes the stock and call option data in terms of current market prices, maturities, and striking prices. On both worksheets, lines 1 through 5 are identical and provide the investor with the net cost of the time spread's initial position. Like Worksheets 5–1 and 5–3, Worksheet 5–5 is completed by the liquidation data and by the profit or loss computations. In Worksheet 5–6 the roll forward section exhibits the transition from the Gap December–March 35 time spread to the Gap January–March 35 time spread. Note that the value for the roll forward cash flow is obtained by purchasing the December option and selling the January option. In this situation there was no need to tamper with the long position in the March 35 call option. This resulted in the largest possible cash inflow at this time.

Worksheet 5–5 Time Spread Purchase Worksheet

A. Position Data						
Underlying Stock	Gap					
Current Stock Price	34 ½					$34.50
Days until Nearby Option Expires	61					
Nearby Options' Maturity Month	January					
Nearby Options' Strike Price	35					
Nearby Options' Intrinsic Value	0					
Nearby Options' Time Value	2 3⁄16					
Nearby Options' Premium	2 3⁄16					$218.75
Days until Deferred Option Expiration	124					$218.75
Deferred Options' Maturity Month	March					
Deferred Options' Strike Price	35					
Deferred Options' Intrinsic Value	0					
Deferred Options' Time Value	3					
Deferred Options' Premium	3					$300.00
B. Initial Position						
1. Sell	1	nearby option	at	2 3⁄16	for	$218.75
2. Less Commissions			at	0	for	$0.00
3. Buy	1	deferred option	at	3	for	$300.00
4. Plus Commissions			at	0	for	$0.00
5. Net Cost						$81.25

C. Position Profit or Loss

Stock Price at Liquidation	34					$34.00
Days until Option Expiration	1					
Nearby Options' Maturity Month	January					
Nearby Options' Strike Price	35					
Nearby Options' Intrinsic Value	0					
Nearby Options' Time Value	1/16					
Nearby Options' Premium	1/16					$6.25
Deferred Options' Maturity Month	March					
Deferred Options' Strike Price	35					
Deferred Options' Intrinsic Value	0					
Deferred Options' Time Value	1 9/16					
Deferred Options' Premium	1 9/16					$156.25
6. Buy	1	nearby options	at	1/16	for	$6.25
7. Plus Commissions						
8. Sell	1	deferred options	at	1 9/16	for	$156.25
9. Less Commissions						
10. Net Revenues						$150.00
Net Profit or Loss (10) – (5)						$68.75

Worksheet 5–6 Time Spread Roll-Forward Worksheet

A. Initial Position Data							
Underlying Stock	Gap						
Current Stock Price	34 ½						$34.50
Days until Nearby Option Expires	35						
Nearby Options' Maturity Month	December						
Nearby Options' Strike Price	35						
Nearby Options' Intrinsic Value	0						
Nearby Options' Time Value	1 ⅜						
Nearby Options' Premium	1 ⅜						$137.50
Days until Deferred Option Expiration	124						
Deferred Options' Maturity Month	March						
Deferred Options' Strike Price	35						
Deferred Options' Intrinsic Value	0						
Deferred Options' Time Value	3						
Deferred Options' Premium	3						$300.00
1. Sell	1	Nearby option	at		1 ⅜	for	$137.50
2. Less Commissions			at		0	for	$0.00
3. Buy	1	Deferred option	at		3	for	$300.00
4. Plus Commissions			at		0	for	$0.00
5. Net Cost							$162.50
B. Roll-Forward Position Data							
Underlying Stock	Gap						
Current Stock Price	33 ⅞						$33.88
Option's Striking Price	35						
Option Premium	1/16	for maturity	at	December		for	$6.25
Option Premium	1 ⅛	for maturity	at	January		for	$112.50
Option Premium	2 ¼	for maturity	at	March		for	$225.00

6. Buy	1	December Maturity	at	1/16	for	$6.25
7. Plus Commissions			at	0	for	$0.00
8. Sell	1	January Maturity	at	1 1/8	for	$112.50
9. Less Commissions			at	0	for	$0.00
10. Buy		March Maturity	at		for	$0.00
11. Plus Commissions		March Maturity	at		for	$0.00
12. Roll-Forward Cash Flow						$106.25
13. Net Cash Flow (12) – (5)						$56.25
C. Position Profit or Loss						
Stock Price at Liquidation	34					$34.00
Days until Nearby Option Expiration	1					
Nearby Option's Maturity Month		January				
Nearby Option's Strike Price	35					
Nearby Option's Option Intrinsic Value	0					
Nearby Option's Premium	1/16					$6.25
Deferred Option's Maturity Month		March				
Deferred Option's Strike Price	35					
Deferred Option's Intrinsic Value	0					
Deferred Option's Time Value	1 9/16					
Deferred Option's Premium	1 9/16					$156.25
14. Buy	1	January Maturity	at	1/16	for	$6.25
15. Plus Commissions			at	0	for	$0.00
16. Sell	1	March Maturity	at	1 9/16	for	$156.25
17. Less Commissions			at	0	for	$0.00
18. Net Revenues						$150.00
Net Profit or Loss (18) + (13)						$93.75

Conclusion

This chapter has introduced three basic spreads: the bull spread, the bear spread, and the time spread. Detailed examples, graphs, and worksheets were provided throughout the chapter to aid in the spreads' explanation. These strategies are similar in that they provide the conservative investor with relatively low risk positions that can be profitable given any type of stock price behavior. Each of these spreads is established by combining a long position and a short position in options of the same class but differ in series. The key to any spread is that the investor establishes the long position in the option that will appreciate most in value. The short position's revenue is used to reduce the cost of the long position and, thus, the spread's total cost.

Problem 5–1 *See Appendix C for solution.*

Suppose that in February the 75-day Adobe April 17 ½ call option has a price of 2 ¾, the 75-day Adobe April 25 call option has a price of ¾, and the price of Adobe's common stock is 18. Since you feel that the price of Adobe's stock will increase in the next 75 days you decide to create a bull spread by purchasing the April 17 ½ call option and selling the April 25 call option. In April, seven days prior to the call options' expiration, the securities are priced as follows:

Adobe Systems common shares, 26

Adobe Systems April 17 ½ call option, 8 ⅝

Adobe Systems April 25 call option, 1 ½

Compute the bull spread's profit assuming it is liquidated seven days prior to the April expiration date.

Problem 5–2 *See Appendix C for solution.*

Suppose that with 25 days until expiration, you observe that Adobe's share price has risen to 24 ⅜, the April 17 ½ call option's price has increased to 7 ¾, the April 25 call option is selling for 2 ⅛, and the April 30 call option is trading at 1 ⅜. Compute the profits generated by a roll up from the April 17 ½–25 spread to the April 25–30 bull spread assuming the spread is liquidated seven days before expiration when the securities are valued as follows:

Adobe Systems common shares, 26

Adobe Systems April 25 call option, 1 ½

Adobe Systems April 30 call option, ⅜

Problem 5–3 *See Appendix C for solution.*

Suppose that on August 1, the 135-day General Motors December 45 put option has a price of 2 $\frac{3}{16}$, the 135-day General Motors December 35 put option has a price of $\frac{3}{16}$, and the price of GM's common stock is 46 ⅛. Since you feel that the price of GM's common stock will drop during the next 135 days, you decide to create a bear spread by purchasing the December 45 put option and selling the December 35 put option. In December, four days prior to the call options' expiration, the securities are priced as follows:

GM common shares, 37 ½

GM December 45 put option, 7 ⅝

GM December 35 put option, ½

Compute the bear spread's profit assuming it is liquidated four days prior to the December expiration date.

Problem 5–4 *See Appendix C for solution.*

Suppose that with 35 days until expiration, you observe that GM's share price has fallen to 38 ⅞, the December 45 put option's price has increased to 7 ⅛, the December 35 put option is selling for 2 ⅞, and the December 30 put option is trading at 1 ½. Compute the profits generated by a roll down from the December 45–35 bear spread to the December 35–30 bear spread assuming the spread is liquidated four days before expiration when the securities are valued as follows:

GM common shares, 37 ½

GM December 35 put option, 2 ⅝

GM December 30 put option, 5/16

Problem 5–5 *See Appendix C for solution.*

Suppose that on December 1, the 75-day Exxon February 65 call option has a price of 2 ⅛, the 135-day Exxon April 65 call option has a price of 3 ⅞, and the price of Exxon's common stock is 64 ½. Since you feel that the price of Exxon's common stock will remain stable during the next two months, you decide to create a time spread by purchasing the February 65 call option and selling the April 65 call option. In February, five days prior to the

February 65 call option's expiration, the securities are priced as follows:

Exxon common shares, 63 7/8

Exxon February 65 call option 1/16

Exxon April 65 call option 2 1/16

Compute the time spread's profit assuming it is liquidated five days prior to the February expiration date.

Problem 5–6 *See Appendix C for solution.*

Suppose that with 5 days until the February expiration, you observe that Exxon's share price has fallen to 63 7/8, the February 65 call option's price has decreased to 1/16, the April 65 call option price has dropped to 2 1/16, and the July 65 call option is trading at 3 3/4. Compute the profits generated by a roll forward from the February–April 65 time spread to the April–July 65 time spread assuming the spread is liquidated four days before the April option's expiration when the securities are valued as follows:

Exxon common shares, 65 1/8

Exxon April 65 call option 3/16

Exxon July 65 call option 3 3/16

Chapter Six

Combinations

Earlier chapters concentrated on forming positions by using either call options or put options. The purpose of this chapter is to acquaint the investor with some simple strategies that rely on combining call options with put options.

Definitions

Two basic strategies will be examined in this chapter: straddles and strangles. A *straddle* is formed by taking similar positions in the at-the-money call options and put options of a given stock. An investor is *long a straddle* if an at-the-money call option and an at-the-money put option are purchased. If an investor is *short a straddle,* then the investor has written an at-the-money call option and an at-the-money put option. The term *strangle* was coined by option traders and means that one has taken similar positions in a given stock's out-of-the-money call options and out-of-the-money put options. An investor is *long a strangle* if out-of-the-money call options and put options are purchased. Selling out-of-the-money call options and put options creates a *short strangle* position for the investor.

Underlying Logic

The logic behind both the straddle and strangle is to profit from changes in the underlying stock's price volatility. It is wrong to assume that it is best to purchase straddles and strangles on high volatility stocks and to write straddles and strangles on low volatility stocks. If a stock's options are fairly priced, then their market prices will accurately reflect the volatility of the stock's price. Straddles and strangles work best when there is a great deal of uncertainty about a stock's price volatility. The logic for the straddle and strangle is based on the positive relationship of the underlying stock's price volatility to both the call and put options' premium. In general, this positive relationship means that both call and put option prices will increase when stock price volatility rises and will decrease as stock price volatility declines. This occurs because an increase in stock price volatility can result in a large increase or decrease in the price of the underlying stock while a decrease in volatility will result in a very stable stock price.

If a substantial increase in a stock's price volatility is anticipated, then a straddle should be purchased. This will allow the investor to benefit from the large stock price movement via either the put option or the call option. If the increased volatility results in a large stock price increase, then the call option will increase in value and the put option's value will decline. If the greater volatility causes the stock price to undergo a drastic decrease, then the put option will increase in value while the call option loses value. The maximum amount that can be lost is the cost of the straddle: the total amount paid for both the put option and the call option.

If a significant decrease in stock price volatility is anticipated, it is better to sell a strangle than a straddle. The logic of this strategy is as follows. A decrease in stock price volatility means that the stock's price should remain stable. A stable stock price means that both the out-of-the-money and at-the-money options will probably be worthless at expiration, since their premiums have no intrinsic value and will decay rapidly as maturity approaches. An investor can profit by selling options before their premiums begin to decay. This can be accomplished by selling either a straddle or a strangle. However, in both cases, the seller is writing a naked call option and a naked put option. Thus, both of these strategies are quite risky, since both have the potential for unlimited loss. Writing a straddle, however, is more risky than writing a strangle, because it will result in more rapid losses if the stock price begins to move. Since the strangle writer can withstand greater stock price movement than the straddle writer before incurring any losses, writing strangles is recommended over writing straddles.

Straddle and Strangle Purchasing Strategies

In this section, we will examine the strategies of purchasing straddles and strangles. In the following section, we focus on the corresponding strategies. Exhibit 6–1 provides the data on which we will base our discussion of all four strategies.

STRADDLE PURCHASE The profitability of purchasing a straddle is illustrated quite clearly in Exhibit 6–1. In this situation, a 120-day Hewlett-Packard November 70 straddle has been formed by purchasing an at-the-money Hewlett-Packard call option for 3 ½, or $350, and an at-the-money Hewlett-Packard put option for 1 ½ points or $150. The graph reflects these values and indicates that the November straddle's cost was 5, or $500. In this case, Hewlett-Packard's share price had to move by at least the cost of the straddle, 5, by expiration for the buyer to just break even. If the price of Hewlett-Packard's shares moved by more than 5 points to a value greater than 75, or less than 65, at the options' expiration, then the straddle buyer would have earned a profit. If Hewlett-Packard's share price was between 65 and 75 at the options'expiration, then the straddle buyer would have suffered a loss. If Hewlett-Packard's share price equaled 70 at the options' expiration, then the straddle buyer would have lost the entire amount paid—5 points, or $500. This is illustrated by the "T = 0" line in Exhibit 6–1.

The three remaining lines indicate the straddle's profit or loss at various points in time prior to maturity. For example, if the stock price is 70 with 90 days until expiration, then the position would lose $75 if the investor was forced to liquidate. The loss occurs because the value of the

Exhibit 6–1 Straddle Buy
Hewlett-Packard 70

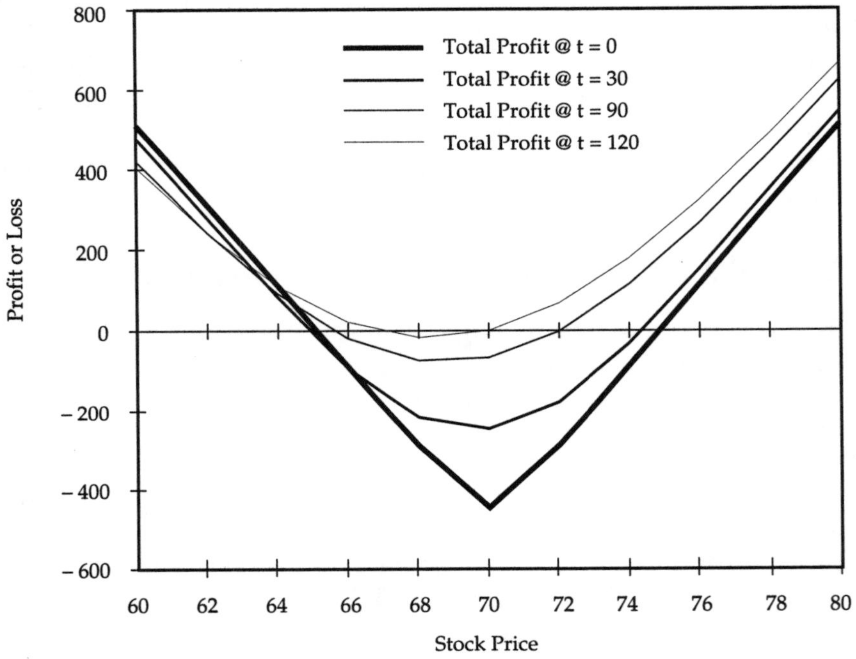

October straddle is 4 ¾—3 ¼ for the November 70 call option and 1 ½ for the November 70 put option—which is ¾ of a point less than the initial cost of 5. If the stock price remained unchanged during the straddle's life, then the losses would be 2 ½ points, or $250, with 30 days until expiration, and finally the entire 5 points or $500 at maturity.

These losses increase as maturity approaches because of the time premium decay. Thus it is extremely important to realize that time is working against the straddle buyer in flat or unchanging markets. On the other hand, since there is no upper limit on the value of the stock, there is no upper limit to the potential profit that could have been earned by the straddle buyer via the call option if the price of Hewlett-Packard kept rising. However, since the stock cannot fall below zero, the maximum profit available to the straddle buyer in a rapidly declining market through the put option is 65 points.

STRANGLE PURCHASE Since a strangle is formed with an out-of-the-money call option and an out-of-the-money put option it is cheaper than a straddle. Therefore, a strangle buyer has less to lose than a straddle buyer. However, the underlying stock's price has to make a very large move before the strangle buyer will earn a profit—indeed, a much greater move than in the case of the straddle buyer.

Exhibit 6–2 can be used to illustrate the profit potential of a strangle buyer. Here a 120-day Hewlett-Packard strangle is constructed by purchasing the out-of-the-money November 75 call option for 1 ⅛, and the out-of-the-money November 65 put option for ⅜, for a total cost of 1 ½ points, or $150. In this situation the "T = 0" line illustrates that Hewlett-Packard's share price must rise or fall by 6 ⅛ points for the strangle buyer to break even at expiration. This large price movement is necessary since either the put option, or the call option, must be in-the-money at expiration before the strangle buyer can break even. A 6 ⅛ point increase in the stock price to 76 ⅛ would result in the November 75 call option taking on 1 ⅛ points of intrinsic value, while a 6 ⅛ point drop in Hilton's share price to 63 ⅞ places the November 65 put option 1 ⅛ points in-the-money. If the price of Hewlett-Packard's common stock is between 65 and 75 at the options' expiration, then both options will expire worthless, since both are out-of-the-money. This is quite different from the 5-point price movement required for the straddle buyer to break even over the same time period. Thus, it is better for an investor to buy a straddle rather than a strangle if an increase in stock price volatility is anticipated.

In order to be consistent with the straddle purchase example, we will assume a constant stock price of 70 with 90 days until expiration, 30 days until expiration, and no time until expiration in our discussion of the strangle's behavior. These maturities are illustrated by the three lines in Exhibit 6–2.

At 90 days until expiration, the November strangle has a value of 1 ⅛ points: ¾ of a point for the November 75 call option and ⅜ of a point for the November 65 put option. If the investor liquidates the position at this point, then a ⅜ point, or $37.50, loss will occur (1 ½ minus 1 ⅛). This

Exhibit 6–2 Strangle Buy
Hewlett-Packard 75 Call, Hewlett-Packard 65 Put

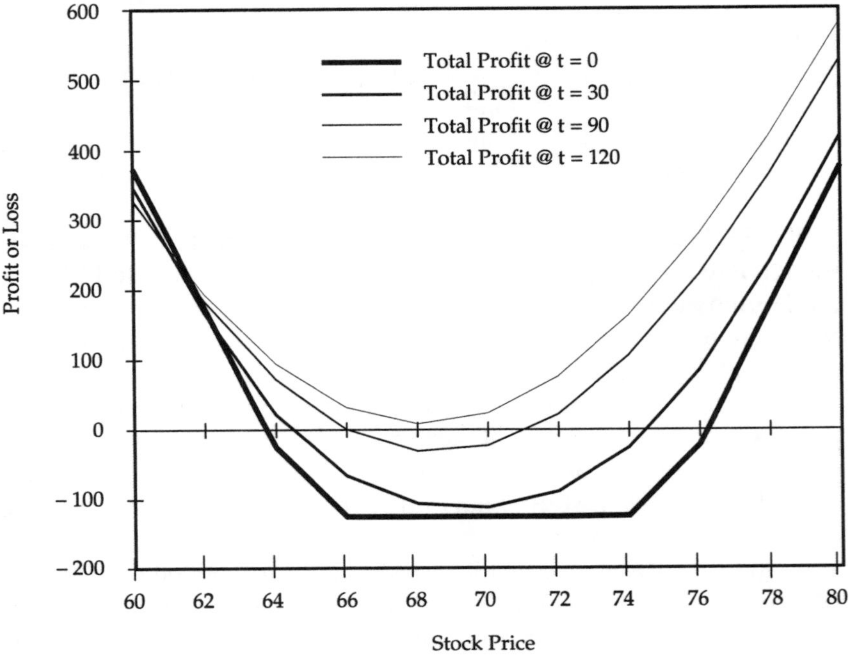

is much less than the ¾ point, or $75, loss that the straddle buyer incurs under the same conditions.

When there are only 30 days left until expiration the strangle's value is ¼—3/16 for the November 75 call and 1/16 for the November 65 put. The strangle buyer suffers a 1 ¼ point loss (1 ½ minus ¼), or $125 if forced to liquidate with Hewlett-Packard's share price at 70. However this is only one-half the 2 ½ point, or $250, loss suffered by the straddle buyer in the same situation.

Finally, at expiration the strangle's value is 0, since both the November 75 call option and the November 65 put option are out-of-the-money. Now, the loss to the strangle buyer is the position's cost, $150, while the straddle buyer incurs a loss of 5 points, or $500.

Note that time works against the strangle buyer just as it does against the straddle buyer. However, the strangle buyer loses less because the position's cost is lower than the straddle's.

Straddle and Strangle Writing Strategies

The same November straddle and strangle used to illustrate the purchase strategies will be used to explain the writing strategies.

STRADDLE WRITE Exhibit 6–3 portrays the profit profile for the writer of the 120-day Hewlett-Packard November 70 straddle. The cash inflow to the straddle writer generated by the sale of the November 70 call option for 3 ½ points and the sale of the November 70 put option for 1 ½ points is 5 points, or $500. According to the maturity line labeled "T = 0," if the price of Hewlett-Packard's shares is 70 at the options' maturity, then both the put option and call option will expire worthless, and the straddle writer will have earned the maximum profit of 5 points.

If the stock's price is anything other than 70 at expiration, then the straddle will have some intrinsic value, which means that the straddle writer must cover the open short position. For example, if the stock's price is greater than 70 at maturity, then the put option will be worthless, but the call option will have intrinsic value. Thus, the straddle writer must cover the short position in the call option by purchasing a call option with an identical striking price and maturity.

If the stock price is less than 70 at expiration, then the call option will be worthless and the put option will have intrinsic value. In this case, the open short position in the put option must be covered by purchasing a put option with an identical striking price and maturity. As long as the price of the Hewlett-Packard stock is between 65 and 75 at the straddle's maturity, the writer will earn a profit. Note that the break-even points of 65 and 75 for the straddle writer are identical to those of the straddle buyer. This is logically consistent since the straddle writer and buyer are taking similar but opposite positions in the same options.

The other maturity lines in Exhibit 6-3 show the straddle writer's profit or loss at various points in time during the straddle's life. For example, if the stock price is 70 with 90 days until expiration, then the straddle writer would gain $75 if forced to liquidate. The gain occurs

Exhibit 6–3 Straddle Write
Hewlett-Packard 70

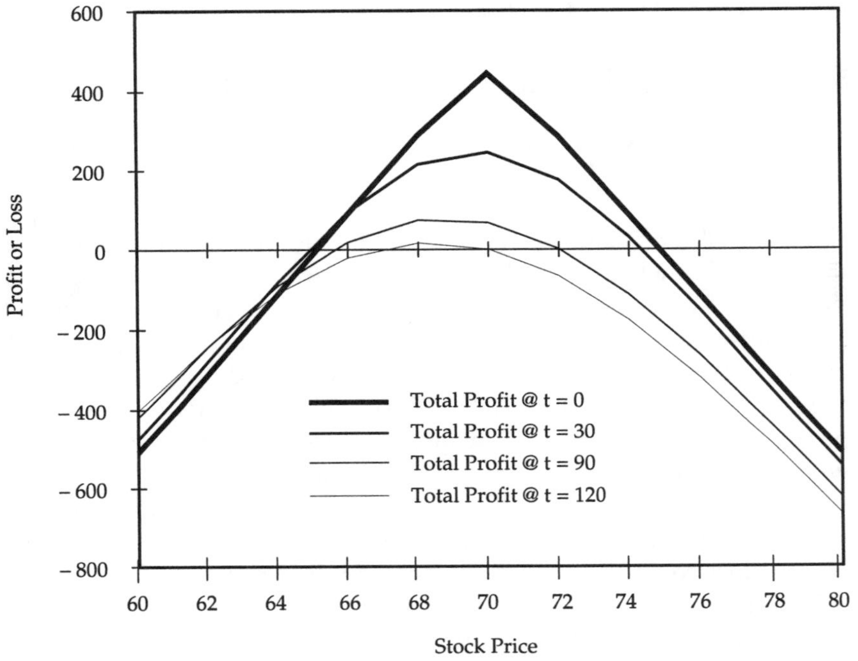

because the value of the October straddle is 4 ¾ (¼ for the November 70 call option and 1 ½ for the November 70 put option) which is ¾ of a point less than the value of the writer's initial cash inflow of 5 points. If the stock price remained unchanged during the straddle's life, then the writer's gains would be 2 ½ points, or $250, with 30 days until expiration and the entire 5, points or $500, at expiration. The straddle writer's profits rise as maturity approaches because of the time premium decay. Remember, the straddle writer sold options that had no intrinsic value. Thus, the entire initial value of the straddle, and the writer's liability, will erode with the passage of time if the price of the underlying stock remains unchanged.

It is very important to realize that in flat or unchanging markets, time works against the straddle buyer, but benefits the straddle writer. In

Exhibit 6–4 Strangle Write
Hewlett-Packard 75 Call, Hewlett-Packard 65 Put

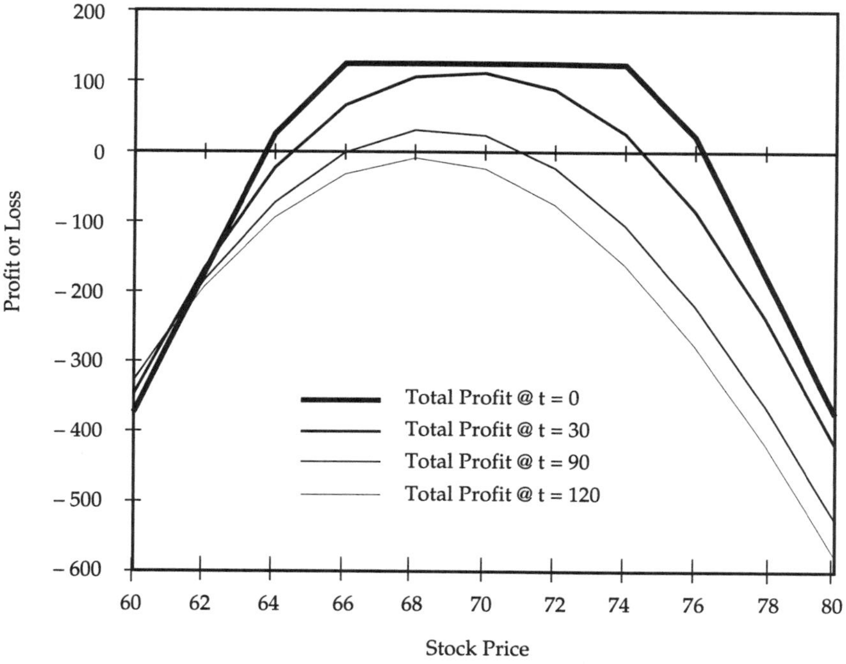

active markets, characterized by rising stock prices, the loss potential for the straddle writer is unlimited since there is no theoretical upper limit to the liability associated with the naked call position. In falling markets, the straddle writer's maximum loss equals the put option's striking price minus the initial value of the straddle and is realized if the market price of the stock falls to zero.

STRANGLE WRITE Exhibit 6–4 can be used to illustrate the profit potential of a strangle seller. Here a 120-day Hewlett-Packard strangle is sold by writing the out-of-the-money November 75 call option for 1 ⅛, and the out-of-the-money November 65 put option for ⅜, for a total cash inflow of 1 ½ points, or \$150. The "T = 0" maturity line illustrates that if Hewlett-Packard's share price rises or falls by 6 ⅛ points at expiration, then the strangle writer will break-even. Price movement less than 6 ⅛ points results in a profit for the writer, since both options will expire out-of-the-money, which allows the strangle writer to keep the entire initial cash flow. Price movement of more than 6 ⅛ points will cause either the put option or call option to be in-the-money at expiration, which translates to a liability for the strangle writer that must be offset. Thus, a loss will be incurred by the strangle writer when the liability is eliminated via the purchase of an option that has an identical striking price and maturity to those of the in-the-money option, since the purchased option will have a value greater than the initial cash inflow of 1 ½ points. This is quite different from the 5-point price movement that the straddle writer can withstand before suffering a loss. Thus, it is better for an investor to write a strangle rather than a straddle if a decrease in stock price volatility is anticipated.

The remaining lines in Exhibit 6–4 provide the strangle's profit or loss at various times prior to maturity. For example, with 90 days until expiration, the November strangle has a value of 1 ⅛ points—¾ of a point for the November 75 call option and ⅜ of a point for the November 65 put option. If the investor liquidated the position at this point, then a ⅜ point, or $37.50, gain would be realized (1 ½ minus 1 ⅛). This is much less than the ¾ point, or $75, gain that the straddle writer enjoys under the same conditions.

When there are only 30 days left until expiration the strangle's value is ¼—³⁄₁₆ for the November 75 call and ⅛ for the October 65 put. Here, the strangle writer earns a 1 ¼ point gain (1 ½ minus ¼), or $125, if forced to liquidate with the Hewlett-Packard share price at 70. However, this is only one-half the 2 ½ point, or $250, profit achieved by the straddle writer in the same situation.

Finally, at expiration the strangle's value is zero, since both the November 75 call option and the November 65 put option are out-of-the-money. Now, the strangle writer's gain is the entire 1 ½ points, or $150, while the straddle writer earns 5 point, or $500.

Note that time works for the strangle writer just as it works for the straddle writer. However, the strangle earns less profit since the strangle's initial cash inflow is lower than the straddle's initial cash inflow.

LIMITATIONS OF OPTION WRITING STRATEGIES It must be emphasised that these option writing strategies will yield profits only if one can correctly anticipate a declining stock price volatility. If the volatility forecast is wrong and the stock price volatility does not shrink, then large losses can occur. Since both of these option writing strategies have limited profit potential but unlimited loss potential, they are not recommended for the conservative investor. If one is determined to implement a strategy that will earn a profit in a stable market, then the call option time spread should be used. Although this spread requires a cash outflow to establish, as opposed to a cash inflow generated by writing a straddle or a strangle—purchasing a time spread is safer and more conservative than writing either the straddle or strangle since the time spread's maximum loss is limited. Furthermore the spread's profit compares quite favorably with the profitability of the strangle and straddle writing strategies.

Illustrations of the Straddle and Strangle Positions

In this section we will examine some examples of the concepts discussed above, and use worksheets to compute the profitability of each of the four positions. These examples are based on the turmoil that surrounded United Airlines Corporation in 1989. This uncertainty created an ideal environment for trading straddles, strangles, and time spreads. The United Airlines data contained in Exhibit 6–5 provide the basis for the examples in this section.

STRADDLE AND STRANGLE PURCHASE In the third quarter of 1989 United Airlines Corporation (UAL) became a takeover target. During this time two bidders were engaged in assembling the components necessary for a successful takeover of UAL. In July, the market began anticipating the eventual takeover of UAL. Average daily trading volume for UAL shares began to increase steadily and UAL's share price started to increase by leaps and bounds. On July 3, UAL shares closed at 144 ½, and by the end of the week they had risen to 166 and showed no sign of falling in the near future. For the next three weeks UAL's share prices traded between 164 and 184. Finally, in early August, Marvin Davis launched a takeover bid for United Airlines Corporation by offering $275 per share for UAL's outstanding shares. UAL's stock was at 164 on Friday August 4, when the offer was made; it closed at 210 on the following Monday, August 7, and jumped to 257 by the end of trading on Friday, August 11. UAL's board of directors did not consider Davis's offer to be in the shareholders' best interest, and, thus, rejected it. However, UAL's stock remained above 250 because another syndicate was readying a bid for UAL.

This second buy-out group was known as Airline Acquisition Corporation and was composed of UAL management, the pilots' union, and British Airways. Shortly after the board of directors rejected the Davis offer, the management-pilot group offered $300 per share for all of UAL's outstanding shares; a deal worth approximately 6.5 billion dollars. The offer was good until midnight, Eastern Time, October 26, 1989.

Given these events, we have chosen to illustrate the combination strategies as of August 16. Exhibit 6–5 shows that the November options are the best choice for the conservative investor since they will not expire until well after the proposed takeover has been settled.

With UAL stock at 251 ¾, the November straddle could have been bought for 35 points, or $3500, by purchasing the November 250 call option for 19 ½ and the November 250 put option for 15 ½. These prices dictate that UAL stock must move by at least 35 points up or down for the investor to break-even. While this may seem like a huge move, recall that the share price had risen from 144 on July 3 to 251 ¾ in just six weeks. The explosion in volatility was driving UAL stock and until UAL's board approved a takeover, there was no reason to expect that volatility would decline.

If one thinks that the November straddle is much too expensive, the less costly alternative is the UAL November strangle. The option prices in Exhibit 6–5 show that the November 260 call option could have been bought for 13 ⅝ and the November 240 put option could have been purchased for 10 ¼, for a total cost of 23 ⅞ points, or $2387.50. Although this is cheaper than the straddle, we do not recommend this strategy since it requires a much greater move in UAL's price than does the long straddle position.

Between August 16 and September 1, UAL shares moved by more than 35 points from 251 ¾ to 287 ¼. With 78 days remaining until expiration, the November 250 straddle also had increased from 35 to 50 ½, and the November strangle had risen to 40 from its earlier level of 23 ⅞. Exhibit 6–5 shows that the November 250 call option had risen to

Exhibit 6–5 Option Prices for the UAL November Straddle and Strangle

November Options' Maturity: T = 93 Days
August 16

Option & NY Close	Striking Price	Calls – Last			Puts – Last		
UAL		Aug	Sep	Nov	Aug	Sep	Nov
251 ¾	240	–	18 ⅞	27	–	5	10 ¼
251 ¾	250	–	11 ½	19 ½	–	8	15 ½
251 ¾	260	–	6 ⅜	13 ⅝	–	13	20 ½

November Options' Maturity: T = 78 Days
September 1

Option & NY Close	Striking Price	Calls – Last			Puts – Last		
UAL		Sep	Oct	Nov	Sep	Oct	Nov
287 ¼	240	48	–	53	¾	–	4
287 ¼	250	39	43 ½	45	⅞	3	5 ½
287 ¼	260	29	34 ½	36	1 ½	4 ⅜	6 ½
287 ¼	270	20 ⅛	25 ¾	28 ½	2	6	8 ¾
287 ¼	280	12 ¼	18	21 ⅛	3 ⅞	9	11 ¼
287 ¼	290	5 ⅞	11	14	7 ¾	12 ¼	15

November Options' Maturity: T = 37 Days
October 12

Option & NY Close	Striking Price	Calls – Last			Puts – Last		
UAL		Oct	Nov	Feb	Oct	Nov	Feb
285	240	–	–	–	–	4	–
285	250	35	40	–	⅝	4 ⅝	7 ½
285	260	26 ¼	30	–	1 ⅛	6	–
285	270	16 ¾	22	23	1 ¼	6 ½	10 ¾
285	280	7 ½	14 ½	16	2 ⅝	9	13 ¾
285	290	1 ⅛	6 ½	8	5 ½	12 ¾	15

November Options' Maturity: T = 32 Days
October 16

Option & NY Close	Striking Price	Calls – Last			Puts – Last		
UAL		Oct	Nov	Feb	Oct	Nov	Feb
223	240	–	11	17	–	35	30
223	250	2 ½	7	14	27	43 ½	45
223	260	1 ¼	4 ¼	9	38 ¼	42	52

45, the November 260 call option had risen to 36, while the November 250 put option had fallen to 5 ½ and the November 240 put option had settled to 4. The fact that UAL's price did not move to the management-pilot group's $300 per share level is a clear indication of the market's skepticism regarding the possibility of the takeover.

Although the market was not convinced that UAL would be taken over at $300 per share, there was ample time for the management-pilot group to negotiate with UAL's board. There was no compelling reason to believe that the deal would not be consummated since the management-pilot group had a strong vested interest in the company and the necessary financing seemed to be in place with a consortium of several large U.S. and Japanese banks. The only question that remained was how close would the final price be to the $300 per share offer.

STRADDLE AND STRANGLE SALE A strong argument can be made for leaving the long combinations intact since there was still the possibility of a 13-point rise in UAL stock before October 26. However, an equally persuasive argument can be made in favor of selling a straddle and strangle since it appeared that the volatility had shrunk and that the share price would not move much from its present level. Therefore, an investor could have capitalized on this shrinking volatility by selling a 78-day November straddle or strangle on September 1.

Exhibit 6–5 shows that a November 290 straddle could have been sold for 29 points, or $2900, by shorting the November 290 call option for 14 and the November 290 put option for 15. Alternatively, the November 290 call option could have been sold for 14 and the November 270 put option could have been sold for 8 ¾ which results in the investor being short a strangle at 22 ¾, or $275. We recommend the more conservative strangle over the straddle since the strangle provides the investor with a much greater cushion than the straddle.

For the next six weeks UAL's share price fluctuated between 290 and 274, settling at 284 on Monday, October 9. With less than three weeks to go until the management-pilot offer's expiration, the takeover appeared to be in trouble. During this week the consortium of U.S. and Japanese banks began to have severe reservations regarding the creditworthiness of management and the pilot's union. The structure of the proposal put the banks in a very risky position at a $300 per share price. Consequently, they began to withdraw their support for the takeover. Rumors that the management-pilot offer was in trouble began to circulate on Tuesday. However, UAL's price remained stable, although trading volume increased a bit. By Thursday, October 12, word that the banks were unwilling to go through with the takeover in its current form began spreading. With the stock price at 285 and 37 days until the November options expired, it was time to close out the short straddle and strangle positions.

The data in Exhibit 6–5 indicate that the UAL November 290 straddle was valued at 19 ¼ points—6 ½ points for the November 290 call option and 12 ¾ points for the November 290 put option. This $1925 liquidation value translates to a 9 ¾ point, or $975, profit for the straddle seller—the 29 point initial value less the 19 ¼ liquidation value. The prices for the November strangle show a liquidation value of 17 ¼ points—6 ½ points for the November 290 call option and 10 ¾ points for the November 270 put option. Consequently the strangle writer's profit is 5 ½ points, or $550.

At 2:30 P.M., Eastern Time, on Friday, October 13, there was no doubt that the management-pilot UAL takeover bid was doomed. The inevitable collapse of the takeover and its $300 per share value prompted heavy selling. At 2:54 P.M. the management-pilot group announced formally that they did not have sufficient financing for their takeover bid. Trading in UAL shares was halted with UAL at 279 ¾. UAL did not trade on the New York Stock Exchange for the remainder of the day but was quoted off the exchange at 230 late Friday afternoon. Obviously those that were long straddles and strangles were benefitting from the explosion in volatility.

On Monday, October 16, UAL opened at 230 per share, dropped to 213 during the day, and settled at 223. Even though there were still 32 days until the November options expired, it was extremely prudent for the straddle and strangle holders to liquidate. The prices for the November options in Exhibit 6-5 show that the November 250 straddle had a 50 ½ point liquidation value—7 points for the November 250 call option and 43 ½ points for the November 250 put option. This $5050 liquidation value leaves the straddle buyer with a 15 ½ point, or $1550, profit. Similarly, the November strangle's liquidation value was 39 ¼ points—4 ¼ points for the November 260 call option and 35 points for the

November 240 put option. In this case, the strangle buyer's profit is 15 ⅜ points, or $1537.50: the 39 ¼ point liquidation value less the original cost of 23 ⅞.

Given the rapid decrease in the stock's price, and the resulting increase in the put options' prices, it is appropriate to dicusss legging out of the long straddle and strangle positions. In general, the term, *legging out* refers to closing out one side of a spread or combination because one is attempting to maximize the net gains associated with the anticipated security price movement. It is important to understand that when one legs out of a combination, a relatively higher level of risk is being assumed since the new position is an open position in the remaining option. The conservative investor should be extremely cautious about legging out of a combination based on the anticipated price movement. Remember, the basic logic of the combination, either straddle or strangle, is that one is attempting to profit from a change in the underlying stock's price volatility; one is not attempting to predict the direction of the underlying stock's price movement. Thus, the combination's purpose is defeated if one legs out prematurely.

In these examples, the straddle and strangle buyers might be tempted to leg out of their position on October 16 because it does not appear that the management-pilot buy-out group will be able to salvage anything remotely resembling their original offer, which should result in further decreases in the prices of both UAL's common shares and call options and increases in UAL put options. If the straddle buyer legs out of the positions by selling the November 250 call option for 7, then the resulting value of the long November 250 put position is 43 ½, with a net cost of 28—35 paid for the straddle less the 7 received for selling the call option. Moreover, if the strangle buyer legs out of the position by selling the November 260 call option for 4 ¼, then the value of the long November 240 put position is 35, with a net cost of 19 ⅝—23 ⅞ paid for the strangle less the 4 ¼ received from the sale of the call option.

COMBINATION WORKSHEETS Worksheet 6–1 (see pages 134–135) has been completed to illus-trate the potential gains and losses for the UAL November 250 straddle purchase. The first portion of the worksheet, entitled position data, summarizes the relevant information for the straddle buyer. In this case the straddle's initial value was 35 points with 93 days until expiration. The worksheet's second section, labeled initial position, allows the buyer to compute the straddle's exact cost, including commissions. The final section of the worksheet enables the investor to compute the straddle's profit or loss, and is completed at liquidation, or expiration, of the position, whichever occurs first. In this example, the straddle buyer did not wait for expiration, but decided to liquidate the position for 50 ½ points, with 32 days remaining until expiration, to reap a net profit of $1550.

Worksheet 6–2 (see pages 136–137) shows the gains and losses for the UAL November strangle purchase. The first portion of the worksheet, entitled position data, provides the relevant information for the strangle purchaser. Here, the strangle's initial value was 23 ⅞ points with 93 days until expiration. The second section of the worksheet, labeled initial position, enables the buyer to compute the strangle's cost, with commissions included. The third section of the worksheet allows the investor to compute the straddle's profit or loss, and is completed at liquidation, or expiration, of the position, whichever occurs first. Like the straddle buyer, the strangle buyer did not wait for expiration, but decided to liquidate the position for 39 ¼ points, with 32 days remaining until expiration, resulting in a net profit of $1537.50.

Worksheet 6–3 (see pages 138–139) portrays the gains and losses for the UAL November 250 straddle seller. The first section of the worksheet, position data, is identical to Worksheet 6–1, the long straddle position, and summarizes the appropriate information for the straddle writer. In this case the straddle's initial value was 29 points with 78 days until expiration. In the worksheet's second section, the initial position section, the buyer computes the straddle's revenues, including commissions. Finally, the last section of the worksheet enables the investor to determine the straddle's profit or loss, and like the other worksheets, is completed at liquidation or expiration of the position. Here, the straddle seller did not wait for expiration, but liquidated the position for 19 ¼ points, with 37 days remaining until expiration. The worksheet shows that the straddle seller earned a $975 profit.

Worksheet 6–4 (see pages 140–141) is the final combination worksheet and shows the gains and losses associated with the UAL November strangle sale. The first part of the worksheet shows the information needed by the strangle seller and indicates that the strangle seller can write a 78-day strangle for 22 ¾ points. The initial portion of the worksheet

Worksheet 6–1 Straddle Purchase Worksheet

A. Position Data								
Underlying Stock	UAL							
Current Stock Price	251 ¾							$251.75
Days until Call Option Expiration	93							
Call Options' Maturity Month	November							
Call Options' Strike Price	250							
Call Option's Intrinsic Value	1 ¾							
Call Options' Time Value	17 ¾							
Call Options' Premium	19 ½							$1950.00
Put Options' Maturity Month	November							
Days until Put Option Expiration	93							
Put Options' Strike Price	250							
Put Options' Intrinsic Value	0							
Put Options' Time Value	15 ½							
Put Options' Premium	15 ½							$1550.00
Straddle Value	35							$3500.00
B. Initial Position								
1. Buy	1	strike =	250	call option	at	19 ½	for	$1950.00
2. Plus Commissions					at	0	for	$0.00
3. Buy	1	strike =	250	put option	at	15 ½	for	$1550.00
4. Plus Commissions					at	0	for	$0.00
5. Net Cost								$3500.00

C. Position Profit or Loss

Stock Price at Liquidation	223							$223.00
Days until Call Option Expiration	32							
Call Options' Maturity Month	November							
Call Options' Strike Price	250							
Call Options Intrinsic Value	0							
Call Options' Time Value	7							
Call Options' Premium	7							$700.00
Put Options' Maturity Month	November							$700.00
Days until Put Option Expiration	32							
Put Options' Strike Price	250							
Put Optionss Intrinsic Value	27							
Put Options' Time Value	16 ½							
Put Options' Premium	43 ½							$4350.00
Straddle Value	50 ½							$5050.00
6. Sell	1	strike =	250	call option	at	7	for	$700.00
7. Less Commissions					at	0	for	$0.00
8. Sell	1	strike =	250	put option	at	43 ½	for	$4350.00
9. Less Commissions					at	0	for	$0.00
10. Net Revenues								$5050.00
Net Profit Or Loss (10) – (5)								$1550.00

Worksheet 6–2 Strangle Purchase Worksheet

A. Position Data

Underlying Stock	UAL	
Current Stock Price	251 ¾	$251.75
Days until Call Option Expiration	93	
Call Options' Maturity Month	November	
Call Options' Strike Price	260	
Call Options' Intrinsic Value	0	
Call Options' Time Value	13 ⅝	
Call Options' Premium	13 ⅝	$1362.50
Put Options' Maturity Month	November	
Days until Put Option Expiration	93	
Put Options' Strike Price	240	
Put Options' Intrinsic Value	0	
Put Options' Time Value	10 ¼	
Put Options' Premium	10 ¼	$1025.00
Strangle Value	23 ⅞	$2387.50

B. Initial Position

1. Buy	1	strike =	260	call option	at	13 ⅝	for	$1362.50
2. Plus Commissions					at	0	for	$0.00
3. Buy	1	strike =	240	put option	at	10 ¼	for	$1025.00
4. Plus Commissions					at	0	for	$0.00
5. Net Cost								$2387.50

C. Position Profit or Loss								
Stock Price at Liquidation	223							$223.00
Days until Call Option Expiration	32							
Call Options' Maturity Month	November							
Call Options' Strike Price	260							
Call Options' Intrinsic Value	0							
Call Options' Time Value	4 ¼							
Call Options' Premium	4 ¼							$425.00
Put Options' Maturity Month	November							
Days until Put Option Expiration	32							
Put Options' Strike Price	240							
Put Options' Intrinsic Value	17							
Put Options' Time Value	18							
Put Options' Premium	35							$3500.00
Strangle Value	39 ¼							$3925.00
6. Sell	1	strike =	260	call option	at	4 ¼	for	$425.00
7. Less Commissions					at	0	for	$0.00
8. Sell	1	strike =	240	put option	at	35	for	$3500.00
9. Less Commissions					at	0	for	$0.00
10. Net Revenues								$3925.00
Net Profit Or Loss (10) – (5)								$1537.50

Worksheet 6–3 Straddle Sale Worksheet

A. Position Data								
Underlying Stock	UAL							
Current Stock Price	287 ¼							$287.25
Days until Call Option Expiration	78							
Call Options' Maturity Month	November							
Call Options' Strike Price	290							
Call Options' Intrinsic Value	0							
Call Options' Time Value	14							
Call Options' Premium	14							$1400.00
Put Options' Maturity Month	November							
Days until Put Option Expiration	78							
Put Options' Strike Price	290							
Put Options' Intrinsic Value	2 ¾							
Put Options' Time Value	12 ¼							
Put Options' Premium	15							$1500.00
Straddle Value	29							$2900.00
B. Initial Position								
1. Sell	1	strike =	290	call option	at	14	for	$1400.00
2. Less Commissions					at	0	for	$0.00
3. Sell	1	strike =	250	put option	at	15	for	$1500.00
4. Less Commissions					at	0	for	$0.00
5. Net Revenues								$2900.00

C. Position Profit or Loss

Stock Price at Liquidation	285							$285.00
Days until Call Option Expiration	37							
Call Options' Maturity Month	November							
Call Options' Strike Price	290							
Call Options' Intrinsic Value	0							
Call Options' Time Value	6 ½							
Call Options' Premium	6 ½							$650.00
Put Options' Maturity Month	November							
Days until Put Option Expiration	37							
Put Options' Strike Price	290							
Put Options' Intrinsic Value	5							
Put Options' Time Value	7 ¾							
Put Options' Premium	12 ¾							$1275.00
Straddle Value	19 ¼							$1925.00
6. Buy	1	strike =	250	call option	at	6 ½	for	$650.00
7. Plus Commissions					at	0	for	$0.00
8. Buy	1	strike =	250	put option	at	12 ¾	for	$1275.00
9. Plus Commissions					at	0	for	$0.00
10. Net Costs								$1925.00
Net Profit Or Loss (5) – (10)								$975.00

Worksheet 6–4 Strangle Sale Worksheet

A. Position Data								
Underlying Stock	UAL							
Current Stock Price	287 ¼							$287.25
Days until Call Option Expiration	78							
Call Options' Maturity Month	November							
Call Options' Strike Price	290							
Call Options' Intrinsic Value	0							
Call Options' Time Value	14							
Call Options' Premium	14							$1400.00
Put Options' Maturity Month	November							
Days until Put Option Expiration	78							
Put Options' Strike Price	270							
Put Options' Intrinsic Value	0							
Put Options' Time Value	8 ¾							
Put Options' Premium	8 ¾							$875.00
Strangle Value	22 ¾							$2275.00
B. Initial Position								
1. Sell	1	strike =	290	call option	at	14	for	$1400.00
2. Less Commissions					at	0	for	$0.00
3. Sell	1	strike =	270	put option	at	8 ¾	for	$1500.00
4. Less Commissions					at	0	for	$0.00
5. Net Revenues								$2275.00

C. Position Profit or Loss

Stock Price at Liquidation	285							$285.00
Days until Call Option Expiration	37							
Call Options' Maturity Month	November							
Call Options' Strike Price	290							
Call Options' Intrinsic Value	0							
Call Options' Time Value	6 ½							
Call Options' Premium	6 ½							$650.00
Put Option' Maturity Month	November							
Days until Put Option Expiration	37							
Put Optiosn' Strike Price	270							
Put Options' Intrinsic Value	0							
Put Options' Time Value	10 ¾							
Put Options' Premium	10 ¾							$1075.00
Straddle Value	17 ¼							$1725.00
6. Buy	1	strike =	290	call option	at	6 ½	for	$650.00
7. Plus Commissions					at	0	for	$0.00
8. Buy	1	strike =	270	put option	at	10 ¾	for	$1075.00
9. Plus Commissions					at	0	for	$0.00
10. Net Costs								$1725.00
Net Profit Or Loss (5) – (10)								$550.00

Worksheet 6–5 Time Spread Purchase Worksheet

A. Position Data						
Underlying Stock	UAL					
Current Stock Price	287 ¼					$287.25
Days until Call Option Expiration	50					
Nearby Options' Maturity Month	October					
Nearby Options' Strike Price	290					
Nearby Options' Intrinsic Value	0					
Nearby Options' Time Value	11					
Nearby Options' Premium	11					$1100.00
Days until Deferred Option Expiration	78					
Deferred Options' Maturity Month	November					
Deferred Options' Strike Price	290					
Deferred Options' Intrinsic Value	0					
Deferred Options' Time Value	14					
Deferred Options' Premium	14					$1400.00
B. Initial Position						
1. Sell	1	nearby option	at	11	for	$1100.00
2. Less Commissions			at	0	for	$0.00
3. Buy	1	deferred option	at	14	for	$1400.00
4. Plus Commissions			at	0	for	$0.00
5. Net Cost						$300.00

C. Position Profit or Loss

Stock Price at Liquidation	285					$285.00
Days until Nearby Option Expiration	10					
Nearby Options' Maturity Month	October					
Nearby Options' Strike Price	290					
Nearby Options' Intrinsic Value	0					
Nearby Options' Time Value	1 ⅛					
Nearby Options' Premium	1 ⅛					$112.50
Deferred Options' Maturity Month	November					
Deferred Options' Strike Price	290					
Deferred Options' Intrinsic Value	0					
Deferred Options' Time Value	6 ½					
Deferred Options' Premium	6 ½					$1075.5
6. Buy	1	nearby option	at	1 ⅛	for	$112.00
7. Plus Commissions			at	0	for	$0.00
8. Sell	1	deferred Option	at	6 ½	for	$650.00
9. Less Commissions			at	0	for	$0.00
10. Net Revenues						$537.50
Net Profit Or Loss (10) – (5)						$237.50

enables the seller to compute the strangle's revenues, with commissions included. The third section of the worksheet permits the investor to compute the straddle's profit or loss, and is completed at the position's liquidation, or expiration. Here, the strangle seller did not wait for expiration, but decided to close the position for 17 ¼ points, with 37 days remaining until expiration, resulting in a net profit of $550.

Earlier it was mentioned that purchasing a time spread was recommended over the sale of either a straddle or a strangle if one is attempting to profit from a flat, or stable, market in the underlying stock. Worksheet 6–5 (see pages 142–143) contains the calculations for an investor who purchased an October–November 290 call option time spread on September 1, and closed out the position on October 12. Notice that the 2 ⅜ point profit is considerably smaller than the 5 ½ point profit earned by the strangle writer but the maximum possible loss of 3 for the spread buyer is much less than the strangle writer's unlimited loss.

Conclusion

This chapter has introduced some basic strategies known as straddles and strangles. The first part of the chapter explained the positions'underlying logic and provided a graphical analysis of their behavior over time. The remainder of the chapter was devoted to examining the profits and losses of various positions via the turmoil that surrounded United Airlines Corporation in the third and fourth quarters of 1989. Worksheets were provided to facilitate the explanation of each trading strategy.

Both the straddle and strangle strategies combine call options with put options, are subject to unlimited gains as well as unlimited losses, and are predicated upon estimating the underlying stock's volatility more accurately than the market as a whole. The basic difference between the strategies is that the straddle uses at-the-money options, while the strangle employs out-of-the-money options. Given this fundamental difference, straddles are much more sensitive to changes in the underlying stock's price than are strangles.

Problem 6–1 *See Appendix C for solution.*

Suppose that in early May, Storage Technology's common stock is trading at 25 ½. You believe that a large price move is imminent, but you do not know whether it will take the form of an increase or a decrease. Therefore, you decide to buy a Storage Technology straddle. At this time, the 105-day Storage Technology September 25 call option has a 5-point premium and the 105-day Storage Technology September 25 put option is selling for 4 ⅛. In mid-August, approximately five weeks prior to the options' expiration, Storage Technology common stock has reached 36, the September 25 call option is trading at 13, and the September put option's price has fallen to a value of ¾. Compute the profits generated by your straddle purchase.

Problem 6–2 *See Appendix C for solution.*

Use the information provided for Storage Technology in problem 6–1 to compute the losses that a straddle writer would incur.

Problem 6–3 *See Appendix C for solution.*

Suppose that in early January, Digital Equipment Corporation's common stock is trading at 38 ¼. You believe that the share price will remain relatively stable, as it has for the last quarter, but you want to protect yourself as much as possible from Digital's notoriously erratic price changes. Thus, you decide to sell a Digital Equipment strangle. At this time, the 108-day April Digital 40 call option is selling for 2 ⅝, and the 108-day April Digital 35 put option is selling for 1 ¾. In mid-March, approximately four weeks prior to the options' expiration, Digital Equipment's common stock rose to 52 ⅛, the April 40 call option was trading at 13 ¾, and the April 35 put option was changing hands at ¼ point. Compute the losses generated by the sale of your strangle.

Problem 6–4 *See Appendix C for solution.*

Use the information provided for Digital Equipment in problem 6–3 to compute the gains that a strangle purchaser would enjoy.

Chapter Seven

ADVANCED OPTION STRATEGIES

In this chapter, we will use a different approach than in previous chapters. Here we will utilize more than one strategy at the same time, building on the basic strategies covered in Chapters One through Six. We recommend that you have a thorough grasp of the fundamental strategies before proceeding with this chapter.

The first three strategies are all bullish in nature, but each entails a unique perspective.

Buying Stock and Selling Puts Simultaneously

DEFINITION AND LOGIC The strategy of *buying stock and simultaneously selling puts* is feasible when the investor is fundamentally bullish on a company but wants to purchase only a percentage of the desired position. In other words, the investor wants to dollar cost average the position. After buying a percentage of the position, the investor incurs the obligation to average down, that is, purchase more stock at a lower price.

To utilize this strategy, the investor purchases at least 100 shares of stock and simultaneously sells a put option on that stock with a striking price at or below the current stock price. By selling a put option, the investor makes an obligation to purchase the stock at the striking price until the option's expiration date. In return for this obligation, the investor receives a premium. If the stock is at or above the striking price at expiration, the option will expire worthless and the investor will have earned the premium as profit and at the same time realized a gain from the long stock position. If the stock is below the striking price at expiration, the option will most likely be exercised and the investor will have to purchase the stock at the striking price. However, the cost basis on the stock that is put to the investor will be the striking price less the premium received.

ILLUSTRATION: DEAN FOODS CORPORATION To better understand this strategy, let us take a look at a realistic situation. Suppose you like the long-term prospects for Dean Foods Corporation. The company has a history of consistent sales and earnings growth. The stock looks attractive, but you are not sure that you want to purchase a full position on it at its current price level. You observe that Dean Foods common stock is trading at $27 a share and the put options are priced as follows:

Dean Foods 6-month 25 put, 1 ½

Dean Foods 6-month 30 put, 4 ½

If your intention is to own 400 shares of Dean Foods, you execute the following strategy: Purchase 200 shares of Dean Foods for $27 a share, and simultaneously sell two 6-month out-of-the-money puts with a striking price of 25 for 1 ½ points each. Thus, your cost basis on these first 200 shares is 25 ½ per share:

27 (stock price per share) – 1 ½ (put option premium)

If the stock is at or above 25 at expiration, the put will expire worthless and your profit will be any amount above 25 ½. If Dean Foods common stock declines to below 25 at expiration, you will have to fulfill your obligation and purchase 200 shares at $25 each. Thus, your cost basis on all 400 shares will be 25 ¼:

27 (original stock price) – 1 ½ (option premium) + 25 (put striking price)

This strategy is intended to run throughout the option's life. However, remember that you may cancel your obligation at any time by purchasing a put option in the options market with the same striking price and expiration date. In this scenario, your cost basis would be 25 ¼, which is 1 ¾ points below what you were originally willing to pay for Dean Foods common stock.

Note that all collateral requirements for the naked puts are probably fulfilled by the long stock position. We recommend that you consult your broker for the most current option margin requirements.

Worksheet 7–1 illustrates the computations involved in this strategy. Worksheet 7–2 fills in the data for our Dean Foods example.

Covered Combinations

Our next strategy—selling covered combinations—is also bullish. It builds on the strategy of buying stock and simultaneously selling puts.

DEFINITION AND LOGIC Selling a covered combination is more conservative than our previous strategy of buying stock and selling puts simultaneously, because the investor receives more option premium and contracts to sell the stock at a predetermined price. In fact, a covered combination strategy is similar to covered call writing but somewhat more aggressive, because it obligates the investor to purchase more stock at a lower price.

In simplified terms, a *covered combination* is a covered call write with the simultaneous sale of puts. An investor utilizes this strategy when he or she is bullish on a particular stock but is willing to lock in a profit at a specific price and incur an obligation to average down in price. Technically, a covered combination involves the purchase of a common stock, the sale of a put with a striking price at or below the current stock price, and the sale of a call with a striking price at or above the current stock price. The maximum profit potential is the premiums received from the sale of the options plus the call striking price minus the initial stock price. On the downside, the investor is protected by the amount of premiums received for the sale of the put and call.

ILLUSTRATION: DEAN FOODS CORPORATION To better understand the mechanics and philosophy of this strategy, let us examine a real-life situation,

Worksheet 7–1 Buying Stock and Selling Puts Simultaneously: Greentree Financial

A. Initial Position Data

Underlying Stock	______					
Current Stock Price	______					______
Put Options' Maturity Month	______					
Put Options' Striking Price	______					
Put Options' Premium	______					
Days until Option Expires	______					
1. Buy	______ # of shares	______ stock	at	__	for	______
2. Plus Commissions			at	__	for	______
3. Net Stock Position			at	__	for	______
4. Sell	______ #	Puts	at	__	for	______
5. Less Commissions			at	__	for	______
6. Net Put Options' Proceeds						______
7. Net Cost of Position (3) – (6)						______
8. Net Cost per Share (7)/(# of shares)						______

B. Result of Position If Put Is Exercised (occurs if stock is below strike price)

9. Buy	______ # of shares	______ stock	at	__	for	______
10. Plus Commissions			at	__	for	______
11. Cost of Shares Put to You			at	__	for	______
12. Cost of Original Shares Purchased (7)			at	__	for	______
13. Net Cost of Total Shares			at	__	for	______
14. Net Cost per Share (13)/(# of shares)	______		at	__	for	______

If stock is at or above strike price, your cost basis is (8).

Worksheet 7–2 Buying Stock and Selling Puts Simultaneously: Dean Foods Corporation

A. Initial Position Data						
Underlying Stock	Dean Foods					
Current Stock Price	27					$27.00
Put Options' Maturity Month	June					
Put Options' Striking Price	25					
Put Options' Premium	1 ½					
Days until Option Expires	182					
1. Buy	200	Dean Foods	at	27	for	$5400.00
2. Plus Commissions			at	0	for	$0.00
3. Net Stock Position			at	0	for	$5400.00
4. Sell	2	Puts	at	1 ½	for	$300.00
5. Less Commissions			at	0	for	$0.00
6. Net Call Options' Proceeds						$300.00
7. Net Cost of Position (3) – (6)						$5100.00
8. Net Cost per Share (7)/(# of shares)	200					$25.50
B. Result of Position If Put Is Exercised (occurs if stock is below strike price)						
9. Buy	200	Dean Foods	at	25	for	$5000.00
10. Plus Commissions			at	0	for	$0.00
11. Cost of Shares Put to You			at	0	for	$5000.00
12. Cost of Original Shares Purchased (7)			at	0	for	$5100.00
13. Net Cost of Total Shares			at	0	for	$10100.00
14. Net Cost per Share (13)/(# of shares)	400		at	0	for	$25.25

again using Dean Foods Corporation. You observe that Dean Foods common stock is trading at $27 a share and the options are priced as follows:

Dean Foods 6-month 25 put, 1 ½

Dean Foods 6-month 30 put, 4 ½

Dean Foods 6-month 25 call, 4

Dean Foods 6-month 30 call, 2

If your intentions are to own 400 shares of Dean Foods, you execute the following strategy: Purchase 200 shares of Dean Foods for $27 a share, and simultaneously sell two 6-month out-of-the-money puts with a striking price of 25 for 1 ½ points and two out-of-the-money calls with a striking price of 30 for 2 points. Thus, your cost basis for this position will be 23.5:

27 (stock price per share) – 1 ½ (put option premium)

2 (call option premium)

You have made an obligation to purchase 200 more shares if the stock is below $25 at expiration and to relinquish, or sell, the long position of 200 shares of Dean Foods at $30 a share if the stock is at or above 30. If called away at $30 a share, you will realize a gain of 6 points, or 27.6 percent unannualized:

$$\frac{30 \text{ (striking price)} - 23\tfrac{1}{2} \text{ (cost basis)}}{23\tfrac{1}{2} \text{ (cost basis)}}$$

In addition, your return will be enhanced by the $54 received in dividends.

This strategy is potentially more appealing than a covered call write, because you contract to sell stock at the same price yet increase your return since you receive the premium from the sale of the out-of-the-money puts, which obligates you to purchase more stock at a lower price.

Worksheet 7–3 illustrates the computations for use in the covered combination strategy. Worksheet 7–4 fills in the data from our Dean Foods example.

Worksheet 7–3 Selling Covered Combinations

A. Initial Position Data

Underlying Stock	_____					
Current Stock Price	_____					_________
Put Options' Maturity Month	_____					
Put Options' Striking Price	_____					
Put Options' Premium	_____					
Call Options' Maturity Month	_____					
Call Options' Striking Price	_____					
Call Options' Premium	_____					
Days until Option Expires	_____					
1. Buy	_____ # of shares	_____ stock	at	__	for	_________
2. Plus Commissions			at	__	for	_________
3. Net Stock Position			at	__	for	_________
4. Sell	_____ #	Calls	at	__	for	_________
5. Less Commissions			at	__	for	_________
6. Net Call Options' Proceeds						_________
7. Sell	_____ #	Puts	at	__	for	_________
8. Less Commissions			at	__	for	_________
9. Net Put Options' Proceeds						_________
10. Net Investment (3) – (6) – (9)						_________

B. Maximum Profit If Stock Is > Strike Price

11. Sell	____ amount in (1)	____ stock	at	___	for	________
12. Less Commissions			at	___	for	________
13. Plus Dividends Received			at	___	for	________
14. Net Proceeds			at	___	for	________
15. Profit (14) – (10)			at	___	for	________
16. Return on Investment (15)/(10)						________
17. Return Annualized (365)/# of Days until Expiration × (23)						________

C. Profit if Stock < Strike

18. Buy	____ amount in (1)	____ stock	at	___	for	________
19. Plus Commissions			at	___	for	________
20. Net Cost of New Shares						________
21. Average Cost of All Shares (per share) [(10) + (20) – (13)]/(# of shares)						________

D. Profit if Stock Is Unchanged

22. Profit (current value of shares) + (13) – (10)	________
23. Return on Investment (22)/(10)	________
24. Return Annualized (365)/Days until Expiration × 23	________

Worksheet 7–4 Selling Covered Combinations: Dean Foods Corporation

A. Initial Position Data

Underlying Stock	Dean Foods					
Current Stock Price	27					$27.00
Put Options' Maturity Month	June					
Put Options' Striking Price	25					
Put Options' Premium	1 ½					
Call Options' Maturity Month	June					
Call Options' Striking Price	30					
Call Options' Premium	2					
Days until Option Expires	182					
1. Buy	200	Dean Foods	at	27	for	$5400.00
2. Plus Commissions			at	0	for	$0.00
3. Net Stock Position			at	0	for	$5400.00
4. Sell	2	Calls	at	2	for	$400.00
5. Less Commissions			at	0	for	$0.00
6. Net Call Options' Proceeds						$400.00
7. Sell	2	Puts	at	1 ½	for	$300.00
8. Less Commissions			at	0	for	$0.00
9. Net Put Options' Proceeds						$300.00
10. Net Investment (3) – (6) – (9)						$4700.00

B. Maximum Profit

11. Sell	200	Dean Foods	at	30	for	$6000.00
12. Less Commissions			at	0	for	$0.00
13. Plus Dividends Received			at	0	for	$54.00
14. Net Proceeds			at	0	for	$6054.00
15. Profit (14) – (10)			at	0	for	$1354.00
16. Return on Investment (15)/(10)						28.81 %
17. Return Annualized (365)/Days until Expiration × (23)						57.78 %

C. Profit if Stock < Strike

18. Buy	200	Dean Foods	at	25	for	$5000.00
19. Plus Commissions			at	0	for	$0.00
20. Net Cost of New Shares						$5000.00

21. Average Cost of All Shares (per share) [(10) + (20) – (13)]/(# of shares)

$24.12

D. Profit if Stock Is Unchanged

22. Profit (current value of shares) + (13) – (10)	$754.00
23. Return on Investment (22)/(10)	16.04 %
24. Return Annualized (365)/(182) × 23	32.17 %

Hedged Covered Call Write

In this section, we demonstrate a bullish yet defensive strategy that is advantageous in an increasingly volatile stock market—the hedged covered call write.

DEFINITION AND LOGIC A *hedged covered call* gives the investor upside potential as well as protection against a severe decline in the stock's price. The basic strategy involves purchasing a minimum of 100 shares of stock, selling an out-of-the-money call, and using the proceeds from the sale to pay for a put that will act as an additional shield.

ILLUSTRATION: COMPAQ CORPORATION In order to fully appreciate the hedged covered call strategy, let's take a look at a realistic situation. Suppose you are bullish on Compaq Corporation. It appears that Compaq has earnings momentum, but the common stock has already increased substantially. Compaq common stock is trading at $52 a share, and the options are priced as follows:

Compaq 6-month 50 put, 2 ½

Compaq 6-month 55 put, 5 ½

Compaq 6-month 50 call, 6 ½

Compaq 6-month 55 call, 3 ½

To use the hedged covered call strategy, you purchase 200 shares of Compaq for $52 a share, buy two 6-month 50 puts, and sell two 6-month 55 calls. Your cost basis is 51:

52 (stock price) – 3 ½ (call premium) + 2 ½ (put premium)

This is actually 1 point below the current market price.

Recall that the put gives you the right to sell Compaq at $50 a share and thus limit your risk to $1 a share. At the same time, you are making an obligation to sell Compaq for $55 a share. If called away, you will have a profit of 4 points [55 (call option striking price) – 51 (cost basis) + dividends]. This strategy is essentially a covered call write in which you are using the call option premium to pay for the put option or insurance.

Worksheet 7–5 presents the computations for the hedged covered call write. Worksheet 7–6 completes our example with data for Compaq Corporation.

Worksheet 7–5 Hedged Covered Call Write

A. Initial Position Data

Underlying Stock	______					
Current Stock Price	______					______
Put Options' Maturity Month	______					
Put Options' Striking Price	______					
Put Options' Premium	______					
Call Options' Maturity Month	______					
Call Options' Striking Price	______					
Call Options' Premium	______					
Days until Option Expires	______					
1. Buy	______ # of share	______ stock	at	__	for	______
2. Plus Commissions			at	__	for	______
3. Net Stock Position			at	__	for	______
4. Sell	______ #	Calls	at	__	for	______
5. Less Commissions			at	__	for	______
6. Net Call Options' Proceeds						______
7. Buy	______ #	Puts	at	__	for	______
8. Plus Commissions			at	__	for	______
9. Net Put Options' Proceeds						______
10. Net Investment (3) – (6) + (9)						______

B. Maximum Profit If Stock > Call Strike Price

11. Sell	________ amount in (1)	________ stock	at	—	for	________
12. Less Commissions			at	—	for	________
13. Plus Dividends Received			at	—	for	________
14. Net Proceeds			at	—	for	________
15. Profit (14) – (10)			at	—	for	________
16. Return on Investment (15)/(10)						________
17. Return Annualized (365)/(182) × (23)						________

C. Maximum Risk

18. Sell	________ amount in (1)	________ stock	at	—	for	________
19. Less Commissions			at	—	for	________
20. Plus Dividends Received						________
21. Net Proceeds						________
22. Potential Loss (10) – (21)						________
23. Percentage Risk (22)/(10)						________

D. Breakeven at Expiration

22. (10) – (13) + (commission/# of shares) ________

Worksheet 7–6 Hedged Covered Call Write: Compaq Corporation

A. Initial Position Data						
Underlying Stock	Compaq					
Current Stock Price	52					$52.00
Put Options' Maturity Month	June					
Put Options' Striking Price	50					
Put Options' Premium	2 ½					
Call Options' Maturity Month	June					
Call Options' Striking Price	55					
Call Options' Premium	3 ½					
Days until Option Expires	182					
1. Buy	200	Compaq	at	52	for	$10,400.00
2. Plus Commissions			at	0	for	$0.00
3. Net Stock Position			at	0	for	$10,400.00
4. Sell	2	Calls	at	3 ½	for	$700.00
5. Less Commissions			at	0	for	$0.00
6. Net Call Options' Proceeds						700.00
7. Buy	2	Puts	at	2 ½	for	$500.00
8. Plus Commissions			at	0	for	$0.00
9. Net Put Options' Proceeds						$500.00
10. Net Investment (3) – (6) + (9)						$10,200.00

B. Maximum Profit						
11. Sell	200	Compaq	at	55	for	$11,000.00
12. Less Commissions			at	0	for	$0.00
13. Plus Dividends Received			at	0	for	$0.0
14. Net Proceeds			at	0	for	$11,000.00
15. Profit (14) – (10)			at	0	for	$800.00
16. Return on Investment (15)/(10)						7.84 %
17. Return Annualized (365)/(182) × (23)						15.72 %
C. Maximum Risk						
18. Sell	200	Compaq	at	50	for	$10,000.00
19. Less Commissions			at	0	for	$0.00
20. Plus Dividends Received						$0.0
21. Net Proceeds						$10,000.00
22. Potential Loss (10) – (21)						($200)
23. Percentage Risk (22)/(10)						1.96 %
D. Breakeven at Expiration						
22. (10) – (13) + (commission/# of shares)						51

Synthetic Stock Position

By using put and call options, it is possible for an investor to create a position that is essentially the same as a long stock position, namely a synthetic stock position.

DEFINITION AND LOGIC The *synthetic stock position* offers the same appreciation potential or risk of loss as in the case of purchasing common stock. The major benefit of the synthetic stock position is that it requires less cash than the long stock position. The major shortcoming is that the position is subject to time premium decay. The synthetic stock strategy has the same margin requirements as the short put position discussed in Chapter Four.

The mechanics of the synthetic stock position involve the purchase of a call and the sale of a put with the same striking price and expiration dates. Recall that the short put position obligates the investor to purchase the underlying stock at the striking price, while the long call position gives the investor the right to purchase the stock at the striking price. Thus, if the stock increases in value and is above the striking price at expiration, the put will expire worthless and the call will appreciate in value. If the stock drops in value to a level below the striking price at expiration, the put will be exercised and the investor will be obligated to purchase the stock at the put option striking price. If the stock is at the striking price at expiration, both the put and the call will expire worthless.

ILLUSTRATION: GLAXO HOLDINGS To illustrate the synthetic stock strategy, we will use Glaxo Holdings. Suppose that you are bullish on the prospects for Glaxo, since they are awaiting FDA approval on a new drug. You observe that Glaxo common stock is trading at 20 points and the options are priced as follows:

Glaxo 6-month 20 put, 2 ½
Glaxo 6-month 20 call, 2 ½

Since you are bullish on Glaxo, you can either purchase 100 shares of stock, or sell one 6-month 20 put for 2 ½ points and use the premium from the put option to purchase a 6-month 20 call option. The short put option position creates the obligation to purchase Glaxo at 20, while the long call option position gives you the right to purchase 100 shares of Glaxo at 20.

Following is a comparison of the synthetic stock strategy and the long stock position that should help you appreciate the risks and rewards involved:

Initial Position

Glaxo Holdings = 20

June 20 GLX call = 2 ½

June 20 GLX put = 2 ½

Stock Position	*Synthetic Stock Position*	*Debit*	*Credit*
Buy 100 GLX @ 20 = $2000	Sell 1 GLX June 20 ½ put		+ 250
	Buy 1 GLX June 20 ½ call	– 250	
	Net investment	0	

*Collateral is required for naked put position

Stock Increases 20% to $24 per Share at Expiration:

Profit of 4 points, or $400	June 20 put expires worthless		—
	Sell June 20 call, which can be sold for 4 points or		+ 400
	Gain		+ 400

Stock Decreases 20% to $16 per Share at Expiration:

Loss of 4 points, or $400	June 20 put will be exercised and the stock will be put to you at $20 per share, resulting in a $400 loss [20 (cost of shares) less 16 (current price)]
	The June 20 call will expire worthless

Stock Stays at $20 per Share:

No gain or loss	June 20 put will expire worthless
	June 20 call will expire worthless

As you can see, a 20 percent increase in the stock's price will result in a $400 profit for both the long stock position and the synthetic stock position, while a 20 percent decrease will create a $400 loss for both positions.

If you use the synthetic stock strategy, you can avoid having the stock put to you by purchasing a put with the same expiration date and striking price in the options market. If the stock remains at 20 at expiration, both the put and the call will expire worthless. In this scenario, you will neither profit nor gain. In a situation in which you had a net debit, you would incur a loss equal to the debit.

It is also important to note that the synthetic stock strategy does not pay dividends, which in some cases may improve your total return.

In this example, the put and call premiums are the same. However, this obviously will not always be the case. Worksheet 7–7 will allow you to run through some of your own ideas to see if they are worthwhile. Worksheets 7–8 and 7–9 complete the illustration of the synthetic stock strategy using our Glaxo example.

Repair Strategy

DEFINITION AND LOGIC An investor uses a *repair strategy* to lower the break-even point in a long stock position that is not working with his or her original investment objective.

ILLUSTRATION: PFIZER CORPORATION Suppose you purchased 100 shares of Pfizer at $62 a share. Just a few weeks later, drug stocks decline on healthcare reform news and the stock falls to $50 a share.

Now you face a dilemma. Although you still remain bullish on the long-term outlook for Pfizer, it would take a 24 percent increase in the value of the stock just for you to break even. As long as you are still bullish on Pfizer, there is one strategy you can employ to lower your break-even point on the stock. First, let's review the current call options available on Pfizer. They are priced as follows:

Pfizer 6-month 50 call, 5

Pfizer 6-month 60 call, 2 ½

The first step in your repair strategy is to purchase one Pfizer 6-month 50 call for 5 points, or $500. Next, you sell two 6-month 60 calls for 2 ½ points, or $250, each. Your new position will look as follows:

Long 100 shares Pfizer Short one 6-month 60 call	Covered call
Long one 6-month 50 call Short one 6-month 60 call	Bull spread

As you can see, you have now created a covered call and a bull spread without paying out any more money except for commissions.

The proceeds from the 6-month 60 calls offset the debit for the 6-month 50 call. As discussed in previous chapters, the two short calls are covered because of one long stock position and one long call option position. In some situations, an additional debit is created, and as an investor you have to decide whether or not you want to contribute more to this investment.

Now let's look at some possible results from your new position. Suppose Pfizer rebounds to 56, or 12 percent, by expiration. In that case, you will have a 6-point, or $600, loss on your original 100 shares. However, you will have a 6-point, or $600, gain on your bull spread. You may now sell the 50 call for 6 points, while the two short 60 calls will expire worthless. Thus, you will have lowered your break-even point on Pfizer from 62 to 56.

If the stock rises to 61, you will have an $800 profit as opposed to a $200 loss had you done nothing. You can sell the long call of the bull spread for 11 points, or $1100, and close out the short position by paying $100. Thus, you will net out $1000 on the bull spread position. The stock will be called away at $60 a share, resulting in a 2-point, or $200, loss on the original stock position. Thus, your net profit will be $800 versus a $100 loss had you done nothing. The point to keep in mind is that you will have recouped a 12-point loss on a 6-point move.

To summarize, an investor has little to lose by using the repair strategy on a currently losing stock position. If the stock rallies at all, the investor will recoup his or her loss much more quickly than by doing nothing. If the stock continues to drop, the investor will lose commission dollars plus any debit incurred. The only situation in which the investor would be better off not employing this strategy is when the stock rallies sharply over a very short time period.

Worksheet 7–10 will help you in creating your own repair strategies. Worksheet 7–11 fills in the data from our Pfizer example.

Worksheet 7–7 Synthetic Stock Position

A. Initial Position Data

Underlying Stock	________					
Current Stock Price	________					______
Put Options' Maturity Month	________					
Put Options' Striking Price	________					
Put Options' Premium	________					
Call Options' Maturity Month	________					
Call Options' Striking Price	________					
Call Options' Premium	________					
Days until Option Expires	________					
1. Buy	________	Call(s)	at	__	for	______
2. Plus Commissions			at	__	for	______
3. Net Debit			at	__	for	______
4. Sell	________	Put(s)	at	__	for	______
5. Less Commissions			at	__	for	______
6. Net Credit						______
7. Net Position						______

B. Liquidating Position

Days until Expiration	______					
8. Sell	______	Call(s)	at	__	for	______
9. Less Commissions			at	__	for	______
10. Net Call Sale						______
11. Gain (Loss) on Call Position (10) – (3)						______
12. Buy	______	Put(s)	at	__	for	______
13. Plus Commissions			at	__	for	______
14. Net Put Purchase			at	__	for	______
15. Gain (Loss) on Put Position						______
16. Net Gain (Loss) (7) + (11) + (15)						______

C. Cost Per Share

Days until Expiration	0				
17. Buy	______	at	__	for	______
18. Plus Commissions		at	__	for	______
19. Less Credit or Plus Debit in (7)		at	__	for	______
20. Net Investment		at	__	for	______
21. Average Cost per Share (20)/(#shares in 17)					______

Worksheet 7–8 Synthetic Stock Position: Glaxo Holdings Stock Increase at Expiration

A. Initial Position Data						
Underlying Stock	Glaxo Holdings					
Current Stock Price	20					$20.00
Put Options' Maturity Month	June					
Put Options' Striking Price	20					
Put Options' Premium	2 ½					
Call Options' Maturity Month	June					
Call Options' Striking Price	20					
Call Options' Premium	2 ½					
Days until Option Expires	182					
1. Buy	1	Call(s)	at	2 ½	for	$250.00
2. Plus Commissions			at	0	for	$0.00
3. Net Debit			at	0	for	$250.00
4. Sell	1	Put(s)	at	2 ½	for	$250.00
5. Less Commissions			at	0	for	$0.00
6. Net Credit						$250.00
7. Net Position						$0.00

B. Liquidating Position

Days until Expiration	0					
8. Sell	1	Call(s)	at	4	for	$400.00
9. Less Commissions			at	0	for	$0.00
10. Net Call Sale						$400.00
11. Gain (Loss) on Call Position (10) – (3)						$150.00
12. Buy	1	Put(s)	at	0	for	$0.00
13. Plus Commissions			at	0	for	$0.00
14. Net Put Purchase			at	0	for	$0.00
15. Gain (Loss) on Put Position						$0.00
16. Net Gain (Loss) (7) + (11) + (15)						$150.00

C. Cost Per Share If Put Is Exercised

Days until Expiration	0					
17. Buy		Glaxo Holdings	at	0	for	$0.00
18. Plus Commissions			at	0	for	$0.00
19. Less Credit or Plus Debit in (7)			at	0	for	$0.00
20. Net Investment			at	0	for	$0.00
21. Average Cost per Share (20)/(# of shares in 17)						$0.00

Worksheet 7–9 Synthetic Stock Position: Glaxo Holdings Stock Decrease at Expiration

A. Initial Position Data						
Underlying Stock	Glaxo Holdings					
Current Stock Price	20					$20.00
Put Options' Maturity Month	June					
Put Options' Striking Price	20					
Put Options' Premium	2 ½					
Call Options' Maturity Month	June					
Call Options' Striking Price	20					
Call Options' Premium	2 ½					
Days until Option Expires	182					
1. Buy	1	Call(s)	at	2 ½	for	$250.00
2. Plus Commissions			at	0	for	$0.00
3. Net Debit			at	0	for	$250.00
4. Sell	1	Put(s)	at	2 ½	for	$250.00
5. Less Commissions			at	0	for	$0.00
6. Net Credit						$250.00
7. Net Position						$0.00

B. Liquidating Position						
Days until Expiration	0					
8. Sell		Call(s)	at	0	for	$0.00
9. Less Commissions			at	0	for	$0.00
10. Net Call Sale						$0.00
11. Gain (Loss) on Call Position (10) – (3)						$0.00
12. Buy	1	Put(s)	at	0	for	$0.00
13. Plus Commissions			at	0	for	$0.00
14. Net Put Purchase						$0.00
15. Gain (Loss) on Put Position						$0.00
16. Net Gain (Loss) (7) + (11) + (15)						$0.00
C. Cost Per Share If Put Is Exercised						
Days until Expiration	0					
17. Buy	100	Glaxo Holdings	at	20	for	$2000.00
18. Plus Commissions			at	0	for	$0.00
19. Less Credit or Plus Debit in (7)			at	0	for	$0.00
20. Net Investment			at	0	for	$2000.00
21. Average Cost per Share (20)/(# of shares in 17)						$20.00

Worksheet 7–10 Stock Repair Strategy

A. Initial Position Data						
Underlying Stock	____					
Original Price Paid	____					
Original Stock Price	____					____
Call Options' Maturity Month (Lower Strike)	____					
Call Options' Striking Price	____					
Call Options' Premium	____					
Call Options' Maturity Month (Higher Strike)	____					
Call Options' Striking Price	____					
Call Options' Premium	____					
1. Bought	____ #	____ stock	at	__	for	____
2. Plus Commissions			at	__	for	____
3. Net Original Position			at	__	for	____
4. Net Cost per Share (1)/(# of shares)			a			____
B. Repair Position						
5. Original Position (3)						____
6. Buy	1	Call(s) (month)	at	__	for	____
7. Sell	2	Call(s) (month)	at	__	for	____
8. Net Commissions for Options						____
9. Net Cost of Repair (6) – (7) net in (8)			at	__	for	____

C. Amount Recovered

10. Sell ____ amount ______ stock at ___ for ______
11. Less Commissions in (1) ______ at for ______
12. Plus Dividends Received ______
13. Net Proceeds from Covered Write ______
14. Sell (6) Position at Market Price ______
15. Less Commissions ______
16. Net Proceeds from Lower Striking Price Call ______
17. Purchase ½ of (7) Position ______
18. Plus Commissions ______
19. Net Cost to Close Short Call Position ______
20. Profit (Loss) on Original Stock Position (13) – (3) ______
21. Profit from Bull Spread (16) + (19) ______
22. Net Profit (Loss) (20) + (21) – (9) ______
23. Current Value of Stock ______
24. Dividends Received ______
25. Original Stock Position (3) ______
26. Sell (6) Position at Market Price ______
27. Less Commissions ______
28. Net Proceeds from Lower Striking Price Call ______
29. Buy (7) Position at Market Price ______
30. Plus Commissions ______
31. Net Cost to Close Short Call Position ______
32. Change in Original Stock Position Value ______
    (23) + (24) – (25) + (28) – (31)

Worksheet 7–11 Stock Repair Strategy: Pfizer Corporation

A. Initial Position Data						
Underlying Stock	Pfizer					
Original Price Paid	62					
Original Stock Price	50					$50.00
Call Options' Maturity Month (Lower Strike)	June					
Call Options' Striking Price	50					
Call Options' Premium	5					
Call Options' Maturity Month (Higher Strike)	June					
Call Options' Striking Price	60					
Call Options' Premium	2 ½					
1. Bought	100	Pfizer	at	62	for	$6200.00
2. Plus Commissions			at	0	for	$0.00
3. Net Original Position			at	0	for	$6200.00
4. Net Cost per Share (1)/(# shares)			a			$62.00
B. Repair Position						
5. Original Position (3)						$6200.00
6. Buy	1	Call(s) (June 50)	at	5	for	$500.00
7. Sell	2	Call(s) (June 60)	at	2 ½	for	$500.00
8. Net Commissions for Options						$0.00
9. Net Cost of Repair (6) – (7) net in (8)			at	0	for	$0.00

C. Amount Recovered

10. Sell	100	Pfizer	at	60	for	$6000.00
11. Less Commissions			at		for	$0.00
12. Plus Dividends Received						$84.00
13. Net Proceeds from Covered Write						$6084.00
14. Sell (6) Position at Market Price						$1100.00
15. Less Commissions						$0.00
16. Net Proceeds from Lower Striking Price Call						$1100.00
17. Purchase ½ of (7) Position						($100.00)
18. Plus Commissions						$0.00
19. Net Cost to Close Short Call Position						($100.00)
20. Profit (Loss) on Original Stock Position (13) – (3)						($116.00)
21. Profit from Bull Spread (16) + (19)						$1000.00
22. Net Profit (Loss) (20) + (21) – (9)						$884.00
23. Current Value of Stock						$0.00
24. Dividends Received						$0.00
25. Original Stock Position (3)						$0.00
26. Sell (6) Position at Market Price						$0.00
27. Less Commissions						$0.00
28. Net Proceeds from Lower Striking Price Call						$0.00
29. Buy (7) Position at Market Price						$0.00
30. Plus Commissions						$0.00
31. Net Cost to Close Short Call Position						$0.00
32. Change in Original Stock Position Value (23) + (24) – (25) + (28) – (31)						$0.00

Conclusion

In this chapter, we built on the fundamental options strategies to help us achieve a variety of investment objectives. If you use your imagination and are proficient in the fundamentals covered in Chapters One through Six, there are an infinite number of options strategies that you can use to better achieve your investment objectives.

Problem 7–1 *See Appendix C for solution.*

Suppose that on December 1 Greentree Financial's common stock is at 51 and the 70-day Greentree February 50 put options have a price of 1 ¾. Since you are bullish on Greentree's long-term prospects, you simultaneously buy 200 shares of Greentree common stock and sell two February 50 put options. In February, one day after the put options' expiration date, Greentree's common stock is at 49 and the February 50 put option is exercised. Compute your cost basis for all 400 shares of Greentree Financial common stock.

Problem 7–2 *See Appendix C for solution.*

Suppose that in January General Motors Corporation's common stock is at 43, the 75-day General Motors March 45 call options are priced at 2 ¾, and the 75-day General Motors March 40 put options have a price of 1 ½. Since you feel that General Motors will either stay stagnant or increase modestly over the next few months, you employ the covered combination strategy. You do this by purchasing 200 shares of common stock for 43 and simultaneously selling two March 45 call options and two March 40 put options. In March, one day after the options' expiration date, General Motors common stock is at 48 and the March 45 call option is exercised. Assuming that you have received one quarterly dividend of $.20 per share, compute the annualized return on your investment.

Problem 7–3 *See Appendix C for solution.*

Suppose that in April Blockbuster's Entertainment common is at 27, the 120-day Blockbuster August 30 call options have a price of 1 ¾, and the 120-day Blockbuster August 25 put options are valued at 1. Since you are bullish on Blockbuster near-term prospects but concerned about a correction in the stock market, you employ a hedged covered call strategy. You do this by purchasing 400 shares of Blockbuster common stock for 27 and simultaneously selling four August 30 call options and buying four August 25 put options. Assuming that you receive two quarterly dividends of $.025 a share, compute your break-even point, maximum profit, and maximum risk.

Problem 7–4 *See Appendix C for solution.*

Suppose that on December 1 the 120-day CUC International April 30 call option has a price of 2, the 120-day CUC April 30 put option is priced at 1, and the price of CUC common stock is 30. Since you feel that CUC's common stock price will increase during the next 120 days, you decide to create a synthetic stock position. You establish this by purchasing an April 30 call option and selling an April 30 put option. In late March, 20 days prior to the options' expiration, the securities are priced as follows:

CUC common stock, 36

CUC April 30 call, 6 ⅜

CUC April 30 put, ¼

Compute the profit generated by the synthetic stock position if liquidated 20 days prior to the April expiration date.

Problem 7–5 *See Appendix C for solution.*

Suppose you purchased 100 shares of Motorola common stock at 85 in April. It is now November, and Motorola common stock is at 70, the 120-day March 70 call options have a price of 3, and the 120-day March 75 call options are priced at 1 ¾. Suggest a repair strategy that you may use to lower your break-even point on Motorola. Given the new position, calculate your net profit or loss if one month prior to expiration. Motorola common stock is at 78, the March 70 call options are priced at 8 ½, and the March 75 call options are at 3 ½. Assume that you have received three quarterly dividends of $.11 a share.

Chapter Eight

LEAPS

Long-term equity anticipation securities (LEAPS) are calls and puts with maturities of up to three years. LEAPS were created to satisfy investors' needs for longer-term maturity options. LEAPS are available on most of the blue chip stocks and some of the more actively traded over-the-counter stocks. The strategies for LEAPS do not significantly differ from shorter-term options. There are, however, some subtleties that should be taken into account when devising strategies using LEAPS.

The intent of this chapter is not to reinvent the preceding chapters, but to show you a few strategies that we think make sense using LEAPS. From there you can use your creativity and the foundation built in Chapters One through Seven to develop other strategies to meet your investment objectives.

Purchase LEAPS Call versus Purchase Long Stock

In Chapter Three, we discussed in great detail the advantages of purchasing call options versus purchasing stock. One of the major deterrents of purchasing calls is that they are a depleting asset—that is, their value diminishes over time if the underlying stock does nothing. Thus, with the purchase of a call expiring in one, two, or three years, one does not need to be as precise on the shorter-term action of the stock as compared to a shorter-term call option. The time value portion of the option erodes at a slower pace than shorter-term options. You are, however, paying more premium for more time. In order to better understand this concept, let's look at a real-life situation.

Suppose you are bullish on the prospects for Microsoft Corporation over the next year. Microsoft common stock is trading at $76 a share and the two-year Microsoft 80 LEAPS calls are at 15. You may want to purchase one call for $1500 versus $7600 for the common stock. Another thought would be to purchase two LEAPS for $3000 as compared to $7600 for 100 shares of Microsoft common. The reason for this is that the delta of the LEAPS may be .60 which means that option will move approximately 60¢ for every dollar move on the stock. By purchasing two calls, you will mimic the stock's move more accurately. Keep in mind that when you purchase LEAPS, you should not intend on holding them for the duration of the contract. Ultimately LEAPS become short-term options, where the time decay becomes very significant.

Suppose in six months Microsoft has reported two very good quarters and the stock has increased 25 percent, or 19 points, to $95 a share. Now if you had purchased the two LEAPS calls they would be worth the intrinsic value 19 points (95–76) plus some time value. Since these are long-term options with one and one-half years still remaining on the contract, they will hold a good percentage of their time value. We can assume that these LEAPS will still have at least 11 points of time value. Let's compare the profit on the LEAPS versus stock if Microsoft increased 25 percent.

	Stock Increases 25	Profit	
100 MSFT at 76 = $7600	100 MSFT at 95 = $9500	$1900	+25%
two 80 LEAPS calls at 15 = $3000	two 80 LEAPS calls at 26 = $5200	$2200	+73%

The LEAPS calls would have given you a return of 73 percent versus 25 percent from the stock purchase. Conversely, if Microsoft had two poor, disappointing quarters and the stock declined 25 percent, or 19 points, to 57 what would the LEAPS do? Since there is still one and one-half years left until expiration, they would maintain a fair amount of time value. Given some historical data, they would probably still be worth about 10 points. Below we compare the LEAPS purchase versus stock if Microsoft declines 25 percent.

	Stock Decrease 25%	Loss	
100 MSFT at 76 = $7600	100 MSFT at 57 = $5700	($1900)	(25%)
two 80 LEAPS calls at 15 = $3000	two 80 LEAPS calls at 10 = $2000	($1000)	(50%)

As you can see, the LEAPS calls offer you an alternative to purchasing the common stock by using less capital. By selling the LEAPS contracts long before expiration, the position is not subject to as much time decay as traditional options.

Purchase of Put LEAPS versus Stock Short Sale

In Chapter Four, we compared the purchase of a put option versus the stock short sale. The main advantage of purchasing puts is that the potential loss is limited by the cost of the option. You are not subject to the margin requirements and rules by which the short seller must abide. Yet, the short seller is not under the same time constraints as the put option purchaser. Thus, if you are bearish on a particular stock, you may want to consider the put LEAPS expiring a year or later so that you do not have to be as precise on the timing. For example, suppose you believe that the semiconductor book to bill ratio will decline over the next six months. Hence, you are bearish on Intel Corporation. Intel common is trading at $65 a share and the two-year Intel 65 LEAPS puts are at 9. Suppose your semiconductor scenario proves to be correct and Intel common declined 20 percent or 13 points to 52. Let's compare the short seller position versus the put LEAPS purchaser. The short seller of the 100 shares would have profited 13 points or 20%. The put LEAPS purchaser would see the put increase by the amount it was in-the-money, 65 minus 52 plus any time premium remaining in the LEAPS. Since these are long-term options with one and one-half years remaining, a fair amount of time premium will still exist even though they are deep-in-the-money. In this scenario, the put will be worth roughly 18, which is 13 points intrinsic value plus 5 points time value. In summary, the benefit of using a long-term put option is that you don't have to be as precise in your timing and as long as you sell them long before expiration, they will hold their time premium.

Covered Call Writing with LEAPS

In Chapter Three, we discussed covered call writing and some of the possible follow-up strategies. You will recall that the covered call writer buys a stock that he or she is comfortable owning and simultaneously sells or writes a call option against that position. This is a bullish strategy that is more conservative than the outright purchase of a stock since the downside risk is reduced by the amount of the premium received. At the same time you have limited your upside potential gain by the striking price at which you have agreed to sell the stock.

By writing a covered call LEAPS you may lock in the desired static return, return if called away, and downside protection with less potential maintenance. Since time is one component of option pricing, it stands to reason that the LEAPS will offer a higher premium than short-term options. Thus, you may achieve your desired return with one stock and option transaction, rather than with two or three over the same period of time. To better understand this, let's look at a realistic situation and the possible consequences. Suppose you think AT&T is a fairly conservative investment over the next year. While you don't think there is much risk, you also think the upside potential is somewhat limited. AT&T common stock is selling for $60 per share and the one-year LEAPS calls are priced as follows:

T	1 year	60 call	6 points
T	1 year	65 call	3 points
T	1 year	70 call	1 ½ points

Exhibit 8–1 shows a covered write using the one-year 65 call LEAPS. As you can see, the investor is potentially getting a respectable return, with some downside protection. At the same time, there is less maintenance than with shorter-term options.

Combinations in a Covered Combination

In Chapter Seven, we discussed advanced strategies including covered combinations. We defined a covered combination as a covered call write with the simultaneous sale of puts. An investor utilizes this strategy when he or she is bullish on a particular stock but is willing to lock in a profit at a specific price and incur an obligation to average down in price.

A variation of this strategy would be to purchase a stock, sell a three- or six-month put with a strike price at or below the current stock price, and sell a LEAPS call with a striking price above the current stock price. In this situation, we are making a shorter-term obligation to purchase more stock at lower prices. One may not want to be obligated to purchase more stock over the next year or two, but may be willing to make that obligation over the shorter term. At the same time, given the premiums on the LEAPS calls, one may be willing to obligate to sell his or her stock at a predetermined price going out one year or more. To better understand the mechanics and philosophy of this strategy, let us examine a real-life situation. Suppose you like the long-term prospects for Motorola Corporation. The company is well positioned to benefit from the telecommunications boom. The stock looks attractive, but it has had a pretty good run. You are willing to purchase 100 shares at current levels, and wouldn't mind buying another 100 if it pulled back in the near term. At the same time, given the current market environment, you would be willing to lock in your upside if you could take in some decent premium. Motorola common is trading at 92, the six-month 85 put is 4, and the one year 100 call LEAPS is 10. By purchasing 100 shares of Motorola and simultaneously selling the six-month out-of-the-money put and a one-

Worksheet 8–1 Sample Covered Call Writing Worksheet

A. Initial Position Data						
Underlying Stock	AT&T					
Dividends (quarterly)	0.33					$0.33
Days until Expiration	365					
1. Buy	500	AT&T	at	60	for	$30000.00
2. Plus Commissions			at	0	for	$0.00
3. Total Cost of Stock			at	0	for	$30000.00
4. Sell	5	January (1995) 65 Calls	at	3	for	$1500.00
5. Less Commissions			at	0	for	$0.00
6. Net Proceeds from Sale of Calls			at	0	for	$1500.00
7. Net Investment (6) – (3)						$28500.00
B. Return If Stock > Strike						
8. Sell	500	AT&T	at	65	for	$32500.00
9. Less Commissions			at	0	for	$0.00
10. Net Proceeds from Sale of Stock			at	0	for	$32500.00
11. Plus dividends Received	4		at	0.33	for	$660.00
12. Total Balance						$33160.00
13. Net Profit (12) – (7)						$4660.00

14. Percentaghe Return (13)/(7)	16.35 %
15. Annualized Return (365)/(days until expiration) × (14)	16.35 %
C. Return If Stock is Unchanged	
16. Net Option Income	$1500.00
17. Dividends Received	$660.00
18. Total Income	$2160.00
19. Total Cost of Stock	$30000.00
20. Rate of Return (18)/(13)	7.20 %
21. Annualized Rate of Return (365)/(365) × (20)	7.20 %
D. Breakeven Point on Stock	
22. Total Cost of Stock	$30000.00
23. Less Proceeds From Sale of Calls	$1500.00
24. Less Dividends Received	$660.00
25. Subtotal	$27840.00
26. Breakeven Price per Share (25)/(# of shares)	$55.68

year out-of-the-money LEAPS call, your cost for the position would be 78.5. [92 (stock price per share) – 3 ½ (put options premium) – 10 (LEAPS call option premium)]. You have made an obligation to purchase 100 more shares if the stock is below 85 at expiration (in six months) and to relinquish, or sell, the long position of 100 shares of Motorola at $100 a share if the stock is above 100 (in a year). If the stock is called away at 100 you will realize a gain of 21.5 points, or 27.4 percent.

$$\frac{100 \text{ (striking price)} - 78.5 \text{ (cost basis)}}{78.5 \text{ cost basis}}$$

In addition, your return will be enhanced by the $44 received in dividends. If the stock declined and you were forced to fulfill your obligation and purchase another 100 shares at 85 your cost basis for the full position would be 81.75 per share.

$$\frac{78.5 \text{ (original 100 shares)} + 85 \text{ (put strike price)}}{2}$$

If the Motorola remained at 92 over the year, both the options would expire worthless and your static return would be the 13 ½ points of received premium from the options, or 14.7 percent (92 ÷ 13 ½).

Conclusion

We have provided you with a few examples where LEAPS strategies make sense. However, the opportunities using LEAPS and shorter-term options with equities are infinite. We hope that you use your creativity and knowledge obtained from chapters 1 through 7, to tailor other strategies to meet your specific investment objectives.

Appendix A

Bibliography

Bookstaber, Richard M. *Option Pricing and Strategies in Investing.* Chicago: Probus Publishing Company, 1987.

Cox, John C., and Mark Rubenstein. *Options Markets.* Englewood Cliffs, NJ: Prentice-Hall, 1985.

Engel, Louis, and Brendon Boyd. *How to Buy Stocks.* Boston: Bantam, 1982.

Hirt, Geoffrey, with Stanley Block and Fred Jury. *The Investor's Desktop Portfolio Planner.* Chicago: Probus Publishing Company, 1986.

Malkiel, Burton G. *A Random Walk Down Wall Street.* New York: Norton, 1980.

McMillan, Lawrence G. *Options as a Strategic Investment.* New York: New York Institute of Finance, 1986.

Natenberg, Sheldon. *Option Volatility and Pricing Strategies.* Chicago: Probus Publishing Company, 1988.

Appendix B

Glossary

AT-THE-MONEY—A condition in which an underlying stock is trading at the options' striking (exercise) price.

AVERAGE DOWN—A strategy used to lower the average cost of a stock by purchasing more shares at a lower price.

BEAR SPREAD (PUT)—The simultaneous purchase of a put option with a higher striking price and sale of a put option with a lower striking price.

BEARISH—Describes the belief that the market or an individual stock will fall in value.

BULL SPREAD (CALL)—The simultaneous purchase of a call option with a lower striking price and sale of a call option with a higher striking price.

BULLISH—Describes the belief that the market or an individual stock will rise in value.

CALENDAR SPREAD—*See* Time Spread.

CALL OPTION—A contract that gives the purchaser the right to buy a stock at a predetermined price and obligates the seller to deliver the stock at a predetermined price.

COVERED CALL WRITE—A bullish strategy that involves the purchase of common stock while simultaneously selling an equal amount of call options.

COVERED COMBINATION—A bullish strategy in which an investor purchases a stock and simultaneously buys an equal amount of calls and sells an equal amount of puts with different strike prices or expiration dates.

COVERED OPTION—A written option position that has a corresponding stock or option position.

DELTA—A measurement of how much an option price will move relative to the movement of the underlying stock's price. Call options have positive deltas (between 0 and 1); put options have negative deltas (between 0 and 1).

EXERCISE—To use the rights available in an options contract, i.e., to buy the underlying stock (call option) or sell the underlying stock (put option) at the striking price.

EXERCISE PRICE—*See* Striking Price.

FUNDAMENTAL ANALYSIS—A type of analysis that attempts to assess a security's potential by examining data such as sales, earnings, balance sheets, income statements, debt, assets, management, and products.

GOOD TILL CANCELLED (GTC)—An order to buy or sell a security that remains in effect until it is executed (or cancelled).

HEDGE—An offsetting position used to limit risk or loss.

IN-THE-MONEY—With a call option, the condition where the stock's current market price is above the striking price; with a put option, the condition where the stock's current market price is below the striking price.

INTRINSIC VALUE—For an in-the-money option, the difference between the striking price and the stock's current market value. (Out-of-the-money options have no intrinsic value.) For call options, intrinsic value-stock price – striking price; for put options, intrinsic value = striking price-stock price.

LIMIT ORDER—An order placed with a broker to buy or sell a security at a specified or better price.

LONG POSITION—Ownership of a stock or an opening buy transaction on an option position.

MARGIN ACCOUNT—A brokerage account set up to allow an investor to borrow money for the purchase of securities or securities loaned for short stock sales. Minimum margin requirements may consist of depositing cash or certain marginable securities. These accounts are governed by Regulation T of the Federal Reserve System.

MARKET ORDER—An order to buy or sell a security at the best current market price.

NEUTRAL POSITION—A position that will perform well if the underlying security undergoes little or no change.

OPTIONS CLEARING CORPORATION (OCC)—A corporation that is owned in equal proportions by the option exchanges. It handles all option transactions and guarantees the fulfillment of all rights and obligations involved in a trade. Also issues a prospectus explaining the risks, rules, and ethical standards concerning option accounts.

OUT-OF-THE-MONEY—With a call option, the condition in which the stock's current market price is below the striking price; with a put option, the condition in which the stock's current market price is above the striking price.

PARITY—A condition where the option premium is equal to its intrinsic value (i.e., time value is not a factor).

PREMIUM—The price paid for an option that is equal to the sum of the option's intrinsic value and time value.

PUT OPTION—A contract that gives the purchaser the right to sell a stock at a predetermined price and obligates the seller to purchase the stock at a predetermined price.

RESISTANCE—A term used by technical analysts to describe the price level at which a stock will stop rising or meet resistance based on its previous trading history.

ROLLING DOWN—Simultaneously closing out one option position at a higher striking price and opening another position at a lower striking price.

ROLLING FORWARD—Simultaneously closing out an option position with a near-term expiration date and opening a position with a later expiration date.

ROLLING UP—Simultaneously closing out one position at a lower striking price and opening another position at a higher striking price.

SHORT POSITION—A position that involves selling stock short or an opening sell transaction on an option position.

SHORT STOCK SALE—A bearish strategy in which the initial position is the sale of a security based on the seller's anticipation of a price decline. The investor borrows the security from a broker-dealer at the time of the short sale. If the stock declines, the investor purchases it back at a lower price, thereby gaining a profit. If the stock rises, the investor buys it back at a higher price, thus incurring a loss.

STOP-LIMIT ORDER—An order placed with a broker to buy or sell a security at a specified or better price; a combination of a stop order and a limit order.

STOP ORDER—An order placed with a broker to buy or sell a security that is currently trading away from the market. Once the security hits the stop price, the stop order becomes a market order.

STRADDLE—The purchase or sale of an equal number of puts and calls on the same underlying stock with the same striking prices and expiration dates.

STRANGLE—The simultaneous purchase or sale of an equal number of out-of-the-money call and put options.

STRIKING PRICE—The price at which a call option holder may elect to exercise the right to buy the underlying security or a put option holder may choose to exercise the right to sell the underlying security.

SUPPORT LEVEL—A term used by technical analysts to describe the price level at which a stock will stop falling or meet support based on its prior trading history.

SYNTHETIC STOCK POSITION—A bullish option strategy that involves the sale of a put option and the purchase of a call option to obtain the equivalent of ownership of the underlying stock.

TECHNICAL ANALYSIS—A type of analysis that attempts to predict future stock or market price movements by using historical data such as past prices, trading volume, number of advancing shares, and short-selling activity.

TIME SPREAD—The simultaneous sale of a near-term option and purchase of a longer-term option. If the striking prices are the same, it is considered a horizontal spread; if different, it is called a diagonal spread.

TIME VALUE—The total option premium less the option's intrinsic value.

UNCOVERED (NAKED) OPTION—A written option position that does not have a corresponding position in the underlying stock.

VOLATILITY—The degree to which a security's price rises or falls within a specific time period.

Appendix C

Solutions

Problem 5–1 Adobe Systems Bull Spread Purchase Worksheet

A. Position Data						
Underlying Stock	Adobe					
Current Stock Price	18					$18.00
Days until Option Expiration	75					
Options' Maturity Month	April					
Low Strike Price	17 ½					
Low Strike Option Intrinsic Value	½					
Low Strike Option Time Value	2 ¼					
Low Strike Option Premium	2 ¾					$2.75
High Strike Price	25					
High Strike Option Intrinsic Value	0					
High Strike Option Time Value	¾					
High Strike Option Premium	¾					$0.75
Spread Value	2					$200.00
B. Initial Position						
1. Sell	1	high strike options	at	¾	for	$75.00
2. Less Commissions			at	0	for	$0.00
3. Buy	1	low strike options	at	2 ¾	for	$275.00
4. Plus Commissions			at	0	for	$0.00
5. Net Cost						$200.00

C. Position Profit or Loss

Stock Price at liquidation	26					$26.00
Days until Option Expiration	7					
Options' Maturity Month	April					
Low Strike Price	17 ½					
Low Strike Option Intrinsic Value	8 ½					
Low Strike Option Time Value	⅛					
Low Strike Option Premium	8 ⅝					$862.50
High Strike Price	25					
High Strike Option Intrinsic Value	1					
High Strike Option Time Value	½					
High Strike Option Premium	1 ½					$150.00
Spread Value	7 ⅛					$712.50
6. Sell	1	low strike options	at	8 ⅝	for	$862.50
7. Less Commissions						
8. Buy	1	high strike options	at	1 ½	for	$150.00
9. Plus Commissions						
10. Net Revenues						$712.50
Net Profit or Loss (10) – (5)						$512.50

Problem 5–2 Adobe Systems Bull Spread Roll-Up Worksheet

A. Initial Position Data								
Underlying Stock	Adobe							
Current Stock Price	18							$18.00
Days until Option Expiration	75							
Options' Maturity Month	April							
Low Strike Price	17 ½							
Low Strike Option Intrinsic Value	½							
Low Strike Option Time Value	2 ¼							
Low Strike Option Premium	2 ¾							$2.75
High Strike Price	25							
High Strike Option Intrinsic Value	0							
High Strike Option Time Value	¾							
High Strike Option Premium	¾							$0.75
Spread Value	2							$200.00
1. Sell	1	April	high strike options		at	¾	for	$75.00
2. Less Commissions					at	0	for	$0.00
3. Buy	1	April	low strike options		at	2 ¾	for	$275.00
4. Plus Commissions					at	0	for	$0.00
5. Net Cost								$200.00
B. Roll-Up Position Data								
Underlying Stock	Adobe							
Current Stock Price	24 ⅜							$24.38
Days until Option Expiration	25							
Options' Maturity Month		April						
Option Premium	7 ¾		at striking price	17 ½				
Option Premium	2 ⅛		at striking price	25				
Option Premium	1 ⅜		at striking price	30				
Days until Option Expiration	0							
Options' Maturity Month								
Option Premium			at striking price					
Option Premium			at striking price					
Option Premium			at striking price					

6. Sell	1	April	at striking price	17 ½	at	7 ¾	for	$775.00
7. Less Commissions								
8. Buy	2	April	at striking price	25	at	2 ⅛	for	$425.00
9. Plus Commissions					at	0	for	$0.00
10. Sell	1	April	at striking price	30	at	1 3⁄8	for	$137.50
11. Less Commissions					at	0	for	$0.00
12. Sell			at striking price		at		for	$0.00
13. Less Commissions					at	0	for	$0.00
14. Buy			at striking price		at		for	$0.00
15. Plus Commissions					at	0	for	$0.00
16. Sell			at striking price		at		for	$0.00
17. Less Commission					at	0	for	$0.00
18. Roll-Up Cash Flow								$487.50
19. Net Cash flow (18 – 5)								$287.50
C. Total Position Profit or Loss								
Stock Price at Liquidation								$26.00
Days until Option Expiration	7							
Options' Maturity Month		April						
Low Strike Price	25							
Low Strike Option Intrinsic Value	1							
Low Strike Option Time Value	½							
Low Strike Option Premium	1 ½							$1.50
High Strike Price	30							
High Strike Option Intrinsic Value	0							
High Strike Option Time Value	⅜							
High Strike Option Premium	⅜							$0.38
Spread Value	1 ⅛							$112.50
20. Buy	1	April	at striking price	30	at	⅜	for	$37.50
21. Plus Commissions					at	0	for	$0.00
22. Sell	1	April	at striking price	25	at	1 ½	for	$150.00
23. Less Commissions					at	0	for	$0.00
24. Net Revenues								$112.50
Net Profit or Loss (24) + (19)								$400.00

Problem 5–3 GM Bear Spread Purchase Worksheet

A. Position Data							
Underlying Stock	GM						
Current Stock Price	46 1/8						$46.13
Days until Option Expiration	135						
Options' Maturity Month	December						
Low Strike Price	35						
Low Strike Option Intrinsic Value	0						
Low Strike Option Time Value	3/16						
Low Strike Option Premium	3/16						$18.75
High Strike Price	45						
High Strike Option Intrinsic Value	0						
High Strike Option Time Value	2 3/16						
High Strike Option Premium	2 3/16						$218.75
Spread Value	2						$200.00
B. Initial Position							
1. Sell	1	December	low strike options	at	3/16	for	$18.75
2. Less Commissions				at	0	for	$0.00
3. Buy	1	December	high strike options	at	2 3/16	for	$218.75
4. Plus Commissions				at	0	for	$0.00
5. Net Cost							$200.00

C. Position Profit or Loss

Stock Price at Liquidation	37 ½						$37.50
Days until Option Expiration	4						
Options' Maturity Month	December						
Low Strike Price	35						
Low Strike Option Intrinsic Value	0						
Low Strike Option Time Value	½						
Low Strike Option Premium	½						$50.00
High Strike Price	45						
High Strike Option Intrinsic Value	7 ½						
High Strike Option Time Value	⅛						
High Strike Option Premium	7 ⅝						$762.50
Spread Value	7 ⅛						$712.50
6. Buy	1	December	low strike options	at	½	for	$50.00
7. Plus Commissions				at	0	for	$0.00
8. Sell	1	December	high strike options	at	7 ⅝	for	$762.50
9. Less Commissions				at	0	for	$0.00
10. Net Revenues							$712.50
Net Profit or Loss (10) – (5)							$512.50

Problem 5–4 GM Bear Spread Roll-Down Worksheet

A. Initial Position Data								
Underlying Stock	GM							
Current Stock Price	46 ⅛							$46.13
Days until Option Expiration	135							
Options' Maturity Month	December							
Low Strike Price	35							
Low Strike Option Intrinsic Value	0							
Low Strike Option Time Value	3/16							
Low Strike Option Premium	3/16							$18.75
High Strike Price	45							
High Strike Option Intrinsic Value	0							
High Strike Option Time Value	2 3/16							
High Strike Option Premium	2 3/16							$218.75
Spread Value	2							$200.00
1. Sell	1	December	low strike options		at	3/16	for	$18.75
2. Less Commissions					at	0	for	$0.00
3. Buy	1	December	high strike options		at	2 3/16	for	$218.75
4. Plus Commissions					at	0	for	$0.00
5. Net Cost								$200.00
B. Roll-Down Position Data								
Underlying Stock	GM							
Current Stock Price	38 ⅞							$38.88
Days until Option Expiration	35							
Options' Maturity Month		December						
Option Premium	1 ½	December	at striking price	30				

Option Premium	2 ⅞	December	at striking price	35				
Option Premium	7 ⅛	December	at striking price	45				
6. Sell	1	December	at striking price	45	at	7 ⅛	for	$712.50
7. Less Commissions					at	0	for	$0.00
8. Buy	2	December	at striking price	35	at	2 ⅞	for	$575.00
9. Plus Commissions					at	0	for	$0.00
10. Sell	1	December	at striking price	30	at	1 ½	for	$150.00
11. Less Commissions					at	0	for	$0.00
12. Buy			at striking price		at		for	$0.00
13. Plus Commissions					at	0	for	$0.00
14. Roll-Down Cash Flow								$287.50
15. Net Cash Flow								$87.50

C. Total Position Profit or Loss

Stock Price at Liquidation	37 ½							$37.50
Days until Option Expiration	4							
Options' Maturity Month	December							
Low Strike Price	30							
Low Strike Option Intrinsic Value	0							
Low Strike Option Time Value	5⁄16							
Low Strike Option Premium	5⁄16							$31.25
High Strike Price	35							
High Strike Option Intrinsic Value	2 ½							
High Strike Option Time Value	⅛							
High Strike Option Premium	2 ⅝							$262.50
Spread Value	2 5⁄16							$231.25
16. Buy	1	December	at striking price	30	at	5⁄16	for	$31.25
17. Plus Commissions					at	0	for	$0.00
18. Sell	1	December	at striking price	35	at	2 ⅝	for	$262.50
19. Less Commissions					at	0	for	$0.00
20. Net Revenues								$231.25
Net Profit or Loss (20) + (15)								$318.75

Problem 5–5 Exxon Time Spread Purchase Worksheet

A. Position Data						
Underlying Stock	Exxon					
Current Stock Price	64 ½					$64.50
Days until Nearby Option Expires	75					
Nearby Options' Maturity Month	February					
Nearby Options' Strike Price	65					
Nearby Options' Intrinsic Value	0					
Nearby Options' Time Value	2 ⅛					
Nearby Options' Premium	2 ⅛					$212.50
Days until Deferred Option Expiration	135					
Deferred Options' Maturity Month	April					
Deferred Options' Strike Price	65					
Deferred Options' Intrinsic Value	0					
Deferred Options' Time Value	3 ⅞					
Deferred Options' Premium	3 ⅞					$387.50
Spread Value	1 ¾					$175.00
B. Initial Position						
1. Sell	1	nearby option	at	2 ⅛	for	$212.50
2. Less Commissions			at	0	for	$0.00
3. Buy	1	deferred option	at	3 ⅞	for	$387.50
4. Plus Commissions			at	0	for	$0.00
5. Net Cost						$175.00

C. Position Profit or Loss

Stock Price at Liquidation	63 7/8					$63.88
Days until Option Expiration	5					
Nearby Options' Maturity Month	February					
Nearby Options' Strike Price	65					
Nearby Options' Intrinsic Value	0					
Nearby Options' Time Value	1/16					
Nearby Options' Premium	1/16					$6.25
Deferred Options' Maturity Month	April					
Deferred Options' Strike Price	65					
Deferred Options' Intrinsic Value	0					
Deferred Options' Time Value	2 1/16					
Deferred Options' Premium	2 1/16					$206.25
Spread Value	2					$200.00
6. Buy	1	nearby options	at	1/16	for	$6.25
7. Plus Commissions						
8. Sell	1	deferred options	at	2 1/16	for	$206.25
9. Less Commissions						
10. Net Revenues						$200.00
Net Profit or Loss (10) – (5)						$25.00

Problem 5–6 Exxon Time Spread Roll-Forward Worksheet

A. Initial Position Data							
Underlying Stock	Exxon						
Current Stock Price	64 ½						$64.50
Days until Nearby Option Expires	75						
Nearby Options' Maturity Month	February						
Nearby Options' Strike Price	65						
Nearby Options' Intrinsic Value	0						
Nearby Options' Time Value	2 ⅛						
Nearby Options' Premium	2 ⅛						$212.50
Days until Deferred Option Expiration	135						
Deferred Options' Maturity Month	April						
Deferred Options' Strike Price	65						
Deferred Options' Intrinsic Value	0						
Deferred Options' Time Value	3 ⅞						
Deferred Options' Premium	3 ⅞						$387.50
Spread Value	1 ¾						$175.00
1. Sell	1	Nearby option	at		2 ⅛	for	$212.50
2. Less Commissions			at		0	for	$0.00
3. Buy	1	Deferred option	at		3 ⅞	for	$387.50
4. Plus Commissions			at		0	for	$0.00
5. Net Cost							$175.00
B. Roll-Forward Position Data							
Underlying Stock	Exxon						
Current Stock Price	63 ⅞						$63.88
Option's Striking Price	65						
Option Premium	1/16	for maturity	at	February		for	$6.25
Option Premium	2 1/16	for maturity	at	April		for	$206.25
Option Premium	3 ¾	for maturity	at	July		for	$375.00

6. Buy	1	February Maturity	at	1/16	for	$6.25
7. Plus Commissions			at	0	for	$0.00
8. Sell	2	April Maturity	at	2 1/16	for	$412.50
9. Less Commissions			at	0	for	$0.00
10. Buy	1	July Maturity	at	3 3/4	for	$375.00
11. Plus Commissions			at	0	for	$0.00
12. Roll-Forward Cash Flow						$31.25
13. Net Cash Flow (12) – (5)						$143.75
C. Position Profit or Loss						
Stock Price at Liquidation	65 1/8					$65.13
Days until Nearby Option Expiration	4					
Nearby Option's Maturity Month		April				
Nearby Option's Strike Price	65					
Nearby Option's Option Intrinsic Value	1/8					
Nearby Option's Premium	3/16					$18.75
Deferred Option's Maturity Month		July				
Deferred Option's Strike Price	65					
Deferred Option's Intrinsic Value	1/8					
Deferred Option's Time Value	3 1/4					
Deferred Option's Premium	3 3/8					$337.50
Spread Value	3 3/16					$318.75
14. Buy	1	April Maturity	at	3/16	for	$18.75
15. Plus Commissions			at	0	for	$0.00
16. Sell	1	July Maturity	at	3 3/16	for	$318.75
17. Less Commissions			at	0	for	$0.00
18. Net Revenues						$300.00
Net Profit or Loss (18) + (13)						$156.25

Problem 6–1 Storage Technology Straddle Purchase Worksheet

A. Position Data								
Underlying Stock	STK							
Current Stock Price	25 ½							$25.50
Days until Call Option Expiration	105							
Call Options' Maturity Month	September							
Call Options' Strike Price	25							
Call Options' Intrinsic Value	½							
Call Options' Time Value	4 ½							
Call Options' Premium	5							$500.00
Put Options' Maturity Month	September							
Days until Put Option Expiration	105							
Put Options' Strike Price	25							
Put Options' Intrinsic Value	0							
Put Options' Time Value	4 ⅛							
Put Options' Premium	4 ⅛							$412.50
Straddle Value	9 ⅛							$912.50
B. Initial Position								
1. Buy	1	strike =	25	call option	at	5	for	$500.00
2. Plus Commissions					at	0	for	$0.00
3. Buy	1	strike =	25	put option	at	4 ⅛	for	$412.50
4. Plus Commissions					at	0	for	$0.00
5. Net Cost								$912.50

C. Position Profit or Loss

Stock Price at Liquidation	36							$36.00
Days until Call Option Expiration	29							
Call Options' Maturity Month	September							
Call Options' Strike Price	25							
Call Options' Intrinsic Value	11							
Call Options' Time Value	2							
Call Options' Premium	13							$1300.00
Put Options' Maturity Month	September							
Days until Put Option Expiration	29							
Put Options' Strike Price	25							
Put Options' Intrinsic Value	0							
Put Options' Time Value	¾							
Put Options' Premium	¾							$75.00
Straddle Value	13 ¾							$1375.00
6. Sell	1	strike =	25	call option	at	13	for	$1300.00
7. Less Commissions					at	0	for	$0.00
8. Sell	1	strike =	25	put option	at	¾	for	$75.00
9. Less Commissions					at	0	for	$0.00
10. Net Revenues								$1375.00
Net Profit or Loss (10) – (5)								$462.50

Problem 6–2 Storage Technology Straddle Sale Worksheet

A. Pcsition Data								
Underlying Stock	STK							
Current Stock Price	25 ½							$25.50
Days until Call Option Expiration	105							
Call Options' Maturity Month	September							
Call Options' Strike Price	25							
Call Options' Intrinsic Value	½							
Call Options' Time Value	4 ½							
Call Options' Premium	5							$500.00
Put Options' Maturity Month	September							
Days until Put Option Expiration	105							
Put Options' Strike Price	25							
Put Options' Intrinsic Value	0							
Put Options' Time Value	4 ⅛							
Put Options' Premium	4 ⅛							$412.50
Straddle Value	9 ⅛							$912.50
B. Initial Position								
1. Sell	1	strike =	25	call option	at	5	for	$500.00
2. Less Commissions					at	0	for	$0.00
3. Sell	1	strike =	25	put option	at	4 ⅛	for	$412.50
4. Less Commissions					at	0	for	$0.00
5. Net Revenues								$912.50

C. Position Profit or Loss

Stock Price at Liquidation	36							$36.00
Days until Call Option Expiration	29							
Call Options' Maturity Month	September							
Call Options' Strike Price	25							
Call Options' Intrinsic Value	11							
Call Options' Time Value	2							
Call Options' Premium	13							$1300.00
Put Options' Maturity Month	September							
Days until Put Option Expiration	29							
Put Options' Strike Price	25							
Put Options' Intrinsic Value	0							
Put Options' Time Value	¾							
Put Options' Premium	¾							$75.00
Straddle Value	13 ¾							$1375.00
6. Buy	1	strike =	25	call option	at	13	for	$1300.00
7. Plus Commissions					at	0	for	$0.00
8. Buy	1	strike =	25	put option	at	¾	for	$75.00
9. Plus Commissions					at	0	for	$0.00
10. Net Costs								$1375.00
Net Profit or Loss (5) – (10)								($462.50)

Problem 6–3 Digital Equipment Strangle Sale Worksheet

A. Position Data								
Underlying Stock	Digital							
Current Stock Price	38 ¼							$38.25
Days until Call Option Expiration	108							
Call Options' Maturity Month	April							
Call Options' Strike Price	40							
Call Options' Intrinsic Value	0							
Call Options' Time Value	2 ⅝							
Call Options' Premium	2 ⅝							$262.50
Put Options' Maturity Month	April							
Days until Put Option Expiration	108							
Put Optiosn' Strike Price	35							
Put Options' Intrinsic Value	0							
Put Options' Time Value	1 ¾							
Put Options' Premium	1 ¾							$175.00
Strangle Value	4 ⅜							$437.50
B. Initial Position								
1. Sell	1	strike =	40	call option	at	2 ⅝	for	$262.50
2. Less Commissions					at	0	for	$0.00
3. Sell	1	strike =	35	put option	at	1 ¾	for	$175.00
4. Less Commissions					at	0	for	$0.00
5. Net Revenues								$437.50

C. Position Profit or Loss

Stock Price at Liquidation	52 ⅛							$52.13
Days until Call Option Expiration	33							
Call Options' Maturity Month	April							
Call Options' Strike Price	40							
Call Options' Intrinsic Value	12 ⅛							
Call Options' Time Value	1 ⅝							
Call Options' Premium	13 ¾							$1375.00
Put Options' Maturity Month	April							
Days until Put Option Expiration	33							
Put Options' Strike Price	35							
Put Options' Intrinsic Value	0							
Put Options' Time Value	¼							
Put Options' Premium	¼							$25.00
Strangle Value	14							$1400.00
6. Buy	1	strike =	40	call option	at	13 ¾	for	$1375.00
7. Plus Commissions					at	0	for	$0.00
8. Buy	1	strike =	35	put option	at	¼	for	$25.00
9. Plus Commissions					at	0	for	$0.00
10. Net Costs								$1400.00
Net Profit or Loss (5) – (10)								($962.50)

Problem 6–4 Digital Equipment Strangle Purchase Worksheet

A. Position Data								
Underlying Stock	Digital							
Current Stock Price	38 ¼							$38.25
Days until Call Option Expiration	108							
Call Options' Maturity Month	April							
Call Options' Strike Price	40							
Call Options' Intrinsic Value	0							
Call Options' Time Value	2 ⅝							
Call Options' Premium	2 ⅝							$262.50
Put Options' Maturity Month	April							
Days until Put Option Expiration	108							
Put Options' Strike Price	35							
Put Options' Intrinsic Value	0							
Put Options' Time Value	1 ¾							
Put Options' Premium	1 ¾							$175.00
Strangle Value	4 ⅜							$437.50
B. Initial Position								
1. Buy	1	strike =	40	call option	at	2 ⅝	for	$262.50
2. Plus Commissions					at	0	for	$0.00
3. Buy	1	strike =	35	put option	at	1 ¾	for	$175.00
4. Plus Commissions					at	0	for	$0.00
5. Net Cost								$437.50

C. Position Profit or Loss

Stock Price at Liquidation	52 ⅛							$52.13
Days until Call Option Expiration	33							
Call Options' Maturity Month	April							
Call Options' Strike Price	40							
Call Options' Intrinsic Value	12 ⅛							
Call Options' Time Value	1 ⅝							
Call Options' Premium	13 ¾							$1375.00
Put Options' Maturity Month	April							
Days until Put Option Expiration	33							
Put Options' Strike Price	35							
Put Options' Intrinsic Value	0							
Put Options' Time Value	¼							
Put Options' Premium	¼							$25.00
Strangle Value	14							$1400.00
6. Sell	1	strike =	40	call option	at	13 ¾	for	$1375.00
7. Less Commissions					at	0	for	$0.00
8. Sell	1	strike =	35	put option	at	¼	for	$25.00
9. Less Commissions					at	0	for	$0.00
10. Net Revenues								$1400.00
Net Profit or Loss (10) – (5)								$962.50

Problem 7–1 Buying Stock and Selling Puts Simultaneously: Greentree Financial

A. Initial Position Data						
Underlying Stock	Greentree					
Current Stock Price	51					$51.00
Put Options' Maturity Month	February					
Put Options' Striking Price	50					
Put Options' Premium	1 ¾					
Days until Option Expires	70					
1. Buy	200	Greentree	at	51	for	$10,200.00
2. Plus Commissions			at	0	for	$0.00
3. Net Stock Position			at	0	for	$10,200.00
4. Sell	2	Puts	at	1 ¾	for	$350.00
5. Less Commissions			at	0	for	$0.00
6. Net Put Options' Proceeds						$350.00
7. Net Cost of Position (3) – (6)						$9,850.00
8. Net Cost per Share (7)/(# of shares)	200					$49.25
B. Result of Position Data						
9. Buy	200	Greentree	at	50	for	$10,000.00
10. Plus Commissions			at	0	for	$0.00
11. Cost of Shares Put to You			at	0	for	$10,000.00
12. Cost of Original Shares Purchased (7)			at	0	for	$9,850.00
13. Net Cost of Total Shares			at	0	for	$19,850.00
14. Net Cost per Share (13)/(# of shares)	400		at	0	for	$49.63

Problem 7–2 Selling Covered Combinations: General Motors

A. Initial Position Data						
Underlying Stock	GM					
Current Stock Price	43					$43.00
Put Options' Maturity Month	March					
Put Options' Striking Price	40					
Put Options' Premium	1 ½					
Call Options' Maturity Month	March					
Call Options' Striking Price	45					
Call Options' Premium	2 ¾					
Days until Option Expires	75					
1. Buy	200	GM	at	43	for	$8600.00
2. Plus Commissions			at	0	for	$0.00
3. Net Stock Position			at	0	for	$8600.00
4. Sell	2	Calls	at	2 ¾	for	$550.00
5. Less Commissions			at	0	for	$0.00
6. Net Call Options' Proceeds						$550.00
7. Sell	2	Puts	at	1 ½	for	$300.00
8. Less Commissions			at	0	for	$0.00
9. Net Put Options' Proceeds						$300.00
10. Net Investment (3) – (6) – (9)	200					$300.00

B. Maximum Profit

11. Sell	200	GM	at	45	for	
12. Less Commissions			at	0	for	$0.00
13. Plus Dividends Received			at	0	for	$40.00
14. Net Proceeds			at	0	for	$940.00
15. Profit (14) – (10)			at	0	for	$1290.00
16. Return on Investment (15)/(10)						16.65 %
17. Return Annualized (365)/(182) * (23)						81.01 %

C. Profit if Stock < Strike

18. Buy	______	______	at	______	for	______
19. Plus Commissions			at	______	for	______
20. Net Cost of New Shares						______
21. Average Cost of All Shares (per shares)						______

D. Profit if Stock Is Unchanged

22. Profit (current value of shares) + (13) – (10)	______
23. Return on Investment (22)/(10)	______
24. Return Annualized (365)/(182) * 23	______

Problem 7–3 Hedged Covered Call Write: Blockbuster

A. Initial Position Data						
Underlying Stock	Blockbuster					
Current Stock Price	27					$27.00
Put Options' Maturity Month	August					
Put Options' Striking Price	25					
Put Options' Premium	1					
Call Options' Maturity Month	August					
Call Options' Striking Price	30					
Call Options' Premium	1 ¼					
Days until Option Expires	120					
1. Buy	400	Blockbuster	at	27	for	$10,800.00
2. Plus Commissions			at	0	for	$0.00
3. Net Stock Position			at	0	for	$10,800.00
4. Sell	4	Calls	at	1 ¼	for	$500.00
5. Less Commissions			at	0	for	$0.00
6. Net Call Options' Proceeds						500.00
7. Buy	4	Puts	at	1	for	$400.00
8. Plus Commissions			at	0	for	$0.00
9. Net Put Options' Proceeds						$300.00
10. Net Investment (3) – (6) + (9)						$10,700.00

B. Maximum Profit						
11. Sell	400	Blockbuster	at	30	for	$12,000.00
12. Less Commissions			at	0	for	$0.00
13. Plus Dividends Received			at	0	for	$20.00
14. Net Proceeds			at	0	for	$12,020.00
15. Profit (14) – (10)			at	0	for	$1,320.00
16. Return on Investment (15)/(10)						12.34 %
17. Return Annualized (365)/(182) * (23)						37.52 %
C. Maximum Risk						
18. Sell	400	Blockbuster	at	25	for	$10,000.00
19. Less Commissions			at	0	for	$0.00
20. Plus Dividends Received						$20.00
21. Net Proceeds						$10,020.00
22. Potential Loss (10) – (21)						$680.00
23. Percentage Risk (22)/(10)						6.36 %
D. Breakeven at Expiration						
22. (10) – (13) + (commission/#shares)						$26.70

Problem 7–4 Synthetic Stock Position: CUC International Stock Increase at Expiration

A. Initial Position Data

Underlying Stock	CUC International					
Current Stock Price	30					$30.00
Put Options' Maturity Month	April					
Put Options' Striking Price	30					
Put Options' Premium	1 ¾					
Call Options' Maturity Month	April					
Call Options' Striking Price	30					
Call Options' Premium	2					
Days until Option Expires	120					
1. Buy	1	Call(s)	at	2	for	$200.00
2. Plus Commissions			at	0	for	$0.00
3. Net Debit			at	0	for	$200.00
4. Sell	1	Put(s)	at	1 ¾	for	$175.00
5. Less Commissions			at	0	for	$0.00
6. Net Credit						$175.00
7. Net Position						$25.00

B. Liquidating Position

Days Until Expiration	20					
8. Sell	1	Call(s)	at	6 ⅜	for	$637.50
9. Less Commissions			at	0	for	$0.00
10. Net Call Sale						$637.50
11. Gain (Loss) on Call Position (10) – (3)						$437.50
12. Buy	1	Put(s)	at	¼	for	$25.00
13. Plus Commissions			at	0	for	$0.00
14. Net Put Purchase			at	0	for	$25.00
15. Gain (Loss) on Put Position						$150.00
16. Net Gain (Loss) (7) + (11) + (15)						$612.50

C. Cost Per Share

Days until Expiration	________		at		for	
17. Buy		________	at	________	for	________
18. Plus Commissions			at	________	for	________
19. Less Credit or Plus Debit in (7)			at	________	for	________
20. Net Investment			at	________	for	________
21. Average Cost per Share (20)/(#shares in 17)						________

Problem 7–5 Stock Repair Strategy: Motorola

A. Initial Position Data						
Underlying Stock	Motorola					
Original Price Paid	85					
Original Stock Price	70					$70.00
Call Options' Maturity Month (Lower Strike)	March					
Call Options' Striking Price	70					
Call Options' Premium	3 ½					
Call Options' Maturity Month (Higher Strike)	March					
Call Options' Striking Price	75					
Call Options' Premium	1 ¾					
1. Bought	100	Motorola	at	85	for	$8500.00
2. Plus Commissions			at	0	for	$0.00
3. Net Original Position			at	0	for	$8500.00
4. Net Cost per Share (1)/(# shares)			a			$85.00
B. Repair Position						
5. Original Position (3)						$8500.00
6. Buy	1	Call(s) (March 70)	at	3 ½	for	$350.00
7. Sell	2	Call(s) (March 75)	at	1 ¾	for	$350.00
8. Net Commissions for Options						$0.00
9. Net Cost of Repair (6) – (7) net in (8)			at	0	for	$0.00

C. Amount Recovered

10. Sell	100	Motorola	at	75	for	$7500.00
11. Less Commissions			at		for	$0.00
12. Plus Dividends Received						$33.00
13. Net Proceeds from Covered Write						$7533.00
14. Sell (6) Position at Market Price						$850.00
15. Less Commissions						$0.00
16. Net Proceeds from Lower Striking Price Call						$850.00
17. Purchase ½ of (7) Position						($350.00)
18. Plus Commissions						$0.00
19. Net Cost to Close Short Call Position						($350.00)
20. Profit (Loss) on Original Stock Position (13) – (3)						($967.00)
21. Profit from Bull Spread (16) + (19)						$500.00
22. Net Profit (Loss) (20) + (21) – (9)						($467.00)
23. Current Value of Stock						($467.00)
24. Dividends Received						______
25. Original Stock Position (3)						______
26. Sell (6) Position at Market Price						______
27. Less Commissions						______
28. Net Proceeds from Lower Striking Price Call						______
29. Buy (7) Position at Market Price						______
30. Plus Commissions						______
31. Net Cost to Close Short Call Position						______
32. Change in Original Stock Position Value						______
(23) + (24) – (25) + (28) – (31)						______

About the Authors

CARL F. LUFT is an assistant professor of finance at De Paul University. He earned an M.B.A. in international business from De Paul in 1977 and a Ph.D. in finance from Georgia State University in 1983. While completing his doctoral degree, Mr. Luft served as a consultant with the Atlanta branch of Cantor-Fitzgerald Brokerage House. Since returning to Chicago, he has consulted with Cargill Investor Services, Mercury Trading, and Hull Trading, and taught at the Chicago Board Options Exchange's Options Institute, and the Chicago Mercantile Exchange.

RICHARD K. SHEINER is an investment broker and a registered Options Principal with William Blair & Co., a leading investment banking firm headquartered in Chicago. He advises individuals and corporations on investment portfolios of stocks, bonds, and options. Mr. Sheiner has been qualified by the Board of Options Institute to teach option investment strategies to both clients and fellow investment professionals. He occasionally conducts courses in options and investments in the Chicago metropolitan area. Mr. Sheiner is a graduate of the University of Michigan, where his studies emphasized business and psychology.

Index

V

W